Siegel's
WILLS AND TRUSTS

Essay and Multiple-Choice Questions and Answers

Fifth Edition

BRIAN N. SIEGEL
J.D., Columbia Law School

LAZAR EMANUEL
J.D., Harvard Law School

MARSH C. BRILLIANT
J.D., Whittier Law School

Revised by
Karen E. Boxx
Professor of Law
University of Washington School of Law

Copyright © 2013 CCH Incorporated.

Published by Wolters Kluwer Law & Business in New York.

Wolters Kluwer Law & Business serves customers worldwide with CCH, Aspen Publishers, and Kluwer Law International products. (www.wolterskluwerlb.com)

No part of this publication may be reproduced or transmitted in any form or by any means, electronic or mechanical, including photocopy, recording, or utilized by any information storage or retrieval system, without written permission from the publisher. For information about permissions or to request permissions online, visit us at www.wolterskluwerlb.com, or a written request may be faxed to our permissions department at 212-771-0803.

To contact Customer Service, e-mail customer.service@wolterskluwer.com, call 1-800-234-1660, fax 1-800-901-9075, or mail correspondence to:

> Wolters Kluwer Law & Business
> Attn: Order Department
> PO Box 990
> Frederick, MD 21705

The authors gratefully acknowledge the assistance of the California Committee of Bar Examiners, which provided access to questions on which many of the essay questions in this book are based.

Printed in the United States of America.

1 2 3 4 5 6 7 8 9 0

ISBN 978-1-4548-2496-1

This book is intended as a general review of a legal subject. It is not intended as a source of advice for the solution of legal matters or problems. For advice on legal matters, the reader should consult an attorney.

About Wolters Kluwer Law & Business

Wolters Kluwer Law & Business is a leading global provider of intelligent information and digital solutions for legal and business professionals in key specialty areas, and respected educational resources for professors and law students. Wolters Kluwer Law & Business connects legal and business professionals as well as those in the education market with timely, specialized authoritative content and information-enabled solutions to support success through productivity, accuracy and mobility.

Serving customers worldwide, Wolters Kluwer Law & Business products include those under the Aspen Publishers, CCH, Kluwer Law International, Loislaw, Best Case, ftwilliam.com and MediRegs family of products.

CCH products have been a trusted resource since 1913, and are highly regarded resources for legal, securities, antitrust and trade regulation, government contracting, banking, pension, payroll, employment and labor, and healthcare reimbursement and compliance professionals.

Aspen Publishers products provide essential information to attorneys, business professionals and law students. Written by preeminent authorities, the product line offers analytical and practical information in a range of specialty practice areas from securities law and intellectual property to mergers and acquisitions and pension/benefits. Aspen's trusted legal education resources provide professors and students with high-quality, up-to-date and effective resources for successful instruction and study in all areas of the law.

Kluwer Law International products provide the global business community with reliable international legal information in English. Legal practitioners, corporate counsel and business executives around the world rely on Kluwer Law journals, looseleafs, books, and electronic products for comprehensive information in many areas of international legal practice.

Loislaw is a comprehensive online legal research product providing legal content to law firm practitioners of various specializations. Loislaw provides attorneys with the ability to quickly and efficiently find the necessary legal information they need, when and where they need it, by facilitating access to primary law as well as state-specific law, records, forms and treatises.

Best Case Solutions is the leading bankruptcy software product to the bankruptcy industry. It provides software and workflow tools to flawlessly streamline petition preparation and the electronic filing process, while timely incorporating ever-changing court requirements.

ftwilliam.com offers employee benefits professionals the highest quality plan documents (retirement, welfare and non-qualified) and government forms (5500/PBGC, 1099 and IRS) software at highly competitive prices.

MediRegs products provide integrated health care compliance content and software solutions for professionals in healthcare, higher education and life sciences, including professionals in accounting, law and consulting.

Introduction

Although law school grades are a significant factor in obtaining a summer internship or entry position at a law firm, no formalized preparation for finals is offered at most law schools. For the most part, students are expected to fend for themselves in learning how to take a law school exam. Ironically, law school exams may bear little correspondence to the teaching methods used by professors during the school year. At least in the first year, professors require you to spend most of your time briefing cases. This is probably not great preparation for issue-spotting on exams. In briefing cases, you are made to focus on one or two principles of law at a time; thus, you don't get practice in relating one issue to another or in developing a picture of an entire problem or the entire course. When exams finally come, you're forced to make an abrupt 180-degree turn. Suddenly, you are asked to recognize, define, and discuss a variety of issues buried within a single multi-issue fact pattern. Alternately, you may be asked to select among a number of possible answers, all of which look inviting but only one of which is right.

The comprehensive course outline you've created so diligently, and with such pain, means little if you're unable to apply its contents on your final exams. There is a vast difference between reading opinions in which the legal principles are clearly stated and applying those same principles to hypothetical essay exams and multiple-choice questions.

The purpose of this book is to help you bridge the gap between memorizing a rule of law and ***understanding how to use it*** in an exam. After an initial overview describing the exam-writing process, you see a large number of hypotheticals that test your ability to write analytical essays and to pick the right answers to multiple-choice questions. **Read them—all of them!** Then review the suggested answers that follow. You'll find that the key to superior grades lies in applying your knowledge through questions and answers, not through rote memory.

GOOD LUCK!

Table of Contents

Preparing Effectively for Essay Examinations

The "ERC" Process 1
Issue-Spotting 3
How to Discuss an Issue 3
Structuring Your Answer 6
Discuss All Possible Issues 8
Delineate the Transition from One Issue to the Next 9
Understanding the "Call" of a Question 9
The Importance of Analyzing the Question Carefully Before Writing . 10
When to Make an Assumption 11
Case Names 12
How to Handle Time Pressures 12
Formatting Your Answer 13
The Importance of Reviewing Prior Exams 13
As Always, a Caveat 14

Essay Questions

Question 1 (Wills—Validity, Revocation, Revival, Intestacy,
   Interpretation) 19
Question 2 (Wills—Formalities for Making, Proving in Probate,
   Revocation, Protection of Spouse) 20
Question 3 (Wills—Revocation, Execution, Dependent Relative
   Revocation) 21
Question 4 (Wills—Failure of Gift; Trusts—Creation of *Inter Vivos*
   Trust, Ademption) 22
Question 5 (Trusts—Amendment, Joint Tenancy) 23
Question 6 (Wills—Formalities for Making, Revocation;
   Trusts—Constructive Trust) 24
Question 7 (Trusts—Trustee's Duty of Loyalty, Spendthrift
   Trust) 25
Question 8 (Wills—Bequest to Former Spouse, Stock Dividends;
   Trusts—Creation, Revocation, Distribution of Assets) 26

Question 9 (Wills—Omitted Child, Incorporation of Trust by Reference, Antilapse Provision, Interested Witness; Trusts—Modification, Spendthrift) 27

Question 10 (Wills—Holographic Wills, Omitted Heir, Interested Witness, Ademption; Satisfaction) 28

Question 11 (Trusts—Creation of Charitable Trust, Delivery of Trust Res, *Cy Pres* Doctrine) 29

Question 12 (Wills—Ademption, Incorporation by Reference, Deceased Devisee, Stock Dividend, Bequest to Divorced Spouse; Trusts—Totten Trust)... 30

Question 13 (Wills—Omitted Spouse, Revocation of Earlier Will, Effect of Codicil, Testator's Mistake) 31

Question 14 (Wills—Formalities for Making, Interested Witness, Revocation of Particular Bequest, Partial Intestacy; Trusts—Semisecret Trust)... 32

Question 15 (Wills—Formalities for Making, Revocation, Revival Interpretation) 33

Question 16 (Wills—Formalities for Making, Incorporation by Reference, Stock Dividend, Interpretation) 34

Question 17 (Wills—Contractual Wills, Omitted Spouse) 36

Question 18 (Wills—Formalities for Making, Stock from Merger, Intestacy, Pretermitted Spouse, Abatement) 37

Question 19 (Wills—Formalities for Making, Republication, Incorporation by Reference, Events of Independent Significance Doctrine).. 38

Question 20 (Wills—Revocation, Incorporation by Reference, Distribution to "Heirs," Intestate Distribution)......................... 39

Question 21 (Trusts—Failure of Trust, Determination of "Issue").......... 40

Question 22 (Wills—Simultaneous Deaths of Testator and Beneficiary, Class Gift, Antilapse Provision, Factual Mistake by Testator) 41

Question 23 (Trusts—Revocation, Spendthrift Trust, Termination) 42

Question 24 (Wills—Admissibility to Probate, Destruction of Devised Property, Stock Split, Antilapse Statute, Intestacy)............... 43

Question 25 (Wills—Nonprobate Assets, Revocation on Divorce, Lapse, Antilapse, *Cy Pres*, Omitted Spouse)........................... 44

Table of Contents

Question 26 (Trusts—Ascertainable Beneficiaries, Delivery of *Inter Vivos* Gift, Intent to Create Trust, Vested Remainders; Wills—Codicils) 45

Question 27 (Trusts—Power of Sale, Duty of Loyalty, Self-Dealing, Duty of Prudent Investment) 47

Question 28 (Trusts—Creation, Oral Trusts, Duty of Loyalty, Duty to Inform, Actions Against Trustees)............................. 48

Question 29 (Wills—Drafting Testamentary Trust)...................... 49

Question 30 (Wills—Drafting Distribution Provision, Advancement) 50

Essay Answers

Answer to Question 1... 53
Answer to Question 2... 58
Answer to Question 3... 62
Answer to Question 4... 64
Answer to Question 5... 68
Answer to Question 6... 69
Answer to Question 7... 72
Answer to Question 8... 75
Answer to Question 9... 78
Answer to Question 10.. 81
Answer to Question 11.. 85
Answer to Question 12.. 88
Answer to Question 13.. 92
Answer to Question 14.. 96
Answer to Question 15.. 100
Answer to Question 16.. 105
Answer to Question 17.. 113
Answer to Question 18.. 115
Answer to Question 19.. 119
Answer to Question 20.. 124
Answer to Question 21.. 128
Answer to Question 22.. 129
Answer to Question 23.. 135
Answer to Question 24.. 138
Answer to Question 25.. 141
Answer to Question 26.. 144

Answer to Question 27. 147
Answer to Question 28. 150
Answer to Question 29. 153
Answer to Question 30. 155

Multiple-Choice Questions

Questions 1 through 101 159

Multiple-Choice Answers

Answers to Questions 1 through 101 203

Tables and Index

Table of References to the Uniform Probate Code (UPC) 249
Table of References to the Uniform Trust Code 251
Table of References to the Restatement (Second) of Trusts 253
Table of References to the Restatement (Third) of Trusts 255
Alphabetical index, listing issues by the number of the question
 raising the issue. 257

Preparing Effectively for Essay Examinations

To achieve superior scores on essay exams, a law student must (1) learn and understand "blackletter" principles and rules of law for each subject; (2) analyze how those principles of law arise within a test fact pattern; and (3) clearly and succinctly discuss each principle and how it relates to the facts. One of the most common misconceptions about law school is that you must memorize each word on every page of your casebooks or outlines to do well on exams. The reality is that you can commit an entire casebook to memory and still do poorly on an exam. Our review of hundreds of student answers has shown us that most students can recite the rules. The students who do *best* on exams are able to analyze how the rules they have memorized relate to the facts in the questions, and they are able to communicate their analysis to the grader. The following pages cover what you need to know to achieve superior scores on your law school essay exams.

The "ERC" Process

To study effectively for law school exams you must be able to "ERC" (*E*lementize, *R*ecognize, and *C*onceptualize) each legal principle covered in your casebooks and course outlines. *Elementizing* means reducing each legal theory and rule you learn to a concise, straightforward statement of its essential elements. Without knowledge of these elements, it's difficult to see all the issues as they arise.

For example, if you are asked, "What is fraud?" it is *not* enough to say, "Fraud is cheating someone." This layperson description would leave a grader wondering if you had actually attended law school. An accurate statement of the fraud principle would go something like this: "If one person makes a material misrepresentation to another person, the person making the misrepresentation knew it was false at the time of making it or recklessly did not know whether it was true or false and intended the other person to act on the misrepresentation, and the other person in fact acts on the misrepresentation and suffers harm, the person making the misrepresentation is liable for fraud." This formulation correctly shows that there are six separate, distinct elements that must be satisfied before the claim of fraud can be successfully asserted: (1) the there was a material representation communicated; (2) the representation was false; (3) when the representation was made, the speaker knew it was false or made it recklessly without any knowledge of the truth (4) the speaker made the representation with the intent that the other person would act upon it; (5) the other person acted in reliance on the representation; and (6) the other person thereby suffered injury. ***Recognizing*** means perceiving or anticipating which words or ideas within a legal principle are likely to be the source of issues and how those issues are likely to arise within a given hypothetical fact pattern. With respect to the fraud concept, there are six ***potential*** issues. Was the misrepresentation material? Was it false? Did the speaker know it was false, or make the representation recklessly without knowing whether it was true or false? Did the speaker intend that the person to whom the misrepresentation was communicated take action as a result of the misrepresentation? Did the person receiving the misrepresentation act on it? Did he or she suffer harm as a result? ***Conceptualizing*** means imagining situations in which each of the elements of a rule of law can give rise to factual issues. ***Unless you can imagine or construct an application of each element of a rule, you don't truly understand the legal principles behind the rule!*** In our opinion, the inability to conjure up hypothetical fact patterns or stories involving particular rules of law foretells a likelihood that you will miss issues involving those rules on an exam. It's ***crucial*** (1) to ***recognize*** that issues result from the interaction of facts with the words defining a rule of law and (2) to develop the ability to ***conceptualize*** or ***imagine*** fact patterns using the words or concepts within the rule.

For example, a set of facts illustrating the "knowledge of the falsity or reckless disregard of whether the representation is true or false" might be the following:

> Tess lived with her daughter Bonita, and she had another daughter Delilah. Delilah was a recovering alcoholic, and Tess had stated repeatedly that if Delilah began drinking again she would disinherit Delilah. Bonita was out one night and saw a woman come out of a bar and stumble to the ground. The woman looked like Delilah, but Bonita was standing a block away and did not get a good look at the woman's face. The woman had the same build and hairstyle as Delilah, however. Bonita went home and told her mother that she had seen Delilah out "stumbling down drunk wandering the streets of downtown." Tess immediately called her lawyer and had her Will revised to cut out Delilah and leave her entire estate to Bonita. Delilah could assert that the will was a result of Bonita's fraud and should be thrown out. Bonita could argue that she believed what she said. However, Delilah could argue in rebuttal that Bonita's statement to Tess was made with reckless disregard of any verification of whether the woman she saw was Delilah and even whether the woman she saw was drunk. In fact, Delilah was out of town on the night in question.

An illustration of how the requirement that the representation be false might generate an issue is the following:

Simon was the tennis instructor of a wealthy widow. He began to flatter her and spend more and more time with her off the tennis court. He told her in the presence of many witnesses that he loved her. The widow changed her Will, eliminating gifts to her relatives and leaving her entire estate to Simon. On her death, her relatives asserted that Simon had procured the new Will by fraud, by telling the widow he loved her. The relatives asserted that this was a false statement because in fact, Simon had a long-term girlfriend.

"Mental games" such as these must be played with every element of every rule you learn.

Issue-Spotting

One of the keys to doing well on an essay examination is issue-spotting. In fact, issue-spotting is *the* most important skill you will learn in law school. If you recognize a legal issue, you can find the applicable rule of law (if there is one) by researching the issue. But if you fail to see the issues, you won't learn the steps that lead to success or failure on exams or, for that matter, in the practice of law. It is important to remember that (1) an issue is a question to be decided by the judge or jury and (2) a question is "in issue" when it can be disputed or argued about at trial. The bottom line is that *if you don't spot an issue, you can't raise it or discuss it.*

The key to issue-spotting is to learn to approach a problem in the same way an attorney does. Let's assume you've been admitted to practice and a client enters your office with a legal problem involving a dispute. He will recite his facts to you and give you any documents that may be pertinent. He will then want to know if he can sue (or be sued, if your client seeks to avoid liability). To answer your client's questions intelligently, you will have to decide the following: (1) what principles or rules can possibly be asserted by your client, (2) what defense or defenses can possibly be raised to these principles, (3) what issues may arise if these defenses are asserted, (4) what arguments each side can make to persuade the fact finder to resolve the issue in his favor, and (5) finally, what the *likely* outcome of each issue will be. *All of the issues that can possibly arise at trial will be relevant to your answers.*

How to Discuss an Issue

Keep in mind that *rules of law are the guides to issues* (i.e., an issue arises where there is a question whether the facts do, or do not, satisfy an element of a rule); a rule of law *cannot dispose of an issue* unless the rule can reasonably be *applied to the facts*.

Mini-Hypothetical

Dahlia has just died intestate. She is survived by Horatio, whom she married a year before her death. She had filed for divorce a month before her death but the divorce was not yet finalized. She is also survived by two grown children from a prior marriage, Sid and Nancy. Neither Sid nor Nancy have any children. Dahlia was killed while riding in a car driven by Nancy, who fell asleep at the wheel as a result of her prescription drug addiction. How should her estate be distributed?

Pertinent Principles of Law:

1. If If a person dies intestate, leaving a surviving spouse and one or more descendants who are not also the descendants of the surviving spouse, under the UPC the estate is distributed as follows: the first $150,000 of the estate plus one-half of the balance to the surviving spouse, and the remaining one-half of the balance to the descendants of the decedent, by representation.

2. A person's status as heir is determined as of the date of decedent's death, and a person remains a spouse until the dissolution of the marriage is final.

3. A person who feloniously and intentionally kills the decedent forfeits his or her interest in the estate of the decedent, including an intestate share. The share of that person passes as if the person disclaimed his or her interest in the estate of the decedent.

First Student Answer

Who are Dahlia's heirs?

Under the UPC, Horatio's share of the estate is the first $150,000 and one-half of the rest, because Dahlia had two descendants, Sid and Nancy, who were not descendants of Horatio. Sid and Nancy, Dahlia's descendants, take the remaining one-half.

Does Nancy lose her interest in the estate because she caused the death of Dahlia?

No. In order for the slayer statute to apply, Nancy would have to intentionally kill Dahlia. What Nancy did was likely a crime, and Dahlia's death was her fault, but it wasn't intentional, so she still receives her share of the estate.

Second Student Answer

Who are Dahlia's intestate heirs?

Because Dahlia died without a will, the takers of her estate are determined under the intestacy statutes. At the time of her death, Dahlia was still married to Horatio even though they had filed for divorce, so he still qualifies as a surviving spouse. Under the UPC, because Dahlia left descendants who were not also descendants of Horatio, Horatio's share as surviving spouse is the first $150,000 plus one-half of the balance of the estate. The remaining one-half is to be divided among the surviving descendants, Sid and Nancy, by representation, and because they are both in the same generation, they divide the remaining estate equally.

Did Nancy forfeit her share by causing the death of Dahlia?

If a person intentionally and feloniously kills another person, that person forfeits his or her interest in the estate of the victim. This includes the killer's share in the estate if the victim dies intestate. If this rule applies to Nancy, then she would not receive her one-half share of the remaining one-half of Dahlia's estate. It would instead pass as if she disclaimed her interest in the estate. Disclaimed property passes as if the disclaimant predeceased the decedent. If Nancy had children, then those children would receive her share of the estate. However, because she did not leave children, her one-half would instead pass to Sid as Dahlia's sole (presumed) surviving descendant.

The issue is whether Nancy's actions were felonious and intentional. Driving while under the influence of drugs is a crime, and a resulting death is also a crime, probably a felony. However, the killing must be *both* felonious and intentional and it does not appear that Nancy intended to kill Dahlia. Unless there are other facts, Nancy does not lose her interest in the estate.

Critique

The First Student Answer is too eager to give the answer without stating the rules. The student misses the issue of whether the divorce filing affects Horatio's status as surviving spouse and does not explain how Sid and Nancy would divide the remaining one-half. It is likely that the student knew that the divorce filing was irrelevant and that Sid and Nancy would divide the remaining estate equally, but the student failed to state that in the answer. The student did not "finish off" the answer by explaining how Sid and Nancy would divide the remaining estate. This is a common mistake in trust and estate questions. Once you have stated how a rule applies to the facts in determining who is entitled to assets from an estate, it is important to follow through completely. For example, if it is a Will question and you conclude that the Will is not enforceable, you should state who would receive the property instead.

On the second issue, the First Student is again too quick to draw a conclusion. The First Student did not completely state the rule. The First Student focused on the "intentional" requirement and decided that it was not met, so the slayer statute rule did not apply. However, it is important to identify those parts of a rule that are satisfied by the facts once application of a rule is raised as an issue. The "felonious" requirement may or may not have been met on these facts and should be discussed. Finally, because it is possible that you have drawn the wrong conclusion about application of a rule, you should give some indication of the result if you were wrong about the rule's application. The First Student's conclusory answer does not give the professor a good indication that the First Student knows the slayer statute rule thoroughly.

The Second Student makes the same conclusions as the First Student but takes the time to state the rules fully and follow through on how the property is to be distributed. The Second Student clearly states the applicable rules and then applies them to the facts. The Second Student does not stop at the first stage of division of the estate, between Horatio's share and the children's share, but then addresses how the children's share would be divided between Sid and Nancy. The Second Student also completes the discussion of the potential consequence of Nancy causing Dahlia's death by addressing where Nancy's share would go if she forfeited it.

Structuring Your Answer

Graders will give high marks to a clearly written, well-structured answer. Each issue you discuss should follow a specific and consistent structure that a grader can easily follow.

A format for analyzing each issue is the ***I-R-A-C format***. Here, the ***I*** stands for ***Issue***; the ***R*** for ***Rule of law***; the ***A*** for ***Application of the facts to the rule of law***; and the ***C*** for ***Conclusion***. I-R-A-C is a legitimate approach to the discussion of a particular issue, within the time constraints imposed by the question. The ***I-R-A-C format*** must be applied to each issue in the question; it is not the solution to the entire answer. If there are six issues in a question, for example, you should offer six separate, independent ***I-R-A-C*** analyses.

Another format that may be more appropriate depending on the question is the ***I-R-A-A-O format***. In this format, the ***I*** stands for ***Issue***; the ***R*** for

Rule of law; the first *A* for **one side's Argument**; the second *A* for **the other party's rebuttal Argument**; and the *O* for your **Opinion as to how the issue would be resolved**. The *I-R-A-A-O* format emphasizes the importance of (1) discussing **both** sides of an issue and (2) communicating to the grader that, where an issue arises, an attorney can only advise his or her client as to the **probable** decision on that issue.

We believe that the *I-R-A-C* approach is usually preferable to the *I-R-A-A-O* formula. However, either can be used to analyze and organize essay exam answers. Your choice may depend on how the exam question is asked. Whatever format you choose, however, you should remember the following rules:

First, **analyze all of the relevant facts**. Facts have significance in a particular case **only as they come under the applicable rules of law**. The facts presented must be analyzed and examined to see if they do or do not satisfy one element or another of the applicable rules, and the essential facts and rules must be stated and argued in your analysis.

Second, you must communicate to the grader the **precise rule of law** controlling the facts. In their eagerness to commence their arguments, students sometimes fail to state the applicable rule of law first. Remember, the *R* in either format stands for **Rule of law**. Defining the rule of law **before** an analysis of the facts is essential in order to allow the grader to follow your reasoning.

Third, it is important to treat **each side of an issue with equal detail**. If a hypothetical describes how a dying elderly woman tried to change her Will to benefit the kind neighbor who selflessly took care of her for years, your sympathies might understandably fall on the side of the neighbor, to validate the attempt at a Will. The grader will nevertheless expect you to see and make every possible argument for the other side. Don't permit your personal viewpoint to affect your answer! A good lawyer never does! When discussing an issue, always state the arguments for each side.

Finally, don't forget to **state your opinion or conclusion** on each issue. Keep in mind, however, that your opinion or conclusion is probably the **least** important part of an exam answer. Why? Because your professor knows that no attorney can tell his or her client exactly how a judge or jury will decide a particular issue. By definition, an issue is a legal dispute that can go either way. An attorney, therefore, can offer the client only his or her best opinion about the likelihood of victory or defeat on an issue. Because the decision on any issue lies with the judge or jury, no attorney can ever be absolutely certain of the resolution.

Discuss All Possible Issues

As we've noted, a student should draw **some** type of conclusion or opinion for each issue raised. Whatever your conclusion on a particular issue, it is essential to anticipate and discuss **all of the issues** that would arise if the question were actually tried in court.

Let's assume that a Wills question raises issues regarding revocation, interpretation, and ademption. If the Will was in fact revoked, then the other issues become moot. Nevertheless, even if you feel strongly that the will was in fact revoked, you *must* go on to discuss the other potential issues as well. If you were to terminate your answer after a discussion of revocation only, you'd receive an inferior grade.

Why should you have to discuss every possible issue if you are relatively certain that the outcome of a particular issue would be dispositive of the entire case? Because at the commencement of litigation, neither party can be **absolutely positive** about which issues he or she will prevail upon at trial. We can state with confidence that every attorney with some degree of experience has won issues he or she thought he or she would lose, and has lost issues on which victory seemed assured. Because one can never be absolutely certain how a factual issue will be resolved by the fact finder, a good attorney (and exam writer) will consider **all** possible issues.

To understand the importance of discussing all of the potential issues, you should reflect on what you will do in the actual practice of law. If you represent the plaintiff in a will contest, for example, it is your job to raise every possible claim that would invalidate the Will (assuming the claims are not frivolous). If there are five potential claims, and your pleadings rely on only three of them (because you're sure you will win on all three), and the other side is somehow successful on all three issues, your client may well sue you for malpractice. Your client's contention would be that you should be liable because if you had only raised the two additional issues, you might have prevailed on at least one of them, and therefore liability would have been avoided. It is an attorney's duty to raise **all** legitimate issues. A similar philosophy should be followed when taking essay exams.

What exactly do you say when you've resolved the initial issue that the Will in fact was revoked, and discussion of any additional issues about the Will would seem to be moot? The answer is simple. You begin the discussion of the next issue with something like, "Assuming, however, the court finds that the Will was not revoked, the next issue would be . . . ." The grader will understand and appreciate what you have done.

The corollary to the importance of raising all potential issues is that you should avoid discussion of obvious nonissues. Raising nonissues is detrimental in three ways: First, you waste a lot of precious time; second, you usually receive absolutely no points for discussing an issue that the grader deems extraneous; and third, it suggests to the grader that you lack the ability to distinguish the significant from the irrelevant. The best guideline for avoiding the discussion of a nonissue is to ask yourself, "Would I, as an attorney, feel comfortable about raising that particular issue or objection in front of a judge?"

Delineate the Transition from One Issue to the Next

It's a good idea to make it easy for the grader to see the issues you've found. One way to accomplish this is to cover no more than one issue per paragraph. Another way is to underline each issue statement. Provided that time permits, we recommend that you use both techniques. The essay answers in this book contain numerous illustrations of these suggestions.

One frequent student error is to write two separate paragraphs in which all of the arguments for one side are made in the initial paragraph, and all of the rebuttal arguments by the other side are made in the next paragraph. This organization is *a bad idea*. It obliges the grader to reconstruct the exam answer in his or her mind several times to determine whether all possible issues have been discussed by both sides. It will also cause you to state the same rule of law more than once. A better-organized answer presents a given argument by one side and follows that immediately in the same paragraph with the other side's rebuttal to that argument.

Understanding the "Call" of a Question

The statement *at the end* of an essay question or of the fact pattern in a multiple-choice question is sometimes referred to as the "call" of the question. It usually asks you to do something specific such as "discuss," "discuss the rights of the parties," "list X's rights," "advise X," "give the best grounds on which to find the statute unconstitutional," "recommend how the estate should be distributed," and so forth. The call of the question should be read carefully because it tells you exactly what you're expected to do. If a question asks, "what claims can X assert against Y?" or "what is Y liable to X for?" you don't have to spend a lot of time on Y's claims against Z. You will usually receive absolutely no credit for discussing issues or facts that are not required by the call. On the other hand, if the call of an essay question is simply "discuss" or "discuss the rights of the parties," then **all** foreseeable issues must be covered by your answer.

Students are often led astray by an essay question's call. For example, if you are asked for "X's claims against Y" or to "advise X," you may think you may limit yourself to X's viewpoint with respect to the issues. This is **not correct**! You cannot resolve one party's claims against another party without considering the issues that would arise (and the arguments the other side would assert) if litigation occurred. In short, although the call of the question may appear to focus on the claims of one of the parties to the litigation, a superior answer will cover all the issues and arguments that person might *encounter* (not just the arguments he or she would *make*) in attempting to pursue his or her claims against the other side.

The Importance of Analyzing the Question Carefully Before Writing

The overriding *time pressure* of an essay exam is probably a major reason why many students fail to analyze a question carefully before writing. Five minutes into the allocated time for a particular question, you may notice that the person next to you is writing furiously. This thought then flashes through your mind: "Oh my goodness, he's putting down more words on the paper than I am, and therefore he's bound to get a better grade." It can be stated *unequivocally* that there is no necessary correlation between the number of words on your exam paper and the grade you'll receive. Students who begin their answer after only five minutes of analysis have probably seen only the most obvious issues and missed many, if not most, of the subtle ones. They are also likely to be less well organized.

Opinions differ as to how much time you should spend analyzing and outlining a question before you actually write the answer. We believe that you should spend at least 12 to 18 minutes analyzing, organizing, and outlining a one-hour question before writing your answer. This will usually provide sufficient time to analyze and organize the question thoroughly **and** enough time to write a relatively complete answer. Remember that each word of the question must be scrutinized to determine if it (1) suggests an issue under the operative rules of law or (2) can be used in making an argument for the resolution of an issue. Because you can't receive points for an issue you don't spot, it is usually wise to read a question *twice* before starting your outline.

When to Make an Assumption

The instructions for a question may tell you to *assume* facts that are necessary to the answer. Even when these instructions are *not* given, you may be obliged to make certain assumptions about missing facts in order to write a thorough answer. Assumptions should be made only when you are told or when you, as the attorney for one of the parties described in the question, would be obliged to solicit additional information from your client. On the other hand, assumptions should *never be used to change or alter the question*. Don't ever write something like "if the facts in the question were . . . , instead of . . . , then . . . would result." If you do this, you are wasting time on facts that are extraneous to the problem before you. Professors want you to deal with *their* fact patterns, not your own.

Students sometimes try to "write around" information they think is missing. They assume that their professor has failed to include every piece of data necessary for a thorough answer. This is generally *wrong*. The professor may have omitted some facts deliberately to see if the student *can figure out what to do* under the circumstances. However, in some instances, the professor may have omitted them inadvertently (even law professors are human).

The way to deal with the omission of essential information is to describe (1) what fact (or facts) appears to be missing and (2) why that information is important. As an example, go back to the intestacy hypothetical we discussed above. In that fact pattern, there was no discussion about the relationship between Nancy and Dahlia and the circumstances of their being in the car together. Nancy may have intentionally drugged herself, planning to kill both her and Dahlia. Also not clear was whether Nancy's action's constituted a felony. The last sentences of the Second Student Answer above show that the student understood these subtleties and correctly supplied the essential missing facts and assumptions.

Assumptions should be made in a manner that keeps the other issues open (i.e., they lead to a discussion of all other possible issues). Don't assume facts that would virtually dispose of the entire hypothetical in a few sentences. For example, suppose that in A's Will, A stated that he was disinheriting B because B is a "convicted felon" (a statement that is inherently defamatory—i.e., a statement that tends to subject the plaintiff to hatred, contempt, or ridicule). If A's statement is true, his estate has a complete defense to B's action for defamation. If the facts don't tell whether A's statement was true or not, it would *not* be wise to write something like, "We'll assume that A's statement about B is accurate, and therefore B cannot successfully sue A's estate for defamation." So facile an approach would rarely be appreciated by the grader. The proper way to handle this situation would be to state, "If we assume that A's statement about B is not correct, A' cannot raise the defense of truth." You've communicated to the grader that you recognize the need to assume an essential fact and that you've assumed it in a way that enables you to proceed to discuss all other issues.

Case Names

A law student is ordinarily **not** expected to recall case names on an exam. The professor knows that you have read several hundred cases for each course and that you would have to be a memory expert to have all of the names at your fingertips. If you confront a fact pattern that seems similar to a case you have reviewed (but you cannot recall its name), just write something like "One case we've read held that . . . " or "It has been held that . . . ." In this manner, you have informed the grader that you are relying on a case that contained a fact pattern similar to the question at issue.

The only exception to this rule is in the case of a landmark decision (e.g., *Roe v. Wade*). Landmark opinions are usually those that change or alter established law. These cases are usually easy to identify because you will probably have spent an entire class period discussing each of them. *Hodel v. Irving, Estate of Rothko,* and *Claflin v. Claflin* are examples of landmark cases in Wills and Trusts. In these special cases, you may be expected to recall the case by name, as well as the proposition of law it stands for. However, this represents a very limited exception to the general rule that counsels against wasting precious time trying to memorize and reproduce case names.

How to Handle Time Pressures

What do you do when there are five minutes left in the exam and you have only written down two-thirds of your answer? One thing **not** to do is write something like "No time left!" or "Not enough time!" This gets you nothing but the satisfaction of knowing you have communicated your personal frustrations to the grader. Another thing **not** to do is insert in the exam booklet the outline you may have made on a piece of scrap paper. Professors will rarely look at these.

First of all, it is not necessarily a bad thing to be pressed for time. The person who finishes five minutes early has very possibly missed some important issues. The more proficient you become in knowing what is expected of you on an exam, the greater the difficulty you may experience in staying within the time limits. Second, remember that (at least to some extent) you're graded against your classmates' answers and they're under exactly the same time pressure as you. In short, don't panic if you can't write the "perfect" answer in the allotted time. Nobody does!

The best hedge against misuse of time is to **review as many old exams as possible**. These exercises will give you a familiarity with the process of organizing and writing an exam answer, which, in turn, should result in an enhanced ability to stay within the time boundaries. If you nevertheless find that you have about 15 minutes of writing to do and 5 minutes to do it in, write a paragraph that summarizes the remaining issues or arguments you would discuss if time permitted. As long as you've indicated that you're aware of the remaining legal issues, you'll probably receive some credit for them. Your analytical and argumentative skills will already be apparent to the grader by virtue of the issues that you have previously discussed.

Formatting Your Answer

Make sure that the way you write or type your answer presents your analysis in the best possible light. In other words, if you write, do so legibly. If you type, remember to use many paragraphs instead of just creating a document in which all of your ideas are merged into a single lengthy block of print. Remember, your professor may have a hundred or more exams to grade. If your answer is difficult to read, you will rarely be given the benefit of the doubt. On the other hand, a paper that is easy to read has a very positive mental impact upon the professor.

The Importance of Reviewing Prior Exams

As we've mentioned, it is *extremely important to review old exams*. The transition from blackletter law to essay exam can be a difficult experience if the process has not been practiced. Although this book provides a large number of essay and multiple-choice questions, ***don't stop here***! Most law schools have recent tests online or on file in the library, by course. If they are available only in the library, we strongly suggest that you make a copy of every old exam you can obtain (especially those given by your professors) at the beginning of each semester. The demand for these documents usually increases dramatically as "finals time" draws closer.

The exams for each course should be scrutinized ***throughout the semester***. They should be reviewed as you complete each chapter in your casebook. Sometimes the order of exam questions follows the sequence of the materials in your casebook. Thus, the first question on a law school test may involve the initial three chapters of the casebook; the second question may pertain to the fourth and fifth chapters; and so forth. In any event, ***don't wait*** until the semester is nearly over to begin reviewing old exams.

Keep in mind that no one is born with the ability to analyze questions and write superior answers to law school exams. Like any other skill, it is developed and perfected only through application. If you don't take the time to analyze numerous examinations from prior years, this evolutionary process just won't occur. Don't just ***think about*** the answers to past exam questions; take the time to ***write the answers down***. It's also wise to look back at an answer a day or two after you've written it. You will invariably see (1) ways to improve your organizational skills and (2) arguments you missed.

As you practice spotting issues on past exams, you will see how rules of law become the sources of issues on finals. As we've already noted, if you don't ***understand*** how rules of law translate into issues, you won't be able to achieve superior grades on your exams. Reviewing exams from prior years should also reveal that certain issues tend to be lumped together in the same question. For instance, where a fact pattern involves a younger relative lying to a frail testator, causing the testator to make a Will favoring the younger relative, three potential challenges to the Will are often present—testamentary capacity, undue influence, and fraud. You will need to see if any or all of these legal challenges apply to the facts.

Finally, one of the best means of evaluating if you understand a subject (or a particular area within a subject) is to attempt to create a hypothetical exam for that subject. Your exam should contain as many issues as possible. If you can write an issue-packed exam, you probably know that subject well. If you can't, then you probably haven't yet acquired an adequate understanding of how the principles of law in that subject can spawn issues.

As Always, a Caveat

The suggestions and advice offered in this book represent the product of many years of experience in the field of legal education. We are confident that the techniques and concepts described in these pages will help you prepare for, and succeed at, your exams. Nevertheless, particular professors sometimes have a preference for exam-writing techniques that are not stressed in this book. Some instructors expect at least a nominal reference to the ***prima facie*** elements of all pertinent legal theories (even though one or more of those principles are ***not*** placed into issue). Other professors want their students to emphasize public policy considerations in the arguments they make on a particular issue. Because this book is intended for nationwide consumption, these individualized preferences have **not** been stressed. The best way to find out whether your professor has a penchant for a particular writing approach is to ask him or her to provide you with a model answer to a previous exam. If a model answer is not available, speak to second- or third-year students who received a superior grade in that professor's class.

One final point. Although the rules of law stated in the answers to the questions in this book have been drawn from commonly used sources (casebooks, hornbooks, etc.), it is still conceivable that they may be slightly at odds with those taught by your professor. In the area of wills and trusts law, there are differences from jurisdiction to jurisdiction, and your professor will probably advise you to follow the Uniform Probate Code and the Uniform Trust Code or the laws of the state in which you are located. In instances in which a conflict exists between our formulation of a legal principle and the one taught by your professor, ***follow the latter***! Because your grades are determined by your professors, their views should always supersede the views contained in this book.

Essay Questions

Question 1

On July 1, 2000, Tom properly executed a will, which created a $50,000 trust for Lil, the 65-year-old widow of Tom's brother Bob, who died without issue. The trustee was directed to pay to Lil "as much of the income and, if income be insufficient, as much of the principal, as may be required for her proper support and maintenance, for so long as she lives." After providing for the remainder interest in this trust to go to the American Red Cross on Lil's death, Tom gave "the rest and residue of my estate to the surviving issue of my brothers, per stirpes."

On July 1, 2003, while Tom was confined to the hospital for major surgery, a new will was delivered to Tom in a sealed envelope by two secretaries from his attorney's office. One of them told Tom, "We have a will here that Attorney Smith has asked us to deliver to you for your signature and that we are to witness." Tom opened the envelope, read the document carefully, and then signed it at the end in front of the secretaries. He then handed it to them. The secretaries walked to a small table in the hallway around the corner from Tom's room, signed the paper on the lines provided for their signature, and then immediately returned the paper to Tom. Under the new will, nephew E was made the sole residuary beneficiary; the rest of the will remained the same as the 2000 will. The 2003 will did not expressly revoke the 2000 will.

Tom died in an automobile accident last month. He was never married and left no issue. He is survived by:

1. A and B, grandchildren of his deceased brother Sam and children of Sam's deceased son James;
2. C, son of his deceased brother John;
3. D and E, children of his deceased brother Frank; and
4. Lil, the 65-year-old widow of Tom's brother Bob.

The original of the 2000 will was found in Tom's safe-deposit box. It bears no evidence of acts of revocation. The 2003 will cannot be found, but an unsigned copy is in Attorney Smith's possession. The $50,000 trust produces a net annual income of $6,000.

1. Which will, if either, should be admitted to probate? Discuss.
2. Except for the $50,000 trust, what difference, if any, does it make to the family whether they take under the 2000 will or under the laws of intestacy? Discuss.
3. Lil's support needs are approximately $1,000 per month; she has pension and other income of $500 per month and has been making up the difference by withdrawals from savings. If either will is admitted to probate, should the trustee pay Lil $1,000 per month or $500 per month? Discuss.

Question 2

Henry has recently died, leaving an estate consisting entirely of his separate property, valued at $500,000. He is survived by his wife, Wanda; his mother, Maude; his daughter; Sally (by a previous marriage); and his brother, Budi. A typewritten will that Henry executed on April 15, 2000, has been filed with the court and reads as follows:

Will of Henry

1. I give $5,000 to my daughter, Sally.
2. I give the rest of my estate to my mother, Maude.
3. I appoint my friend Wanda as executrix of my will.

The will was published and signed by Henry in the presence of Wanda and Sally who, in Henry's presence and in the presence of each other, signed as subscribing witnesses.

Wanda and Henry were married on January 15, 2001. Shortly thereafter, Henry's lawyer, Lana, prepared a new will for Henry, and that will was properly executed in Lana's office on January 30, 2001. That will left Henry's entire estate to Wanda. The original of that will has not been found, but a photocopy is in Lana's files, and it contains a clause expressly revoking all prior wills.

If called as a witness, Lana will testify that (1) the photocopy in her file is a correct copy of the 2001 will and (2) in December 2008 she tore up the original of the 2001 will at Henry's direction and in his presence.

If called as a witness, Lana's law clerk, Charles, will testify that (1) he was called into Lana's office one day in December 2008, when Lana and Henry were both present; (2) Lana told him that the scraps of paper on the desk were Henry's 2001 will, which she had destroyed at Henry's request; and (3) Henry then nodded his head affirmatively and said, "Now things are back the way I want them; Wanda won't get a penny of my property."

Assuming Lana and Charles testify as stated above and their testimony is properly admitted, how should Henry's estate be distributed? Discuss.

Question 3

Teddy had a duly executed will that left his estate in trust for his wife, Wilma, for her life, remainder to Wilma's daughter, Taylor. The original will was kept at the lawyer's office. Teddy had essentially raised Taylor as his own daughter, though he never adopted her. Teddy had no other living relatives. While Teddy was on a business trip in San Francisco, he discovered that Wilma was involved in an internet relationship with a man in Denmark and that she was planning to meet him in person, lying to Teddy that she was visiting the orphanage that they had founded in Mexico. Teddy was furious and called his lawyer at home. He told the lawyer that he intended to disinherit Wilma and leave his entire estate in equal shares to Taylor and to their Mexican orphanage. He told the lawyer to immediately shred the existing will and prepare a new will along those lines and that he would be in the lawyer's office the next afternoon to sign the new will. In his hotel room, Teddy also wrote in his journal, "The will must be revoked!" and then signed and dated the entry as he always did. The lawyer shredded the will, prepared the new will, and the next afternoon waited for Teddy, but Teedy didn't show. Teddy unfortunately had been killed that morning in a car accident on the way to the San Francisco airport. Teddy's home state does not recognize holographic wills, but California does. How will Teddy's estate be distributed?

Question 4

Three years ago, Alfred Dinsmore executed a will that contained the following provisions:

1. I give my government bonds to Yale College;
2. I give 10 percent of the balance of my estate to my nephew, John, on the condition that he is still married, at the time of my death, to his present wife, Kathleen;
3. I give the residue of my estate to my niece Barbara.

Early last year, Alfred wrote the following letter to his niece Barbara:

> I have established a trust for your children at ABC Bank. This trust is worth approximately $50,000 and is composed of all my U.S. and state X bonds. You can decide how these funds should be used.

This is the only document evidencing Alfred's intention to establish a trust. Barbara's two children, Carol and David, are minors.

When Alfred wrote his will, he owned U.S. bonds worth $20,000, state X bonds worth $30,000, and state Z bonds worth $50,000. Alfred died a few weeks ago. At his death, all of these bonds were still registered in his name and had never been out of his possession.

John and Kathleen were divorced three months before Alfred's death, which was unexpected.

At his death, Alfred was unmarried and was survived by his nephew John (who had no children), his niece Barbara, and Barbara's two children, Carol and David.

1. What are the rights of John and Barbara and of Barbara's children? Discuss.
2. If the court finds a valid trust was created by Alfred's letter to Barbara, what are Yale's rights? Discuss.

Question 5

Arthur and Phyllis were a middle-aged couple who had been dating for years. Arthur purchased a home, and he and Phyllis moved in together. Arthur then went to an estate planning lawyer and had a revocable living trust prepared, leaving Phyllis a life estate in the residence and the remainder of his estate to his two children from a prior marriage. Arthur was named as trustee, and the lawyer was named as the successor trustee. The trust agreement provided that it could be amended or revoked "by a duly executed document delivered to the trustee." He properly executed the trust and also executed a will leaving all of his property to the trustee of the revocable living trust. He did not transfer any property into the trust except for a few shares of stock. Five years later he contacted the lawyer and said that he wanted to leave the home to Phyllis outright. The lawyer prepared a new page for the trust agreement changing the gift to Phyllis from a life estate to an outright gift, substituted the page in the original trust agreement, which was stored at the lawyer's office, and sent a copy of the trust agreement with the new page to Arthur. Arthur also added Phyllis's name to a bank account as joint tenant with right of survivorship. Arthur died three years later, and his children are claiming that the change to the trust was invalid and that Arthur named Phyllis as joint tenant on the bank account just for convenience, so she should not receive the funds in the bank account. Discuss whether the trust amendment is valid and whether Phyllis is entitled to the bank account as surviving joint tenant.

Question 6

Ten years ago, Daniel, a widower, executed a valid, typed will containing the following dispositive provisions:

1. I give $5,000 to my daughter, Alice.
2. I give $10,000 to my brother, John.
3. I give the residue of my estate to my son, Bill. It is my wish that my son use whatever portion of the residue of my estate he deems appropriate to provide for my sister Karen.

John was one of the two witnesses to Daniel's will.

Shortly before the execution of the will, Daniel and John orally agreed that John would convey any property he would receive under Daniel's will to Daniel's sister, Lois.

One year after executing the will, Daniel drew an ink line through the "$5,000" figure in the bequest to Alice, and then wrote above it in ink the figure "$50,000." Daniel also wrote his initials next to the "$50,000" figure.

For many years prior to his death, Daniel had made regular payments to Karen to help her meet ordinary living expenses.

Daniel recently died and is survived by his children, Alice and Bill; by his brother, John; and by his sisters, Karen and Lois. His net estate is $100,000.

What are the rights of Alice, Bill, John, Karen, and Lois to Daniel's estate? Discuss.

Question 7

Agatha loaned $300,000 to her brother, George. George never repaid any part of the loan. When he died three years later, George left a will that provided that if Agatha forgave the $300,000 debt in writing, a $300,000 trust would be created for her by his executor under his will (Trust #1). Agatha forgave the debt and agreed to look to the trust instrument instead. Under the trust, Agatha is to receive the income for life. Upon her death the corpus is to be distributed to Betty, Agatha's daughter.

After making several other specific bequests, George left his residuary estate in Trust #2, for the benefit of five named beneficiaries. Agatha was not included as a beneficiary of this trust.

Both of the trusts created by George's will contained spendthrift provisions stating that creditors could not reach the income in the trustee's hands.

Nancy, George's accountant, was designated trustee of Trust #1, and Agatha was designated trustee of Trust #2. Each trustee was authorized to sell trust assets.

Before George's death, Agatha borrowed $15,000 from John, a fellow worker. Agatha repaid $5,000 to John and then defaulted. John, who knew about the trust for Agatha, asked her to use her income from the trust to cure the default. She told John that the spendthrift provision prevented her from doing that, but she offered, instead, to sell John 100 shares of TT&A stock from the corpus of Trust #2 for $10,000. The fair market value of the stock was then $21,000. John agreed and purchased the stock from Agatha as trustee of Trust #2 with a check for $10,000.

Six months later, John gave the TT&A stock to his nephew Larry as a wedding present. Larry had no notice of the prior transactions and still has possession of the stock.

What are the rights and liabilities of John, Agatha, and Larry? Discuss.

Question 8

Thirty years ago, Thea executed a trust instrument for "my children," naming State Bank as trustee. At the time of execution, Thea was pregnant with her first child by her husband, Fred.

Thea delivered 80 shares of Disney stock to the Bank under the trust. The trust instrument provided for distribution to Thea's "children" in equal shares upon Thea's death.

Thea died last month. She is survived by her two youngest children. Her oldest child, who was born shortly after the creation of the trust, died two years ago, leaving one son, who also survived Thea.

Eight years ago, Thea executed a valid will in which she gave 100 shares of Disney stock to her husband Fred "out of shares held by me at my death" and "the residue of my estate to my children in equal shares." Six years ago, after she and Fred were divorced, Thea executed a valid codicil. In her codicil, she revoked the gift to Fred and gave 100 shares of Disney stock to her close friend Sal "out of shares held by me at death."

When she executed her will, Thea personally owned 100 shares of Disney stock. After the codicil was executed, a one-for-two stock dividend was declared and issued, and Thea owned 150 shares of Disney stock at her death. After Thea's death, a two-for-three stock dividend was declared, so that her estate held 250 shares at the time of distribution. The trust held 120 shares of Disney stock at Thea's death and, as a result of the two-for-three stock dividend, now holds 200 shares.

Assume that the jurisdiction's applicable statutory provisions are the same as comparable provisions of the Uniform Probate Code.

How should Thea's estate and the trust assets be distributed? Discuss.

Question 9

Alice's husband died more than 20 years ago. Ten years after his death, Alice executed a written instrument transferring $200,000 to Bank in trust for her son Daniel, then 25, and her sister Celia, then 40. Under the terms of the trust, Celia and Daniel were each to receive one-half the income for 10 years, at the end of which each was to receive one-half the principal and any accumulated and undistributed income. If either died during the 10-year period, then, at his or her death, his or her share would be distributed to his or her estate.

Six years ago, Phil, a building contractor, sued Celia for $40,000. While the suit was pending, Alice, Bank, Celia, and Daniel executed a written agreement which amended the trust instrument by adding the following:

> No interest hereunder (i) shall be assigned or alienated by any beneficiary, or (ii) shall be subject to the claims of any creditor of any beneficiary.

After the amendment was executed, Phil obtained a judgment against Celia for $40,000. Celia was insolvent (apart from her interest in the trust) and could not pay the judgment. Phil has tried to attach Celia's interest in the trust to satisfy the judgment.

A year ago, Alice executed a valid will. The will gave $100,000 to Bank as trustee under Alice's trust, $50,000 in cash to Celia, and the remainder of the estate to her old friend Stan. One of the two attesting witnesses to the will was Doris, Celia's daughter. Celia died six months ago. Alice died one month ago.

Alice's only surviving heirs are Doris and Daniel.

In probate proceedings, Daniel asserts the invalidity of Alice's will on the following grounds:

Daniel is not mentioned in the will;

The $100,000 bequest to Bank as trustee should fail because the trust document was not executed in compliance with the Statute of Wills;

The $50,000 bequest to Celia lapsed at her death, and Doris has no claim because she was a witness to the will.

1. How should Alice's estate be distributed? Discuss.
2. Can Phil still reach Celia's interest in the trust? Discuss.

Question 10

Ten years ago, Tina, her husband Hector, and their two adult children Charlie and Sally were residents of the state of Terra. They lived in a house owned by Tina. At that time, Tina wrote, dated, and signed her will entirely in her own handwriting. The will provides as follows:

> I want my house to go to my daughter, Sally. All my other property of any kind is to go to my husband, Hector, if he survives me, and otherwise to Sally.

Sally acted as witness to Tina's signing and dating of the will and then added her signature under the word "witness." Terra requires that a handwritten will be witnessed and signed by two witnesses.

Charlie died eight years ago. He was survived by his one-year-old son, George. Five years ago, Tina and Hector moved to the state of Calco. A year later, Hector died intestate. Shortly thereafter, Tina gave Sally $300,000 for the purchase of a home. At the time of the gift, Tina stated in writing that the gift was an advancement.

Recently, Tina died while still a resident of Calco. She never revoked or modified her will. Tina was survived by Sally and by George, who was living with his mother in Terra and whom Tina had never seen. When Tina died, her house in Calco was worth $200,000. Her other assets were worth a total of $50,000.

You may assume that the Probate Code of the state of Calco is the same as the Uniform Probate Code.

1. Is Tina's will effective in Calco? Discuss.
2. How should the assets of Tina's estate be distributed? Discuss.

Question 11

Tippi, a very wealthy woman, decided to endow a public library in her home city. To carry out her plan, Tippi executed the following documents:

1. A declaration stating her intention to create the Tippi Library for the use of the inhabitants of the city. She designated as trustees three persons to serve on the first Tippi Library Board of Governors (the Board) and provided for the selection of successor members of the Board in the event of death or resignation of a member or members;

2. A deed conveying a block of land Tippi owned near the city center to the Board, "in perpetuity," for the purposes stated in her declaration;

3. A check payable to the Board in the sum of $100,000, as an initial contribution for the library; and

4. A document containing an itemized list of a number of Tippi's stocks and bonds having a market value of $2 million, and a statement that these stocks and bonds were to be delivered to the Board in specified installments over a 2-year period.

The declaration, check, deed, and the securities list have all been delivered to the Board. The Board has recorded the deed, cashed the check, and deposited the proceeds in a bank account entitled "Tippi Library Board." No funds have been withdrawn from, or charged to, the account.

Tippi died three months after all these events occurred but before any of the securities were transferred to the Board under the document for specified installments. Tippi left a valid will naming her only child, Betty, as executrix and sole beneficiary. Tippi's husband predeceased her.

The $100,000 fund held by the Board is not sufficient to construct a library building on the land or to maintain a library. If the specified stocks and bonds are transferred to the Board, a library building can be constructed and the library maintained.

The Board has proposed to use the block of land as a public park if it fails in its efforts to get Tippi's stocks and bonds. The park will be named Tippi Memorial Park. The funds now in the Board's possession are sufficient to maintain the land as a public park for at least ten years.

Betty has brought suit (1) to recover the block of land and all the money in the Tippi Library Board bank account and (2) for a declaratory judgment that all of the stocks and bonds on Tippi's itemized list are free from any claim by the Board. The Board has responded by asserting all applicable rights and defenses.

To what relief, if any, are Betty and the Board entitled? Discuss.

Question 12

Leonard and Fay Woods had two children, Michael and Linda. Michael was married to Wanda, and they had one adopted child, Roberta. Linda was unmarried and childless. On March 25, 1995, Fay executed a will, with the necessary legal formalities, which contained the following provisions:

> To my daughter, Linda, I give my business property at 1125 Main Street, and such of my jewelry as is enumerated on the list that will be found in my jewel box. To my son, Michael, I give my 1,000 shares of XYZ Class A stock. To my husband, Leonard, I give the rest and residue of my estate.

Leonard and Fay were divorced in November 1996. They had not entered into a property settlement agreement. In January 1997, Michael was killed in a plane crash. In April 1997, Fay sold the business property at 1125 Main Street for $20,000 and deposited one-half the proceeds in her commercial account and the other one-half in a savings account in the name of "Fay Woods, Trustee for Linda Woods." In May 1997, XYZ Corporation declared a stock dividend of one-half share of Class A stock and one-half share of Class B stock for each share of Class A stock held by Fay.

Fay died last month. The following typed note was discovered in her jewel box:

> In accordance with the provisions of my will of March 25, 1995, I want my daughter, Linda, to have the following jewelry found herein: Grandmother Barnes's diamond ring, my wedding rings, and my pearl necklace and earrings.

The note was signed and dated March 25, 1995.

All these events took place, and all of Fay's property was located, in the state of Franklin. Fay's estate, after payment of all taxes, expenses, and debts consists of 1,500 shares of XYZ Class A stock; 500 shares of XYZ Class B stock; the jewelry described in the March 25, 1995, note; $10,000 in the savings account in the name of "Fay Woods, Trustee for Linda Woods"; and $15,000 in her commercial account. All property was Fay's separate property.

Assume that (1) the applicable statutory law of Franklin is the same as comparable provisions of the Uniform Probate Code, and (2) Fay's parents are no longer living.

How should Fay's estate be distributed? Discuss.

Essay Questions

Question 13

The following events all occurred in state Y.

On January 5, 1998, Tess executed a valid and attested will naming her mother Martha as her sole beneficiary. In July 2000 Tess married Hubert Jones. Shortly after her marriage, Tess signed a document, entirely in her own handwriting, which reads as follows:

> Codicil to my will of 1/5/98. One-half of my property to my husband Hubert; one-fourth of my property to State University; the rest to my mother.
>
> 8/4/00
> Tess Jones

In January 2008 a son, Sonny, was born to Tess and Hubert. Tess recently became upset by the signs of professionalism in college athletics and especially the fact that State University constantly had national championship teams in several sports. After watching State trounce A&M in the Apple Bowl, she signed a document that was entirely in her own handwriting and that read as follows:

> I revoke my codicil of 8/4/00. Nothing to athletic factories like State University. I want to benefit a college that has no athletic program. The one-fourth of my property is to go to Harvale College for academic scholarships.
>
> Tess Jones

Tess died in an auto accident two weeks after making the second codicil. She is survived by Martha, Hubert, and Sonny. Her estate, after payment of all taxes, debts, and expenses of administration, consists of cash and securities having a total value of $300,000.

Harvale is a private, nonprofit college. Unbeknownst to Tess, the regents of State University had voted to discontinue all intercollegiate athletic programs prior to Tess's execution of the second codicil. However, their decision was not announced until after Tess's death.

Assume that the applicable statutory law of state Y is the same as the comparable provisions of the Uniform Probate Code.

How should Tess's estate be distributed? Discuss.

Question 14

Nelly died a widow, leaving a two-page, handwritten will containing two dispository clauses. Clause 1 provided for bequests of $10,000 "to each of my children, Ann, Brad, and Charlie." Clause 2 provided that all of Nelly's stocks and bonds be given to Brad, "to be used as we have agreed." Nelly's home and personal effects, together worth $60,000, were not disposed of by the will.

Nelly signed her name on the bottom of page 1 of the will. Page 2 contained only the date in her handwriting and Brad's signature under the word "witness." When the will was offered for probate, several lines were drawn through Ann's name in Clause 1.

Brad is prepared to testify that several months after signing the will, Nelly, in his presence, drew lines through Ann's name and told him she wanted to disinherit Ann. Brad is also prepared to testify that he had agreed with Nelly to use the income from the stocks and bonds for Charlie during his life but that the stocks and bonds were to be Brad's after Charlie's death. Charlie died several months before Nelly, leaving no spouse or descendants.

The estate includes, in addition to Nelly's home and personal effects, $10,000 in cash and stocks and bonds worth $70,000.

Assume that the applicable statutory law of the state is the same as the comparable provisions of the Uniform Probate Code.

Is the will valid? Discuss.

How should the estate be distributed? Discuss.

Question 15

The following events all occurred in state A.

In November 2007, T. Tate, a widower, instructed his lawyer to prepare the following document:

> I, T. Tate, a widower, dispose of all my estate as follows: I give my sister Sally one-half and my favorite nephew, Sally's son Ron, the other one-half. I have intentionally omitted all of my other heirs.

After reading the document, Tate told the attorney he wanted to think about the matter some more and took the document with him without signing it. A week later, on December 2, 2007, Tate attended a dinner party at Sally's house. After dinner and a few drinks, Tate announced that he wanted to execute his will and took the document from his pocket. Slightly intoxicated, Tate signed and correctly dated the document in the presence of all the dinner guests. Tate then had Sally and two of her guests sign as witnesses.

On January 20, 2008, Tate again consulted his lawyer and told him he wanted a new will prepared, revoking all prior bequests and leaving his entire estate to the Child Care Foundation (CCF), a recognized charitable organization. While Tate was still in the office, the lawyer had his secretary type a memorandum correctly setting forth Tate's requests. Tate signed that memorandum and gave it to the lawyer.

Tate died of a heart attack three weeks after signing the January 20, 2008, memorandum. The document dated December 2, 2007, was found in Tate's desk. Across the document was the following statement, written in Tate's handwriting: "This will is canceled; I have made a new will. TT."

Tate was survived by his son Art, his sister Sally, and Sally's two sons, Don and Zeke, his only relatives. Tate never had a nephew named Ron.

The applicable statutory law of state A is the same as the Uniform Probate Code.

How should Tate's estate be distributed? Discuss.

Question 16

Tawny, a widow, died a few months ago. In searching through her effects, her children found an undated document in her top desk drawer. The document was in Tawny's handwriting and was signed by her. It stated:

> My wishes for the distribution of my estate are described on two pieces of paper which are in the bottom drawer of my desk.
>
> (Signed) Tawny

In Tawny's bottom desk drawer, the children found the following papers:

Document #1

On a form of deed that Tawny had purchased at a local stationery store, all the necessary ingredients of a valid conveyance of Tawny's house, designating her daughter Ann as grantee. The deed was properly executed. Attached to the deed with a paper clip was a note stating:

> This is for my beloved daughter. I hope that she enjoys it as much as I have.
>
> (Signed) Tawny
> June 1, 2007

The note was typewritten, except for Tawny's signature and the date.

Document #2

A paper, dated June 1, 2008, stating:

> All my money—brother Bob
>
> ABC stock—sister Shirley
>
> Jewelry—Ann

The note was typewritten, except that the words "brother Bob" had a handwritten line drawn through them. Above them, in Tawny's handwriting, was written, "son Sam."

Document #3

A handwritten, undated piece of paper, stating at the top "Page 2" and continuing:

> I meant to mention in the first page of my will that everything else should be divided equally among Bob, Shirley, and Ann.
>
> (Signed) Tawny

Essay Questions

Tawny was survived by her daughter Ann, her son Sam, her brother Bob, and her sister Shirley.

Tawny's estate consists of her house, valued at $250,000; furniture located in the house worth $10,000; $100,000 in cash; and $50,000 worth of stock in ABC Corp. She owned no jewelry but did own a $10,000 diamond- and ruby-studded jewelry box. ABC stock has split three for one.

The applicable statutory law is the same as the Uniform Probate Code.

How should Tawny's estate be distributed? Discuss.

Question 17

Andy and Patty were engaged to be married. Both of them had been married before and had children from their previous marriages. Andy had two sons, and Patty had three daughters. Patty was a lot younger and much poorer than Andy. A week before their wedding, they signed identical wills, leaving everything to each other, and if the other predeceased, in equal shares to Andy's sons and Patty's daughters. They also stated in the wills that the wills were a result of a contract between the two of them, agreeing that the survivor would leave his or her estate equally to Andy's sons and Patty's daughters in consideration of the first to die agreeing to leave everything to the survivor. The wills did not mention that Andy and Patty were planning to marry. They got married a week later. Five years later Andy died without changing his will. The applicable state statute provided: "If, after making a will, a testator marries, and no provision in the will has been made for the possibility of future marriage, the subsequent marriage acts as a revocation on the will." Andy's sons argue that Andy's will is revoked by the statute, so he died intestate, and the applicable intestacy laws would divide his estate between Patty and the two sons. Patty argues that the will is valid and she is entitled to the entire estate. Discuss the arguments for each position.

Question 18

Trisha Tait personally typed this draft of her will:

September 17, 1995

> I, Trisha Tait, being of sound mind, hereby publish this as my last will.
>
> First. To my son, Sal, I give my 150 shares of Minco stock.
>
> Second. To my daughter, Diane, I give my 500 shares of Oilco stock.
>
> Third. My personal effects located in the wall safe in my living room I give to my friend Bill.
>
> Fourth. To my husband, Hoby, I give the rest, residue, and remainder of my estate.

Tait did not execute this will. The following appears in Tait's handwriting across the bottom of the draft:

June 15, 2003

> Being of sound mind, I adopt my draft will, dated September 17, 1995, written above as my last will. TT

On July 1, 2003, Oilco merged with Zebco. The Oilco shareholders received one share of Zebco stock in exchange for each share of Oilco stock.

Tait died last month.

Tait's son Sal died in August 2004. Sal's sole surviving heirs are his father Hoby, his wife Ann, and his adopted daughter Helen. After payment of all expenses of administration, taxes, and debts, Tait's estate included only the following: 50 shares of Abco stock (worth $5,000) in the living room wall safe; $100,000 in various bank accounts; personal jewelry in the living room wall safe; 300 shares of Minco stock (worth $60,000) and 500 shares of Zebco stock (worth $15,000) in a bank safe-deposit box. The personal jewelry was placed in the wall safe on July 1, 2005.

Assume that the applicable statutory law is the same as the comparable provisions of the Uniform Probate Code.

1. Is there a valid will? Discuss.
2. If the will is valid, how should the estate be distributed? Discuss.
3. If the will is not valid, how should the estate be distributed? Discuss.
4. If Hoby predeceased Tait, and Tait had married a man named John one month before her death, how should the estate be distributed? Discuss.

Question 19

The following events all occurred in state Y.

When Timothy Thomas died recently, three documents were found in an envelope in his safe-deposit box.

The first read, in its entirety:

> I, Timothy Thomas, make this will, one-half to my sister Bessie and the other one-half to the Boys Club. Sept. 20, 2005.
>
> Witness: William Wordsworth

The second read:

> I'm changing my previous will—Bessie doesn't need all that—all stocks listed in my black book go to Bessie's child—June 30, 2008.
>
> Timothy Thomas

The third was a black notebook containing accurate records of all of Thomas's purchases and sales of securities. All entries were dated prior to June 30, 2008, with the exception of two entries. These showed a sale of 100 shares of ABC stock and the purchase of 100 shares of XYZ stock, both on July 7, 2008.

Each entry in the black notebook was made by Thomas on the actual date of the corresponding transaction.

All writing in the three documents is in Thomas's handwriting, except the words "Witness: William Wordsworth" in the first document. These words are typewritten.

Thomas was never married. His surviving next of kin are his sister, Bessie, and Bessie's daughter, Dorothy.

Thomas's estate consists of the following: 300 shares of ABC stock purchased prior to June 30, 2008, having a fair market value of $30,000; 100 shares of XYZ stock purchased on July 7, 2008, having a fair market value of $10,000; and $100,000 cash in bank accounts.

Assume that the applicable statutory law of state Y is the same as comparable provisions of the Uniform Probate Code.

As among Bessie, the Boys Club, and Dorothy, how should Timothy Thomas's estate be distributed? Discuss.

Question 20

Ten years ago, Tammy Thor, a widow, validly executed a formal, witnessed will (Will #1) which contained the following dispositive clauses:

> (1) to my friend Robert Rood, $10,000 to be used by him for the education of his daughter Carrie;
>
> (2) the residue of my estate to my friend Doris Drake, trustee, in trust, to pay the income to my daughter Ethel so long as Ethel may live and upon Ethel's death to distribute the trust corpus to my then-living heirs; the trustee may invade the corpus if necessary for the proper care and maintenance of Ethel.

Three years ago, Thor signed a dated, typewritten document purporting to be her last will and testament (Will #2). The document was identical to Will #1, except that the last clause of the residuary bequest, giving the trustee power to invade the corpus, was omitted. This will was attested by only one subscribing witness.

Thor recently died. Will #1 and Will #2 were found in Thor's safe-deposit box. Stapled to Will #1 was the following document, in Thor's handwriting:

> This will is hereby canceled and revoked. I have made a new will.
>
> Tammy Thor

The note was dated, in Thor's handwriting, one day subsequent to the date on Will #2.

Thor was survived by the following heirs and legatees and no others:

A. Ethel, her daughter;

B. Robert Rood, her friend, and Carrie, Robert's 16-year-old daughter;

C. John and Gil, sons of her deceased sister Anne;

D. Warren, grandson of her deceased sister Bessie; and

E. Doris Drake, her friend.

Ethel died before distribution of Thor's estate. By a valid will, Ethel left her entire estate to her friend Sandra.

1. Did Thor die testate or intestate? Discuss.

2. Assuming Thor died testate, what persons are entitled to Thor's estate, and what share or interest will each receive? Discuss.

3. Assuming Thor died intestate, what persons are entitled to Thor's estate, and what share or interest will each receive? Discuss.

Question 21

The testator died in 1936, leaving a will that divided his residuary estate into four trusts, one for each of his four children. The will stated:

> Upon the attainment by each child of his or her 45th year, I direct that the trustee pay absolutely and forever, to said child one-half of the principal of the trust for such child, and thereafter pay to such child the entire income of the remaining one-half of such part so long as such child shall live, and upon the death of such child, pay the remaining principal to the child's then surviving issue. If any of my children predecease me, or if surviving me, die prior to his or her 45th year, then I direct the entire principal of the trust for such child so dying shall be paid to and vest absolutely in the issue of such child so dying, or if there is no such issue, then to the surviving brothers and sisters of such child so dying and the issue of any deceased brother or sister, by right of representation.

In addition the Will stated "the term 'issue' and words of similar import shall not include adopted persons."

Testator's last surviving daughter, Gladys, has just died at age 96. Gladys had two adopted children, one of whom is still living and one of whom predeceased her, leaving two children now living. Gladys's three siblings and all of their descendants are now dead, but Gladys's brother's wife is still alive. How is the remainder of Gladys's trust to be distributed?

Question 22

Betty and Wilma had been business partners and close friends for many years. Both were widows and each had two children.

In 2000, Betty executed a will in which she bequeathed "$100,000 to my close friend Wilma, if she survives me; otherwise, to the natural persons who are beneficiaries of Wilma's last will and testament, and if she dies intestate, to her next of kin." The residue of Betty's estate was bequeathed "to my children, share and share alike." In 1994, both of Betty's children died, survived by issue. Her son, Charles, left two sons, George and Fred. Her daughter, Jane, left a daughter, Alice.

Wilma had drawn a will in 1995 leaving her entire estate "one-half to my children and one-half to State University." In 2005, thinking that her son Bill had failed to thank her for an expensive present (a new Volvo she had given to him), Wilma drew a codicil, providing, "I hereby delete from my will the gift to my son, Bill. Because of his ingratitude, I leave him nothing." In fact, Bill had sent Wilma a "thank you" e-mail, but Wilma had accidentally deleted it without reading it.

Last week, Betty and Wilma were killed in an airplane crash while en route to a convention. Betty's next of kin were her three grandchildren. Wilma's next of kin were her two children, Bill and Mary.

Betty and Wilma each left a net estate of $500,000 in cash and marketable securities.

Assume the applicable statutory law is the same as comparable provisions of the Uniform Probate Code.

How should their estates be distributed? Discuss.

Question 23

Ball transferred $100,000 in trust to Trust Company for the benefit of his son Sam. The income was to be distributed to Sam during Sam's life, and the remainder of the trust was to pass to Sam's children living at the time of Sam's death. Ball could, according to the terms of the trust, revoke the trust, provided that the revocation was in writing signed by him and delivered to the trustee. The trust also contained a spendthrift clause.

After the creation of the trust, Sam married Pearl and they had one child, Carol. Two years after the birth of Carol, Pearl divorced Sam. Pearl took this action because Sam had become a chronic alcoholic. When Ball learned of the divorce and that a large alimony award had been given to Pearl, Ball called the trustee and stated, "I revoke the trust and will confirm this revocation by letter." However, Ball died the following day, before he had written the letter. Ball died intestate. Sam was Ball's only child. Sam has no income apart from that paid to him by the trust.

Trust Company has filed a petition for instructions in the appropriate court. The petition alleges the following:

(A) That Sam has made written demand that the trustee (1) turn over the entire trust estate, free of trust, to the administrator of Ball's estate, or, in the alternative, (2) out of the income and, to the extent necessary, the principal of the trust, pay Pearl the amount now due to her for alimony, and thereafter pay her periodically the amount awarded to her for future alimony.

(B) That Pearl has made written demand that the trustee, out of the income and, to the extent necessary, the principal of the trust, pay her the amount now due to her for alimony and thereafter pay her periodically the amount awarded to her for future alimony. In her demand, Pearl states that she represents Carol, now age three, and, on Carol's behalf, agrees to an invasion of the trust principal for such purpose.

(C) That Sam and Pearl, jointly, have made a written election, on their own behalf and on behalf of Carol, to terminate the trust, if the trustee does not agree to the foregoing demands.

The trustee requests instructions with respect to the following:

1. Whether the trust was effectively terminated by Ball in his lifetime;
2. Whether the trustee is obligated to pay Pearl either past or future alimony, or both, out of the income and, to the extent necessary, principal of the trust;
3. Whether Sam and Pearl have the legal power to terminate the trust.

How should the court instruct the trustee? Discuss.

Question 24

The following events all occurred in state Y.

Theresa Taylor died recently. After her death a typewritten document was found in her safe-deposit box. It read (in its entirety) as follows:

> To Aunt Marie—my home; to my friend Al—my 200 shares of XYZ stock; to my friend Frank—20 shares of IBM stock; to my daughter Doris—NOTHING!

Stapled to the typewritten document was another piece of paper on which was written, in Taylor's handwriting: "The attached is the way I want my property to go; all the rest to sister, Sarah. 5-15-2000. Theresa Taylor."

Taylor was survived by her daughter Doris, Aunt Marie, friends Al and Frank, and a brother, Ben. Her sister Sarah died in October 2007 without issue but with a will that left everything to Sarah's husband Greg.

Taylor's estate consists of $50,000 cash on deposit in banks (the proceeds of fire insurance relating to her home, which was destroyed by fire two months ago); 400 shares of XYZ stock (200 shares of which were the result of a stock split in August 2008); and government bonds having a fair market value of $100,000. Taylor did not have, and never had owned, any IBM stock.

Assume that the applicable statutory law of state Y is the same as comparable provisions of the Uniform Probate Code.

How should Taylor's estate be distributed after payment of debts, taxes, and expenses of administration? Discuss.

Question 25

Herman and Wisteria were married in 1990. Herman owned a life insurance policy that was fully paid up (no more premiums were due) and that was to pay $50,000 on his death. The life insurance policy named Wisteria as the beneficiary.

In 2000, Herman went to see Ava, an attorney, to have his will prepared. He specified that he wanted to give his life insurance policy to his lifelong friend, Sylvia, because Sylvia had once saved his life. He also specified that he wanted to give $5,000 to his cousin Carla, a $5,000 gift to his church to be used for the homeless shelter the church operated, and the rest of his estate to Wisteria. The lawyer drafted the will according to Herman's directions. On the day he went in to sign the will, Herman was having lunch with Sylvia, and because they were still catching up, Sylvia went with Herman to the lawyer's office. They were late, and the only people remaining in the office were the attorney, a blind client, and a temporary receptionist. The lawyer was worried about witnesses, and asked Herman if his friend in the reception area could act as witness. Sylvia was called into the conference room and acted as witness together with the receptionist.

In 2003, Wisteria and Herman divorced, never having had children. Herman married Abigail in 2005. He named Abigail as beneficiary of his retirement plan with his employer because his employer informed him that it was required. Herman died recently, survived by Abigail, Wisteria, Sylvia, and Brad, his brother. He and Brad had not spoken in decades. His cousin Carla was killed in 2005, survived only by her husband George. The church had since closed the homeless shelter and now ran a local day care center for the elderly. The only will Herman had ever executed was the 2000 will.

Discuss distribution of Herman's assets.

Question 26

Tobey was a wealthy confirmed bachelor and a regular on the puzzles tournament circuit. He was a crossword puzzle writer whose puzzles were frequently published. He prepared a will in 1995, with the following provisions:

> I leave my library to my puzzle mentor, Melinda.
>
> I leave $100,000 to my friend Roger.
>
> I leave $50,000 to my personal representative to divide equally among those of my business advisors I am relying on regularly at the time of my death and regular travel companions at the time of my death, such individuals to be identified at the sole discretion of the personal representative.
>
> I give the residue of my estate to be held in trust for my aunt Belinda for her life, and on her death the remainder of the estate shall be distributed to Little College.

He named Roger as the personal representative of the estate. The will was duly signed and witnessed.

By 2006, Tobey's library of books and papers on puzzles was world-renowned. Now in his eighties, he was losing his vision and unable to enjoy the library and was concerned about preserving his legacy. So he began negotiations with the Shortz Puzzle Museum and Institute to donate his library to the Museum, with the understanding that the library would stay intact and would have a dedicated room, and the room would bear Tobey's name. The details were being worked out, but the Museum had a dinner in Tobey's honor, announcing the gift of the library, and Tobey attended. He was too frail to speak at the dinner but was beaming and nodding when the Museum director announced that Tobey had given his library to the Museum. It was agreed that delivery of the books and papers would be made when the new room was ready. The Museum director visited Tobey frequently to discuss with him the design of the room that was to hold his collection.

In late 2008, Tobey suffered a fall and needed in-home nursing care. He became very close to his caregiver, a young immigrant woman who was very kind and respectful to Tobey. He began to write crossword puzzles for her to work on as a way to improve her English.

Tobey has now died. Among his papers was a draft crossword puzzle he had been working on. When Tobey wrote puzzles, he did it completely by hand. He had written in "Half my estate to caretaker Maria" in the spaces for 24 across. At the bottom of the puzzle was his signature and a date one month before his death. Melinda, Roger, and Aunt Belinda (who is now 99) are still alive. Aunt Belinda is Tobey's only living relative. Little College is still in existence, but it is in negotiations to sell its assets to Big University because it lost its endowment in an investment scandal.

Discuss distribution of Tobey's estate.

Question 27

Tommy had been a successful music producer who retired from that business and started an unrelated business with Gary, a musician that Tommy had previously worked with. Tommy's will set up a trust for his daughter, Jan, until she reached the age of 35. The will named Gary as trustee of the trust. At Tommy's death, his estate consisted of a 50 percent share of the business he owned with Gary, valued at $5 million; $2 million in a stock portfolio; and Tommy's home. The home was a historic mansion where Tommy had held legendary parties for famous musicians and other big music industry people. The trust was funded with the business interest and the house. The stock portfolio was used to pay estate taxes and other expenses of the estate.

One month after becoming trustee, Gary sold the mansion to a music producer friend, Alfred, who came to Gary asking to buy the house for $2 million because Alfred had always wanted a place in that part of town, he was a huge fan of Tommy's and would promise to preserve his memory and the history there, and if Gary sold it to Alfred he would save a bundle on the real estate commission. The house was assessed with the county at a value of $2 million. Because Alfred was going through a bad divorce and couldn't get a mortgage until the divorce was final, Gary took a promissory note for the purchase price, which provided that the $2 million would be due in full in 18 months, with no interest. Gary prepared the note, and Alfred signed it. Gary didn't get a mortgage on the mansion to secure the note, but he was sure Alfred was good for it, and Gary was anxious to curry favor with Alfred because he wanted to record another album and was hoping Alfred would work with him.

Gary continued to run the business that was now half-owned by the trust. One year after Tommy's death, a generous offer to purchase the business was made by a competitor, but Gary turned it down because Tommy hated this particular competitor. Whenever Jan asked about the business and about the cash flow, Gary told her things were fine and that she shouldn't worry about it. Within five years after Tommy's death, the business had been forced into bankruptcy by fierce competition from the competitor whose offer had been refused and by Gary's less-than-aggressive business style (he was the idea guy, and Tommy was the business guy).

Did Gary violate fiduciary duties to Jan, and if so, which?

Question 28

Don is a 75-year-old man who has owned and operated his drugstore business for the past 35 years. He is ready to retire, so he signs over ownership in the business, including his rights as a tenant in a long-term lease of the building where the drugstore is located, to Hally, a longtime friend and fellow pharmacist who owns a nearby drugstore. He tells Hally that his grandson Kevin is planning to go to pharmacy school, and he wants her to run the drugstore until Kevin becomes a licensed pharmacist, and then transfer the store to Kevin. He also tells Hally that while she is running the business, she should use the profits to pay herself and to keep up the business, and that she should give any extra money to Kevin to help out with his educational expenses.

Don has a foster daughter, Margaret, who is now grown but with whom he is still close, and he tells her when she asks that he has given the store "to Hally to run for now, and then to give it to Kevin when he's ready." Don doesn't tell Kevin about his deal with Hally.

Don dies six months later without a will, and his surviving family includes Kevin and his only daughter, Tamara (mother of Kevin). Once Don dies, Hally changes the name of Don's drugstore to the same name as her store, changes the focus of the stores to high-end beauty products, and starts offering spa services at the stores, and three years after Don's death, she sells both stores to a spa chain.

Margaret had been out of the country since before Don's death, and when she returned a year after Hally had sold the stores, she told Kevin and Tamara what Don had told her about his intentions with the store.

What causes of action and claims are available to Kevin and Tamara at this point?

Question 29
This is a drafting exercise.

A client comes in to see you. The client is unmarried, with no close family. She is very wealthy and has a very unusual last name. She tells you that she has tried to track down the origins of her last name, but her grandfather was an orphan. She has been able to find only one other person in the United States with her last name. She has found others, but they had either altered their actual last name to the form of her last name, or their last name was the result of a misspelling when their ancestor immigrated to the United States. She continues to search, but she has been diagnosed with a terminal illness and fears she will not have time to locate any others. She is interested in preserving her last name. She wants you to draft a will that gives her estate in four equal parts, one part to the one person who has her same last name provided that person finds three others who legitimately carry her last name as their legal name on their birth certificate and whose family had had that last name for at least five generations. The other three parts are to go to the three others who meet those requirements. She also wants to condition the bequests on an agreement of the beneficiaries to give their last name to any children they may have. Draft a sample clause, and also discuss what you may advise the client about this bequest.

Question 30

This is a drafting exercise.

Your client, Wendy, a widow, has three children: David, Marian, and Gary. She has provided financial support to all three, as follows:

1. In 2007, she purchased a residence for David. The cost of the house was $180,000.
2. She purchased a commercial warehouse in which Marian conducts her business. She took title as "Wendy and Marian as joint tenants with right of survivorship." Wendy paid $200,000 down, and Marian has been making the mortgage payments for the $100,000 balance.
3. She gives Gary cash on a regular basis. She gave him $70,000 to get him out of debt in 2001, and she continues to give him about $10,000 a year.

Wendy wants you to draft a will to provide that on her death, the remainder of her estate will pass to the children equally. However, she wants to equalize the lifetime giving to some extent. She wants the value of the house deducted from David's share, the value of her share of the warehouse deducted from Marian's share, and the value of the support she has given to Gary over the years deducted from his share.

Draft a provision to be included in her will that would equalize the ultimate shares of the children on the death of Wendy. HINT: use the same approach as the hotchpot technique used to determine the distribution of an intestate estate where advancements were made.

Essay Answers

Answer to Question 1

> **Important aspects**
>
> At the start of the answer to each essay question is a listing of the main ideas you should have in mind after you've read the question and begun to think about it. Please go back and read the question another time if there are big differences between these "important aspects" and your own initial reactions to the question.

Important aspects:
Will execution requirements, will revocation, presumption of revocation, revival of revoked will, determining Tom's intestate heirs, support trusts and consideration of beneficiary's other resources.

1. Which will, if either, should be admitted to probate?

Was the 2003 will valid?
The requirements for will execution vary from state to state. The modern trend, reflected in the Uniform Probate Code (UPC), is to liberalize the requirements. Under the UPC, a will is valid if it is witnessed by at least two persons, each of whom signed within a reasonable time after he or she witnessed either the testator's signing of the will or the testator's acknowledgment of (1) his signature or (2) the will itself. (UPC §2-502.) (The UPC has been recently amended to authorize a will that is notarized rather than witnessed by two persons, but that provision is not relevant here.) Because (1) Tom (T) executed the will in front of two legal secretaries who knew the document to be his will, and (2) the secretaries signed the document almost immediately thereafter, the 2003 will was valid when executed. There is (at least, under the UPC and in many jurisdictions) no requirement that the witnesses sign in the presence of the testator (or in the presence of each other), so the fact that the witnesses here signed in the hallway outside T's hospital room does not affect the validity of the will. In some states, the requirements for validity would be more stringent.

If the 2003 will is deemed valid, does it revoke the 2000 will?
A subsequent testamentary instrument need not contain a revocation clause in order to revoke a prior will. A prior will may be revoked either expressly or by inconsistency. (UPC §2-507(a)(1).) Even without a revocation clause, a subsequent will wholly revokes a previous will by inconsistency if the testator intended the subsequent will to replace the old one

rather than supplement it. (UPC §2-507(b).) When the later will disposes of the entire estate, that will is presumed to be entirely inconsistent with the earlier will, even if some provisions remain essentially the same in the two wills. (UPC §2-507(c).) Because the 2003 will purports to dispose of T's entire estate, if it is deemed valid it will supersede the 2000 instrument and will be admitted to probate.

Is the 2003 will deemed revoked by being lost?
If a will that was last in the testator's possession (or control) cannot be found upon his or her death, ordinarily a presumption arises that the testator destroyed the will with the intent to revoke it (in many states, it must also be shown that the testator had capacity until death). The presumption does not arise if the will was last known to be in the possession of a third person. If the presumption arises, it is rebuttable. The UPC is silent on the issue of lost wills.

Here, the facts indicate that (1) the 2003 will was last in the testator's (Tom's) possession (after the witnesses signed the will, they "immediately returned" it to Tom); (2) after Tom's death, the will cannot be found; and (3) Tom had capacity until his death. The presumption arises that Tom revoked the will by act. Once the presumption arises, the burden shifts to those who favor probate of the will to offer a more plausible explanation for why the will cannot be found.

T's nephew E can attempt to rebut this presumption by arguing that T knew how to enlist the assistance of Attorney Smith in connection with his will and would have gone back to Smith if he had actually meant to revoke the 2003 will. However, this argument alone would probably *not* be sufficient to rebut the presumption that T had intended to revoke the 2003 will. The fact that T retained the 2000 will in his safe-deposit box supports the presumption that he meant to revoke the 2003 will. If he had meant to substitute the 2003 will for the 2000 will, arguably he would have removed the 2000 will from the deposit box and replaced it with the 2003 will.

Based on these facts, the better and more probable conclusion is that the 2003 will was revoked, and the copy of the 2003 will should ***not*** be admitted to probate.

If, however, the 2003 will is deemed not to have been revoked, the court might probate the 2003 will under the "lost will" doctrine—which in most jurisdictions requires the proponent to prove the terms of the will by clear and convincing evidence. Here, the unsigned copy of the 2003 will in Attorney Smith's possession, coupled with the testimony of Attorney

Smith and the two secretaries, would probably constitute clear and convincing evidence of the terms of the 2003 will.

If the 2003 will is deemed revoked, is the 2000 will revived?
What happens to an earlier will when a subsequent will that was intended to revoke the earlier will is itself revoked by destruction or loss? In most states the answer is provided by a specific statute. Some states provide that, once revoked, a prior will may not be revived unless it is properly re-executed with full compliance with requirements for a valid will. In other states and under the UPC, the first will is revived when the second will is destroyed, if that is the testator's intent. The UPC provides that where the later will is revoked by act, "[t]he previous will is revived if it is evident from the circumstances of the revocation of the subsequent will or from the testator's contemporary or subsequent declarations that the testator intended the previous will to take effect as executed." (UPC §2-509(a).)

Here, there is no evidence that T intended or desired the 2000 will to be reinstated. Although the will was preserved in his safe-deposit box, it's possible that T simply neglected to dispose of the 2000 will after the 2003 document was created. However, the aggrieved beneficiaries (*i.e.*, those residuary beneficiaries in the 2000 will who were left out of the 2003 will) might prevail, *if* they could show that T was such a careful and prudent person that he would recognize that his intent would be best expressed by preserving one will and destroying or disposing of the other. On this proof, T's retention of the 2000 will would arguably manifest his desire to have that document constitute his testamentary scheme.

The doctrine of dependent relative revocation is not applicable to these facts. The doctrine comes into play where a testator validly revokes a will based on a mistake, and the testator would not have revoked the will but for the mistake. Where such is the case, it is assumed that the testator would want the revoked will reinstated. The doctrine is not applicable here because there is no evidence that Tom revoked either the 2000 will or the 2003 will based upon a mistake.

Summary:
The probable conclusion is that the 2000 will should not be revived and the testator, Tom, died intestate. If the court were to conclude that the presumption that the 2003 will was revoked is overcome, and the terms of the will are established under the lost will doctrine, Tom's nephew E would take his remaining estate after the trust for Lil was established. If the court were to conclude that the 2003 will was revoked and the 2000 will was

revived, the trust would be established for Lil, and the surviving issue of Tom's brothers would take the residue of his estate per stirpes.

2. What is the difference between the disposition of the residue in the 2000 will and intestacy?

[*Note:* For exam questions such as this one (where there are many potential beneficiaries and you are asked to discuss the difference between testamentary and intestate distribution to those beneficiaries), you should diagram the family tree (on scrap paper, not in your exam bluebook) before attempting to answer.] The family tree for this question would look like this:

Under the 2000 will, the surviving issue of T's brothers take as directed by T; that is, per stirpes (*i.e.*, through the roots of each brother). Conceptually, the residue is divided into three shares, one for each brother who has issue, and then into subshares for the issue of each brother. Thus, A and B would each receive one-sixth of T's residuary estate (*i.e.*, they get equal shares of the one-third that James would have gotten as the sole issue of Sam); C would receive a full one-third of T's residuary estate (as the sole issue of John); and D and E would each get one-sixth (sharing equally the one-third that would have gone to Frank). As the facts tell us, brother Bob died without issue.

Under intestacy, that part of a decedent's estate not effectively disposed of by will passes to the decedent's heirs as prescribed by statute in each state. Under the Uniform Probate Code, a testator's intestate property would pass to his "descendants by representation." (UPC §2-103(a)(1).) The Uniform Probate Code has adopted the *per capita at each generation* approach. Under this approach the first division of the decedent's estate is made at the highest level where there are living members—one share for each party who is alive at that level, and one share for each party who is dead but survived by issue. (UPC §2-106(b).) Thus, one equal share each would go to C, D, and E and one to the issue of deceased James. The final result would be that C, D, and E would each get one-fourth of the residuary estate, and A and B would each get one-eighth (splitting James's one-fourth share equally).

3. Should Lil receive $1,000 per month, or $500 per month?

A support trust is a trust that requires the trustee to pay as much income (and, if expressly provided in the trust, principal as well) as necessary for the beneficiary's support. Tom has created a support trust for Lil.

When there are ambiguous provisions in a will or the provisions are capable of different or inconsistent interpretations, the court will attempt to effectuate the testator's intent by inquiring into all the circumstances. Lil could argue that she was intended to be the sole living beneficiary of the trust and that T would naturally prefer her interests to those of a large and well-funded charity. By using the terms "as much of the income, and if income be insufficient, as much of the principal ... ," T manifested a clear directive to support her from the trust, not to cause her to deplete her savings.

On the other hand, T presumably knew that Lil was receiving funds from other sources. He could have requested Attorney Smith to insert the language, "regardless of Lil's other income" if he had wanted to give a free hand to the trustee. Because (1) the principal would be exhausted in a relatively short period of time if Lil received $12,000 per year from the trust, and (2) the trust was apparently to last for her entire life (the trust language states, "for so long as she lives"), it can be argued that T intended to limit Lil to $500 per month from the trust.

Without additional facts, either interpretation of the will's provision would be reasonable.

Answer to Question 2

Important aspects:
Will execution formalities, interested witnesses, lost wills, revocation by revocatory act, revival, omitted spouse, elective share, determination of Henry's intestate heirs

We must first decide whether the 2000 will was validly executed, and, if so, whether it was effectively revoked by the 2001 will and, if it was revoked, whether it was revived by the destruction of the 2001 will.

Was the 2000 will executed with the requisite formalities?
The Uniform Probate Code requires that an attested will be in writing, signed by the testator or in the testator's name by some other person in the testator's conscious presence and by the testator's direction, and that it be either signed by two persons within a reasonable time after execution or notarized. (UPC §2-502.)

Historically, persons interested as legatees or beneficiaries under a will could not serve as witnesses. Today, the rule in most states is still either to (1) automatically disqualify interested witnesses, *or* (2) permit them to qualify, but purge them of their gifts. The UPC and a number of states remove this disqualification. (UPC §2-505(b).) Under the UPC, the 2000 will appears to be valid even though Sally was both a beneficiary and a witness. Wanda's appointment as executor would not affect her qualification as a witness, even in a state that does disqualify interested witnesses. The theory is that the executor has a separate interest as recipient of fees for service as a fiduciary. (*Note:* A lawyer who prepares the will or is present at the execution is a valid witness.)

Can the 2001 will be proved as a testamentary instrument although the original is not produced?
In most jurisdictions, a will that cannot be produced in court can nevertheless be proved. However, the burden is on the proponents of the will to prove its valid execution and its terms—and in most jurisdictions the burden of proof under these circumstances is clear and convincing evidence.

In this case, Lana's testimony proves the revocation of the 2001 will and gives the reason why it cannot be produced in court. Lana's testimony that the photocopy is a true and correct copy of the 2001 will may be used to establish its terms. Her testimony is supported by the testimony of Lana's law clerk, who saw the torn scraps of the will and heard Henry confirm that he considered the 2001 will ineffective.

There is probably sufficient evidence that the 2001 will was properly executed. Its execution revoked the 2000 will.

Was the 2001 will revoked?
The UPC allows revocation by "revocatory act." The definition of a revocatory act includes "burning, tearing, canceling, obliterating, or destroying the will or any part of it." The burning, tearing, or cancelation of a will are revocatory acts even if the acts do not touch any of the words on the will. The acts must be performed by the testator or another person at (1) the testator's direction, and (2) in his "conscious presence," with the intent of revoking it. (UPC §2-507(a)(2).) Lana's testimony, corroborated by Charles, establishes that the will was destroyed by Lana in Henry's presence and at Henry's direction.

Did the revocation of the 2001 will have the effect of reviving the 2000 will?
In many states, revocation of a later testamentary instrument that by its terms revokes a prior testamentary instrument does *not* revive the earlier instrument. The UPC confirms that the previous will "remains revoked, unless it is revived." However, the Code goes on to provide that if the second will was revoked by physical act, the first will is revived if it appears from either (1) the circumstances of the revocation of the second will, or (2) the testator's contemporaneous or subsequent declarations, that the decedent intended the first will to take effect as executed. (UPC §2-509(a).)

Henry's statement that "things are back the way I want them; Wanda won't get a penny of my property" suggests that his intent was to have the 2000 will revived. Wanda will argue, however, that the statement is too ambiguous to prove an intent to revive the 2000 will. Nevertheless, Henry's statement to Lana and Charles would probably be interpreted to mean that he desired reinstatement of the earlier will rather than intestacy.

Assuming the 2000 will is revived, how should the estate be distributed?
Assuming the validity of the first will and its revival, Wanda has two additional arguments she can make to try to gain a share of Henry's estate.

Wanda's first claim would be that she qualifies as an omitted spouse. The UPC provides that if a testator fails to provide for a surviving spouse who married the testator *after* the execution of the will, the omitted spouse receives a modified intestate share (see below), unless (1) it appears from the will or other evidence that the will was made in contemplation of the marriage; (2) the will expresses the intention that it is to be effective notwithstanding any subsequent marriage; or (3) the testator provided for the spouse outside the will with intent that the transfer serve as a substitute for a gift under the will. (UPC §2-301.) The difficult issue here is determining what should be the date of a revived will. The omitted spouse doctrine is based on the assumption that the spouse was "accidentally" omitted from the will. Clearly that was not the case here. The better position is that the date of the revived will should be the date the testator properly revived the will. Here, that is *after* Henry married Wanda. Under this analysis, Wanda would not qualify as an omitted spouse.

On the other hand, the omitted spouse serves a spousal protection purpose of ensuring that surviving spouses are adequately provided for. Wanda will argue that inasmuch as she is not provided for in the 2000 will, and it is the 2000 will that is being probated, the will should be dated as of the date of its original execution, and thus she should qualify as an omitted spouse. If the court were to adopt this analysis, Wanda would receive her omitted spouse share under UPC §2-301, which provides that she receives her intestate share as to that portion of the testator's estate that is devised neither to a child of the testator born before the marriage in question (who is not a child of the surviving spouse) nor to a descendant of such a child. Here, Henry devised $5,000 to his daughter Sally, who is not Wanda's child. Even if Wanda were to qualify as an omitted spouse, she would take her intestate share from the estate passing under the residuary clause only—it would not include the gift to Sally. Under UPC §2-102(4), where one or more of the decedent's surviving descendants are not descendants of the surviving spouse (in this case, his daughter Sally), the surviving spouse's share is $150,000 plus one-half of the balance of the estate ($345,000). Wanda would receive $150,000 plus $172,500, for a total of $322,500. The remaining balance ($172,500) would go to Maude per the terms of the residuary clause. Henry's brother would not share.

Assuming the jurisdiction is a non-community property state, Maude could also claim her elective share. The details of the elective share doctrine vary from state to state. Under the current version of UPC §2-202, the elective share would depend upon how long the parties had been married. For example, if they had been married for nine years, under UPC §§2-202 and 2-203, Wanda is entitled to 27 percent of Henry's augmented estate (under these facts, the "augmented" estate component is not applicable). Wanda would take $135,000.

Wanda is better off if she can qualify as an omitted spouse, but even if she cannot, she is entitled to her elective share amount.

Assuming the 2000 will is not revived, how should the estate be distributed through intestacy?
If it is determined that the first will was not revived, the estate would be distributed by intestate succession. This would result in Wanda's receiving $325,000 (not $322,500 as calculated above because her intestate share would be determined as against Henry's entire estate as opposed to only that portion of the estate not going to Sally). The balance of the estate would be distributed to Sally as Henry's only surviving descendant. Maude and Budi would not share.

Answer to Question 3

Important aspects: revocation by physical act, holographic wills, dependent relative revocation

Was the Will revoked when the lawyer shredded it?

The lawyer's shredding of the will was not a valid revocation because revocation of a will by physical act must be done either by the testator or at the testator's direction and in his or her presence. Teddy did not shred the will himself, and although he directed the lawyer to shred the will, the lawyer did not do it in the presence of Teddy, so it was not a valid revocation.

Was Teddy's conversation with the lawyer sufficient to create a new estate plan?

His conversation with the lawyer about his intentions to change his will is not a valid estate plan because it was not put into writing and signed by Teddy or properly witnessed.

Was the journal entry an effective holographic will?

On the other hand, his journal entry was done in a jurisdiction that recognizes holographic wills, and virtually all states will recognize a will or codicil validly executed under the laws of the jurisdiction where executed. The journal entry could be deemed to be a valid codicil revoking the existing Will and leaving Teddy intestate. However, this result would not be consistent with Teddy's wishes because under all states a surviving spouse would be a significant beneficiary of the deceased spouse's estate. Also, Taylor is only Teddy's stepdaughter and therefore would have no interest in the estate as an intestate heir. Wilma is likely to argue that the journal entry was a valid codicil because if the will is revoked, her intestate share is likely to be Teddy's entire estate because he had no other surviving family members.

Could Taylor argue dependent relative revocation?

If Wilma is successful in arguing that the journal entry is a holographic codicil, then Taylor should argue dependent relative revocation. Under that doctrine, if a testator revokes a will under the belief that a second will or estate plan will take effect, and that second plan fails for some reason, the court may find that the revocation of the first will was conditional on the effectiveness of the second, and because the second plan failed, the revocation of the first will also fails. Dependent relative revocation is discretionary with the court and is applied when the first will (which was revoked) is closer to the testator's intent than intestacy, or whatever disposition of the testator's estate will occur if the revocation of the first will is upheld. In this case, it is clear that the will, which gives Wilma only a life interest, with the remainder going to Taylor, is closer to Teddy's intent than intestacy, which would give his entire estate to Wilma. Therefore, if Wilma succeeds in establishing the journal entry as a codicil, then Taylor should be able to convince the court to apply dependent relative revocation and enforce the will. If Wilma fails to establish the journal entry as a holographic codicil, then the will have not been revoked and Teddy's estate will be distributed under the first will.

Answer to Question 4

Important aspects: Conditional bequests, public policy, creation of trust, necessity of trust property, ademption

1. What are the rights of John and Barbara and of Barbara's children?

As to John: Was the gift to John revoked by failure of the condition?
Barbara will contend that the gift to John was subject to an express condition subsequent that became effective to revoke John's bequest. The condition was that John remain married to Kathleen at Alfred's death.

Unless a condition in a will is deemed against public policy, it will ordinarily be given effect as written. Some conditions are so offensive that they are almost never enforced. Among these are (1) conditions that restrain a person from marrying, or (2) conditions that encourage divorce. The condition in this case accomplished the very opposite: It encouraged John to preserve his marriage to Kathleen. Because Alfred was childless, he was probably especially concerned to encourage stability in his nephew's life. Also, he may have become fond of Kathleen and wished not to harm her. On these facts, it is likely that the court will enforce the condition as written.

The Uniform Probate Code makes specific provision for devises (other than residuary devises) that fail. The Code provides that a gift that fails for any reason becomes part of the residue of the estate. (UPC §2-604(a).) Because the will provides that Barbara take the residue, John's 10 percent interest in the balance of the estate goes to Barbara.

Did Alfred create a valid trust in favor of Barbara's children?
Neither the trust nor Barbara's children are mentioned in the will, and more than two years elapsed between execution of the will and the letter to Barbara. Barbara's children will assert that Alfred had continued to review his affairs and that he intended his letter to Barbara to constitute a valid, *inter vivos*, discretionary trust for their benefit. If a valid living trust existed, then the U.S. and state X bonds would not be part of Alfred's estate when he died, and they would not pass to Yale College.

An *inter vivos* trust requires (1) manifestation of intent by the settlor to create a trust, (2) funding (that an identifiable property interest be transferred to the trust/trustee), (3) ascertainable beneficiaries, and (4) possibly a writing (if real property is part of the trust res). The children will argue that all these requirements were satisfied by the letter. Alfred's intent to create a trust is clear and emphatic ("I have established a trust . . ."). The beneficiaries are ascertainable. The trust is intended to be for Barbara's "children." Although Alfred does not name them, the description is clear enough that there is an objective means of determining who the beneficiaries are. The trust is an *inter vivos* trust, so it does not have to be in writing unless it holds real property—which here it does not. The problem is the funding requirement. An identifiable property interest must be transferred to the trustee. Alfred stated that the trust property was to be "all of my U.S. and state X bonds," but there is no evidence that he transferred them to the trustee.

The best argument in support of a trust is that he was declaring himself to be the trustee, but where the settlor is also the trustee, most courts require clear evidence of the intent to create a trust and/or proof that the settlor has segregated the assets in question from his or her other assets. Alfred wrote that he was going to segregate the assets by establishing the trust at ABC Bank, but there is no evidence that he put the assets in the bank. In the alternative, Barbara's children can argue that he intended Barbara to be the trustee and gave her full discretion to distribute the income and corpus of the trust as she wished.

Yale will argue that (1) Alfred may have thought about creating a trust but changed his mind and finally decided not to; (2) his intent was not to be the trustee himself but to make the bank the trustee, and that his failure to execute the necessary documents at the bank clearly proves his change of heart; (3) that no delivery of the trust res ever occurred (*i.e.*, the U.S. and state X bonds were never delivered to anyone but were retained by Alfred, a clear indication that he meant them to go to Yale as originally planned); and (4) that there is no reasonable basis for concluding that he meant Barbara to be the trustee—the language "I have established a trust . . . " instead of the equally simple language "I am establishing a trust" shows that he did not intend Barbara to be the trustee.

Barbara's children will argue in rebuttal that Alfred's unequivocal language in his letter to Barbara ("I *have* established a trust for your children . . . composed of all my U.S. and state X bonds") should control regardless of the trustee's identity. The retention of the bonds by Alfred simply establishes that he was holding them as both his will and the letter would indicate—the U.S. and state X bonds for the benefit of the children and only the state Z bonds for Yale.

In response, the children will reassert their argument that Alfred intended himself to be the trustee. His statement to Barbara, "You can decide how the funds should be used," meant only that Alfred would consult with

Barbara before expending any funds in the children's behalf. Because the trust res (the U.S. bonds and the X bonds only) was clearly identified in Alfred's letter to Barbara, Alfred was not obliged to segregate the bonds from his other assets.

Because the letter to Barbara so clearly designated the components of the trust and so clearly designated the intent to benefit Barbara's children, it is likely that the children will prevail.

If a trust was created with Alfred as trustee, his subsequent death would not cause the trust to fail. A successor trustee (probably Barbara) would simply be appointed.

If, as seems unlikely, no trust at all was created, then the U.S. and state X bonds remained in Alfred's estate and at his death would go to Yale College along with the state Z bonds.

2. Assuming the creation of a valid trust for Barbara's children, what are the rights of Yale College?

If a valid trust *was* created by Alfred, the court will have to decide what effect that will have on the testamentary gift to Yale. Specifically, does Yale get cash equal to the value of the U.S. and state X bonds at Alfred's death? To the extent Yale gets cash, the residuary gift to Alfred's niece Barbara will be reduced accordingly.

Under the common law, a specific devise is adeemed — rendered ineffective — if the property that is devised is not owned by the testator at death. Under the common law, Yale would not get cash in lieu of the value of the U.S. and state X bonds. Instead, it would get only the state Z bonds.

The more modern approach, reflected in the UPC, is to apply ademption only where the facts indicate that the testator intended to extinguish the gift or when ademption is "consistent with the testator's manifested plan of distribution." (UPC §2-606(a)(6).) Yale will argue that ademption is inconsistent with Alfred's overall testamentary scheme. As evidenced in his will, his intent was to give his government bonds, or the value thereof, to Yale. Assuming he created a valid trust of his U.S. and state X bonds, Yale will argue that it is entitled to the monetary equivalent — that all Alfred was doing was shifting his assets around (transferring some of the bonds to benefit Barbara's children, but money should be shifted to Yale to compensate for the shift in the bonds). Alfred made no attempt at revising or revoking the original gift to Yale, arguably indicating that he still wanted the original gift — or its monetary equivalent — to go to Yale. On the other hand, Barbara will argue that even under the modern trend/UPC "intent of the testator" approach, ademption should apply here. The facts indicate that the bonds were a material part of Alfred's assets; it's unlikely he wanted to drain his estate of a matching amount of cash to Yale, especially as that would come at the sole expense of his niece, Barbara. After the failure of the conditional bequest to his nephew John, Barbara was his principal living heir and we may reasonably presume that he would prefer her.

Whether ademption should apply under the UPC approach is a close call. Because Yale bears the burden of proof, and because applying ademption would favor his family over Yale, the more likely result is that a court would apply ademption. Yale would, however, be entitled to the state Z bonds, because these are included in the term "government bonds" and were excluded from the contents of the trust.

Answer to Question 5

Important aspects: Method of amending trust, legal malpractice, ownership presumption on death of one joint tenant

Was the trust amendment valid?

The validity of the trust amendment depends on how flexibly the trust provision regarding amendments is interpreted. "Duly executed document" seems to require a document prepared or at least signed by the trustor. Arthur's only involvement with the preparation of the trust amendment was his telephone call to the lawyer. A copy of the substituted page was mailed to Arthur, who was also the trustee, so the requirement that the document be delivered to the trustee was met. Whether this will be sufficient depends on state law. Under UTC §603, amendment of a revocable living trust is valid if it "substantially complies" with the method of amendment specified in the agreement, so strict compliance is not necessary. However, the requirement of a "duly executed document" may mean that substitution of a new page is not substantial compliance. Section 603 of the UTC also provides that if the trust agreement's method of amendment is not expressly exclusive, then the trust can be amended by "any other method manifesting clear and convincing evidence of the settlor's intent." As long as there was no language in the trust agreement that made the "duly executed agreement" the exclusive method of amending the trust, the circumstances should be able to meet this standard.

If the trust amendment is not valid, does Phyllis have any other recourse?

If the court holds nevertheless that the amendment is not valid, Phyllis may have a claim against the lawyer for malpractice. She may have some difficulties in bringing this claim, because she was not the lawyer's client and therefore lacks privity to bring a direct claim. However, the modern approach is to allow disappointed beneficiaries to sue attorneys who failed to prepare documents that carried out a client's intent to benefit them.

Is Phyllis entitled to the bank account?

The presumption is that the surviving joint tenant is the owner of the account. In some states this presumption is conclusive. See UPC §6-212. In other states the presumption can be rebutted by evidence that the owner of the funds creating the account intended something different. Even if the presumption was rebuttable, the burden would be on Arthur's children to rebut the presumption, and there are no facts in the question that would indicate Arthur did not want Phyllis to receive the funds on his death.

Answer to Question 6

Important aspects: Interested witness, partial revocation by physical act, holographic wills, harmless error, dependent relative revocation, omitted child, precatory language, promise to convey to another, constructive trust

Is Daniel's will valid?

Does the fact that John, a beneficiary, acted as witness render Daniel's will ineffective? The answer is "no." The fact that John was an interested witness would not cause the will to fail. Nor would it cause the provision in favor of John to fail. (UPC §2-505(b).) The facts do not suggest any undue influence by John on Daniel, and it is only natural to bestow a testamentary gift upon one's brother.

Bequest to Alice:

As residual beneficiary, Bill might be expected to challenge the specific bequests. He will contend that the $5,000 bequest to Alice was revoked by Daniel's cancelation (*i.e.*, drawing a line through it with the intent to revoke it), and (2) that it was not effectively replaced by the $50,000 bequest, which fails as an attested will because it does not comply with the necessary testamentary formalities (*e.g.*, witnesses). See UPC §2-507; §2-502.

Holographic will:

In rebuttal, Alice will argue that the handwritten modification was valid as a holographic will. The statutes controlling holographic wills vary widely from state to state. Some states require that the entire document be in the testator's handwriting, including a full signature. Other states follow the reasoning of the UPC and are much more liberal. In these states writings qualify as holographic wills as long as they contain the handwritten signature of the testator, the "material provisions" are in the testator's handwriting, and the document evidences testamentary intent (the intent that the person intended this document to be his or her last will). (UPC §2-502(b).) Initials will generally suffice as a signature, especially if it is clear that they are in the testator's hand. Bill will argue that the mere insertion of a new number by the testator does not satisfy the "material provisions" requirement. Most courts define the "material provisions" as requiring the testator's handwriting to indicate who takes what. Here, only the amount of the gift is in the testator's handwriting, not who is to take the gift. Most courts would hold that this does not meet the formalities of a holographic will.

Harmless error doctrine:

Even if the court is reluctant to find a holographic will, Alice has a good chance of getting the court to overlook the need for testamentary formalities, under a provision that was added to the UPC in 1990. Under UPC §2-503, the lack of formalities will be treated as harmless by the court if there is "clear and convincing evidence" that the document at issue (or an addition or alteration to the document) was intended as the decedent's will. Here, the line through the old amount, the handwritten new amount, and the initials alongside the new amount—taken together—would probably satisfy this standard. Alice should be entitled to the increased amount.

Doctrine of dependent relative revocation:

In the event a court were to rule (1) that Daniel's handwritten provisions do not constitute a holographic codicil, and (2) that Daniel's line through the original gift to Alice constitutes a valid revocation of the original gift of $5,000, Alice's best argument would be to invoke the dependent relative revocation doctrine. This doctrine permits a mistaken revocation to be nullified. Under the doctrine, when a testator revokes a will, or a provision in a will, and substitutes a new will or provision under the mistaken belief that the new will or provision is valid, the revocation is viewed as having been conditional or "dependent" upon the validity of the new will or provision. Applying this principle, if Daniel's changes are not valid, the earlier bequest of $5,000 is restored. Daniel obviously would prefer that Alice get $50,000, but if that change is invalid, the $5,000 gift should certainly be revived. If Alice loses on the "holographic will" and "testamentary intent" arguments, she will almost certainly be permitted to receive the original $5,000 gift under the doctrine of dependent relative revocation.

Omitted child:

Alice will *not* be able to claim as an omitted child (UPC §2-302) because she was already born when the will was executed. Thus, she is not entitled to an intestate share.

Possible trust in favor of Karen:

Karen will contend that the bequest to Bill was subject to a trust for her benefit; that Bill was obligated to provide for her needs. This contention is supported by the fact that Daniel had helped Karen to meet her living expenses during his life and presumably would want Karen to be cared for in a similar manner after his death. Bill will argue that the phrasing in the will with respect to Karen is only precatory. Precatory phrasing imposes only a moral obligation on the donee (here Bill) to use the gift for the benefit of the third party (here Karen), not a legal obligation. It is a close call here. The phrasing in the will ("it is my *wish* . . . ") is not enough, standing alone, to impose a legal obligation on Bill. But when coupled with Daniel's history of helping to care for Karen, it is a close call. Ultimately it is a question of the testator's (Daniel's) intent. A court could go either way on this issue.

Is Lois entitled to John's $10,000?
The law distinguishes between a beneficiary who receives property under a promise to convey to another but who changes his or her mind *after* the testator's death and one who receives property under a similar promise but who never intended to keep the promise in the first place, or who did intend to keep the promise but changed his or her mind *before* the testator's death. In the former case, the beneficiary is generally allowed to keep the property free of the promise. In the latter case, a constructive trust is generally applied in favor of the person who will benefit from the promise.

Lois will contend that she is entitled to the $10,000 that Daniel left to John, on the theory that a constructive trust arose because Daniel relied on John's promise to convey the money to Lois, even though the promise was oral. Where there is adequate extrinsic evidence of the testator's reliance upon the beneficiary's promise, most courts will impose a *constructive trust* in favor of the intended beneficiary. As we have pointed out, the court is more likely to do this if it believes that John never intended to keep the promise—or that he did intend to keep the promise but changed his mind before the testator's death—than if it believes he originally intended to comply and changed his mind after the testator's death. We don't know from these facts what John's state of mind was, nor are we told that John has manifested an intent not to convey to Lois. If there is a dispute between them, Lois is likely to prevail.

Summary:
Probably, Alice will receive $50,000; either Lois or John will receive $10,000; and Bill will receive $40,000—which may be subject to an obligation to care for Karen.

Answer to Question 7

Important aspects: Duty of loyalty, self-dealing, bona fide purchaser, constructive trust

Beneficiaries of Trust #2 (Beneficiaries) v. Agatha:
The trustee owes a duty of loyalty to the beneficiaries of the trust. She or he may not, for example, sell any trust property to herself or himself, regardless of the fairness or good faith of the transaction, without (1) authorization from the trust, (2) court approval, or (3) approval of the beneficiaries after full disclosure. (Uniform Trust Code [UTC] §802(b).) The duty of loyalty precludes the trustee from making any personal profit from trust transactions. When the duty of loyalty is breached, beneficiaries can recover from the trustee (a) any loss resulting from the breach, (b) any profit resulting from the breach, and (c) any profit the trust would have made if the breach had not occurred. The beneficiaries have several equitable remedies as well (*e.g.*, an injunction to prevent the trustee's breach, an action to appoint a receiver, an action to compel a waiver of the trustee's compensation). In addition, when trust property is wrongfully transferred to a third party, the beneficiaries may trace the property and/or its product into the hands of the third party and secure its return to the trust.

There is little doubt on these facts that Agatha breached her duty of loyalty by utilizing trust property to satisfy a personal obligation. Her actions resulted in a substantial loss to the Beneficiaries. She is therefore liable to the Beneficiaries for at least the loss in the TT&A stock's value to Trust #2 at the time of transfer ($11,000). In many states, she would also be liable for any increase in the stock's value *to the time of trial* (plus any lost dividends).

Beneficiaries of Trust #2 (Beneficiaries) v. Larry:
If the Beneficiaries believe that TT&A stock will continue to increase in value, they can seek to trace the stock and recover the shares directly from Larry.

Under the constructive trust doctrine, when the retention of identifiable property would result in unjust enrichment to the recipient at the expense of the intended beneficiary, the court may deem the item to be held in trust for the benefit of the intended beneficiary. The Beneficiaries will contend that, because Larry received the stock as a gift, the constructive trust doctrine should be applied to require him to return the stock to them.

Larry will respond that he received the stock from his uncle John, a *bona fide* purchaser for value and that he stands in John's shoes. But this argument will probably fail because John did not act in good faith. He knew or should have known that (1) Agatha was transferring trust assets, and (2) the assets were worth much more than he paid for them—that is, enough to enable Agatha to pay off her entire loan balance, plus 10 percent interest. Equity requires that the Beneficiaries prevail against Larry.

If the TT&A stock is recovered by the Beneficiaries, can John invade Trust #1 to satisfy Agatha's obligation to him? If the Beneficiaries obtain a judgment against Agatha, can they invade Trust #1?

If Larry is forced to return the stock to the trust, John will probably stop at nothing in a renewed effort to recover Agatha's $10,000 from the assets of Trust #1. He will argue that there has been a material failure of consideration and that he released Agatha from her obligation without receiving anything in return. The question is whether John can invade Trust #1 to satisfy his $10,000 debt.

Ordinarily, a trust beneficiary may assign or transfer his or her interest in the same way as a fee owner. When the testator wishes to prevent unlimited transfer by the beneficiary, he or she may use one of several restraints. One of these is a spendthrift trust. A spendthrift trust is one that includes an express provision prohibiting alienation of a beneficiary's right to receive a benefit, whether principal or interest or both. The provision may be limited to voluntary transfers, but it may also be written to apply to involuntary transfers. A majority of states enforce spendthrift provisions; a minority do not.

Most spendthrift clauses express two restraints: (1) one that prevents the beneficiary from voluntarily alienating his or her interest in the trust income or corpus, and (2) one that prevents creditors of the beneficiary from reaching the interest of the beneficiary. Most courts that enforce spendthrift clauses will construe a will that contains either restraint as intending both. These courts hold that it is against public policy to permit a settlor to restrain involuntary alienation without also restraining voluntary alienation. Some courts will not enforce a restraint against involuntary transfer unless there is also a restraint against voluntary transfer. These courts permit creditors to reach the beneficiary's interest if the beneficiary is not also restrained.

Both of George's trusts stated that creditors could not reach the income in the trustee's hands. We may reasonably conclude that there was no corresponding provision specifically enjoining voluntary alienation by the beneficiaries. In those states in which a spendthrift provision will not be enforced without such a clause, Agatha's creditors may invade the trust (at least to the extent of her income interest).

In the majority of states, however, the restraint against creditors will be construed as including a restraint against voluntary alienation as well. In those states, John will be prevented from reaching Agatha's interest.

John may have one final ace up his sleeve. The general rule is that a settlor may not create a spendthrift trust for himself or herself. John will argue that the agreement between George and Agatha was a skillful effort to avoid this rule.

John will argue that Agatha really acted as settlor of her own trust by forgiving the $300,000 debt to George's estate and agreeing to substitute the trust instead. He may be able to prove that the arrangement between Agatha and George was a ruse to limit access to Agatha's assets by her creditors.

The same arguments made by John will be made by Agatha's other creditors, including the beneficiaries of Trust #2.

Answer to Question 8

Important aspects: ascertainable beneficiaries, revocation of trust, class gifts, vested remainders and survival requirements, revocation of will on divorce, increase in gifts of stock

Was a valid trust created 30 years ago?
An *inter vivos* trust requires (1) manifestation of intent by the settlor to create a trust, (2) funding (that an identifiable property interest be delivered to the trust/trustee), (3) ascertainable beneficiaries (either immediately or within the period of the Rule Against Perpetuities), and (4) possibly a writing (if real property is part of the trust res). The facts here state that a trust instrument was executed, that State Bank was named trustee, and that 80 shares of Disney stock were delivered to the trustee. Thus, three of the four elements are clearly satisfied. The only issue is whether the ascertainable beneficiaries element is satisfied.

Because Thea had no children "in being" at the time the trust was created, it may be argued that the fourth requirement is not satisfied because there is no living person who may be identified as the beneficiary and therefore no person to ensure the enforceability of the trust. A trust for unborn children, however, is a widely accepted exception to the requirement that there must be ascertainable beneficiaries. Most courts and the Uniform Trust Code permit trusts for unborn children as long as the beneficiaries may become ascertainable within the period of the Rule Against Perpetuities. (UTC §402, Comment.) Moreover, for probate purposes, the traditional rule has been that a child born alive is treated as alive from the moment of conception. Inasmuch as Thea was pregnant when she created the trust, and the child was born alive, there is also the traditional argument that there was an ascertainable beneficiary from the moment the trust was created.

Therefore Thea's trust was validly created 30 years ago.

Did the bequest to Fred in Thea's will revoke the trust?
Sal might contend that the gift of 100 shares to Fred revoked the *inter vivos* trust, on the theory that the "out of shares held by me" language implied that Thea owned more than 100 shares and that only some of her shares would be taken "out of" the total to satisfy the gift to Fred. Because this would be true only if we included the shares in the trust, Thea arguably meant to revoke the trust. But the children are likely to prevail against this argument. They will contend that (1) in most states, an *inter vivos* trust cannot be revoked unless the power to revoke is expressly retained by the

settlor, and (2) even if the power to revoke was specifically reserved in the trust document (the facts are silent on this point), revocation of a trust must be clear and unequivocal. The will stated that Fred was to receive the stock "out of shares held by me at my death." Technically, Thea did not own the shares in the trust; the trust/trustee held legal title to the shares in the trust at the time of her death. Most likely, Thea anticipated the acquisition of more shares of Disney stock prior to her death, but intended nothing more by this language. Furthermore, the will contained no reference to the trust agreement, and we are not told that Thea made any effort to reclaim the Disney stock from State Bank. It's unlikely that the court will decide that the trust agreement was revoked.

To whom should the trust assets be distributed?

This issue is complicated because the fact pattern does not give us all of the facts—in particular, who has what interest, if any, in the trust while the settlor is alive; and do Thea's children hold any interest while Thea is alive, or only upon her death?

When Thea created the trust for the benefit of her "children," she created a class gift. When the term "children" is used in a trust document, it is generally construed as including only the generation immediately following the settlor (*i.e.*, it does not include grandchildren). Her two youngest children will be entitled to shares. The issue is what should happen to the share for her oldest child, who died two years before Thea, leaving a son who survived Thea.

The son will argue that once his parent was born, the interest in Thea's trust vested. As a vested interest, it is inheritable and devisable. If Thea's oldest child died intestate, the interest would pass through intestacy to the child's heirs (including the son—again the facts are incomplete). If Thea's oldest child died testate, the interest would pass under the terms of his or her will (most likely to the residual donee).

The Uniform Probate Code adopts a different approach. Section 2-707 requires holders of future interests to survive to the time of distribution (assuming the right to distribution can be characterized as a future interest—an issue that turns on the precise terms of the trust, which the facts do not provide). If a remainderman does not survive to the time for distribution, the UPC provides for a gift over to the remainderman's issue; and if there are none, the gift fails and is returned to the settlor's estate—unless there is an express default taker who is to take in the event the gift fails. Under the UPC approach, one-third of the trust assets would be distributed to the son of Thea's child who predeceased her. The other two-thirds would be divided equally between her surviving children.

What is the effect of Thea's divorce from Fred?
The UPC provides that the dissolution of a marriage has the effect of revoking a testamentary gift to the former spouse (UPC §2-804(b)), unless the will or a court order or a marital agreement expressly provides to the contrary. Therefore, Fred gets nothing. (This would be so even if there were no codicil or the codicil were, for some reason, invalidated.)

What does Sal receive?
The UPC provides that where a testator devises stock, and at the time the testator executed the will, the testator owned matching shares of stock, if thereafter the stock changes due to action initiated by the corporate entity, the beneficiary receives the benefit of the change—regardless of whether the language of the gift makes it look like a general or specific gift. (UPC §2-605(a)(1).) At the time Thea executed her codicil, she owned matching shares of Disney stock. Therefore, Sal is entitled to the 50-share increase that occurred between the time the codicil was executed and the testator's death. His gift includes the 100 shares allocated to him in the will, plus the additional 50 shares issued as a stock dividend before Thea's death.

What is the effect of the stock dividend that occurred after Thea's death?
Because all interests in the estate became vested at Thea's death, the stock dividend during the period of administration is allocated 100 percent to the party who holds the underlying stock interest. Here, the stock dividend on the shares held in trust will go to the trust beneficiaries; the stock dividend on the shares held by the probate estate will go to the devisee under the will—Sal.

Answer to Question 9

Important aspects: omitted child, testamentary gift to trust, incorporation by reference lapse, interested witness, spendthrift trusts, trust modification

1. How should Alice's estate be distributed?

Does it matter that Daniel was not mentioned in the will?
In general, a testator is free to disinherit a child in his or her will. Some states have attempted to mitigate the effect of this general principle. Thus, in some states a child is barred from taking only if the intent to disinherit is expressed in the will. In some states, only children who are born after the will is executed are protected. The UPC now protects after-born children only, in circumstances that are not relevant under these facts. (UPC §2-302.) But the UPC makes no provision for a child who is alive when the will is executed unless the testator erroneously believes that the child is dead (in which case the child is treated as an omitted after-born child). Daniel's arguments will fall on deaf ears. Alice made adequate provision for Daniel both in the original trust and also through her additional bequest to the trust in her will. There is no reason to conclude that she meant to do anything more for Daniel.

Should the $100,000 bequest to the trustee fail?
According to the facts, Daniel has asserted that the $100,000 bequest to Bank as trustee should fail because the trust document was not executed in compliance with the Statute of Wills. This argument will also fail.

There is nothing in the facts to suggest that the original trust instrument was defective in any way or that it was invalid. The bequest to Bank will simply operate as a gift to an existing valid legal entity. An existing trust is an eligible devisee, and the gift to the trust will be held and distributed pursuant to the terms of the trust. (UPC §1-201(11).) Daniel's challenge of the $100,000 bequest to Alice's trust is without merit.

In the alternative, the beneficiaries under the trust can argue incorporation by reference. The doctrine of incorporation by reference permits a separate writing that is in existence when a will is made to be incorporated within the will, if the language of the will (1) manifests an intent to incorporate the document, and (2) describes the document sufficiently to permit its identification. Although the doctrine is generally applied to informal documents of the testator that he or she wants to include within his or her will, it can be applied to the trust here. The trust agreement (including the amendment signed by Daniel himself) was already in existence when the will was executed, and it was specifically mentioned in the will.

Did the bequest to Celia lapse at her death?
A will is deemed effective as of the date of the testator's death. A gift to a named beneficiary who has died before the testator is therefore deemed invalid. It is said to lapse. Most states have statutes that control the disposition of a lapsed bequest. Under the UPC's antilapse provision, when a beneficiary who is a lineal descendant of the testator's grandparent predeceases the decedent, the gift passes to his or her surviving descendants. (UPC §2-603(b)(1).) As Alice's sister, Celia was protected by this provision. Doris is entitled to receive the $50,000 devise to Celia as Celia's sole surviving descendant.

Is Doris's claim affected by her witnessing of the will?
At common law, any person having a pecuniary interest in the testator's estate was incompetent to act as witness to the testator's will. This impediment has been changed by statute in most states. Under the UPC, "[i]nterest no longer disqualifies a person as a witness, nor does it invalidate or forfeit a gift under the will." (UPC §2-505, Official Comment.) Furthermore, Doris did not have a pecuniary interest at the time she signed the will. Celia was still alive to take the gift and Doris was not an "interested person" as that term is defined in the UPC. (UPC §1-201(24).)

Conclusion:
Based upon the foregoing, (1) Bank, in its capacity as trustee of the trust established by Alice, would receive $100,000 from her estate; (2) Doris would receive $50,000; and (3) the balance would pass to Stan.

2. Can Phil reach Celia's interest in the trust?
In his attempts to reach Celia's assets in the trust, Phil has probably asserted that the spendthrift provisions added to the trust were invalid against him as a pre-existing creditor of Celia.

Phil might have initially argued that an *inter vivos* trust cannot ordinarily be terminated or modified by the settlor, unless this power has been specifically retained by him or her. However, most jurisdictions permit a settlor to terminate or modify an *inter vivos* trust provided the trustee and *all* of the outstanding beneficiaries agree. See Restatement 2d of Trusts, §338(1). Because Bank, Alice, Celia, and Daniel were the trustee, the settlor, and all the beneficiaries, they had the power to modify the trust by adding the spendthrift provision.

Phil might make a second, more powerful, argument that Celia's conduct in securing and participating in the execution of the amendment constituted a *fraud upon Phil as Celia's creditor.* Fraud on creditors occurs when a debtor attempts to place his or her assets beyond the reach of creditors without giving fair value for the assets or while retaining a concealed interest in the assets. Celia was arguably guilty of such conduct because she entered into a modification of the trust only to insulate her interest from Phil, while preserving her ability to receive income from the trust. When a fraud upon a creditor has occurred, the creditor may invade the trust to the extent of his debtor's interest.

The facts don't tell us whether Celia's consent was in fact necessary to effectuate a modification of the trust, or whether her consent was superfluous because Alice reserved the power to amend in the original instrument. If Celia's consent was crucial to the modification, Phil's "fraud upon creditors" argument should prevail. However, if Alice had reserved the power to amend the trust without Celia's consent, Phil's contention would be weaker. Even then, however, if it were shown that Celia induced Alice to make the change for the purpose of defeating Phil's rights as a creditor, a court might find that Phil had been defrauded.

[Note that some states allow certain classes of creditors to reach a beneficiary's interest in a spendthrift trust. In some states a creditor who has rendered basic necessities to the beneficiary may reach the beneficiary's interest. Phil might be able to persuade the court that his services as building contractor should be included in the definition of basic necessities. Other creditors who may reach spendthrift trust interests, depending on the jurisdiction and the approach, are (1) ex-spouses entitled to alimony; (2) children entitled to child support; and (3) federal and state governments entitled to taxes.]

Answer to Question 10

Important aspects: will execution and comity, holographic will, interested witness, omitted child, ademption, advancement, satisfaction

1. Is Tina's will valid in Calco?

Under UPC §2-506, a will is valid if it was executed in compliance with the law of the place where the will was executed, or with the law of the place where the testator was domiciled or had "an abode" at either the time of the execution or at the time of his or her death. Thus, while we are told that Tina's will was not valid under the law of Terra, it is valid in Calco—the place of Tina's domicile at death. The facts tell us that Calco's probate code is the same as the UPC. Tina's will qualifies as a holographic will (*i.e.*, a will that is signed by the testator and the material terms of which are in the testator's handwriting). See UPC §2-502(b). In the alternative, there is also a good chance that the document could be validated as an attested will under the harmless error doctrine. (UPC §2-503.)

Although Sally is an interested person as defined in UPC §1-201(23), her signature does not invalidate the will. First, a holographic will does not need to be witnessed at all, so Sally's signature was irrelevant to the validity of the will. Second, under the UPC, the signing of a will by an interested witness does not invalidate the will or any provision of it. (UPC §2-505(b).) Of course, a person opposing the will may be able to show that the witness—especially one who receives a substantial benefit under the will—exerted undue influence on the testator. See Comment, UPC §2-505.

2. How should Tina's estate be distributed?

Claims on behalf of George:

Can George's guardian claim an interest by George under the omitted child doctrine? UPC §2-302 deals with "omitted children." Was George's father Charlie an omitted child of Tina? The answer is "no." The UPC protects an omitted child only if (1) the testator erroneously believed the child, though alive, was deceased, or (2) the child was born or adopted *after* the execution of the will. Charlie was not an omitted child as that term is defined and George cannot claim through him. Further, the protection accorded to omitted children under UPC §2-302 does not extend to omitted grandchildren. The term "child" specifically excludes grandchildren of a testator. See General Definitions, UPC §1-201(5). A grandchild—even one born or adopted after the will is executed—cannot take advantage of the omitted child provisions of the UPC. George will receive nothing, even though he is an after-born issue of a child of the testator.

Gifts to Sally:
We have determined that Tina's will is valid in Calco. Does Sally's status as witness affect her status as beneficiary under the will? Under UPC §2-505, the signing of a will by an interested witness does not invalidate either the will or any of its provisions. The provisions for Sally's benefit remain intact. Sally was Tina's daughter and the natural object of Tina's affection and her largesse. Nothing in the facts indicates that Sally exercised any undue influence on her mother. On the contrary, we know that Tina later gave Sally enough money to buy a house.

Which house is "the house" referred to in the will?
George's guardian may contend that Tina meant to give Sally only the house in Terra, and that when the Terra house was sold, the doctrine of ademption by extinction applied and made the gift ineffective. At common law, ademption was applied mechanically; if the property referred to in the will was not in the estate at death, the gift failed. The modern trend is to soften the impact of ademption. One device is to construe the will as though it read at the death of the testator, not at the date of execution. Under this device, the original gift is deemed replaced by any substitute that may exist at death. Another device is to read the disposition in its most general sense instead of as referring to specific property. Thus, "my" house becomes not a specific house, but any building in which the testator resides.

The Uniform Probate Code offers relief in the case of substituted real or tangible personal property. UPC §2-606(a) provides: "A specific devisee has a right to the specifically devised property in the testator's estate at death and: . . . (5) real or tangible personal property owned by the testator at death which the testator acquired as a replacement for specifically devised real or tangible personal property . . . ." Under this provision, the Calco house would be substituted for the Terra house under the will.

Even if the specific bequest fails, the Calco house will still go to Sally under the residuary clause.

The significance of the $300,000 "advancement":
Tina did not use the term "advancement" correctly. The term is applied only in the case of total or partial intestacy. An advancement is an *inter vivos* transfer made by a deceased before his or her death to a person who is entitled to take in intestacy, which the testator intended as an advance

against the person's final disposition from the intestate estate. For example, A has two sons, B and C. A dies intestate, leaving $100,000 in cash. Two years before his death, A gave son B $50,000 with the admonition, "This is an advance against your money when I die." Under the advancement doctrine, A's "hotchpot" estate would be $150,000. Inasmuch as B has already received $50,000, his share of the hotchpot is only $25,000. C would take the remaining $75,000 (remember the "real" probate estate is only $100,000, so the math works out fine). Under the UPC, an *inter vivos* gift to an heir of an individual who dies intestate is treated as an advancement only if (1) the testator declares in a contemporaneous writing that the gift is an advancement, or the donee acknowledges it in writing; or (2) a writing of the decedent, or a written acknowledgment of the donee, indicates that the gift is to be taken into account in computing the division and distribution of the intestate estate.

Here, it's clear that by using the word "advancement" Tina meant only that she was giving Sally some money she needed then instead of keeping it for Sally as part of the residue of Tina's estate under her will.

Was the devise of the house to Sally satisfied by the inter vivos gift of $300,000?

When Tina gave Sally $300,000 to purchase the house, did Tina intend for the gift of cash to be in satisfaction of the bequest of the house? The effect of construing the gift as a satisfaction would be to revoke the bequest of the house. At common law, there was authority for the proposition that a substantial *inter vivos* gift to a child who was also a legatee presumably satisfied the legacy if the other beneficiaries of the will were other children of the testator. The presumption was rebuttable by evidence of a contrary intent by the testator.

Under UPC §2-609, an *inter vivos* gift is treated as a satisfaction only if the will provides for deduction, or if the testator declares in writing that the gift is in satisfaction of the devise, or if the devisee acknowledges in writing that the gift is in satisfaction. Although Tina did not use the word "advancement" correctly (as she died testate), one could argue that she was expressing the intent that her *inter vivos* gift to Sally should count against Sally's share of Tina's estate and that satisfaction should apply. The problem with this argument under these facts is that because Hector died before Tina, Sally stands to take all of Tina's estate. Application of the satisfaction doctrine is moot. Sally takes all of Tina's estate as the alternative taker under the residuary clause whether satisfaction applies or not. (Had Hector not predeceased Tina, he would have had a strong argument that satisfaction should apply under these facts and it would have affected Sally's gift under the will.)

Summary:
Sally receives Tina's entire estate.

Answer to Question 11
Important aspects: charitable trusts, charitable purpose, delivery, *cy pres*

Has Tippi created a valid charitable trust?
An *inter vivos* charitable trust requires (1) the settlor's intent to create a charitable trust, (2) funding (delivery of an identifiable property interest to the trust/trustee), and (3) possibly a writing (if the trust is to hold real property). A charitable trust does not require ascertainable beneficiaries because it is deemed to be for the benefit of the public at large or a large subset of the public. (The state attorney general typically has standing to enforce the trust on behalf of the public.)

The intent to create a trust arises any time one person transfers property to a second for the benefit of a third (or if the person uses traditional trust terminology). Here, although the facts do not indicate that Tippi used the term "trust" in her documents, she used the term "trustees," and she transferred the land and $100,000 to the trustees for the benefit of the public at large. Tippi intended to create a trust. She expressed her intent in writing, as required by the Statute of Frauds, because the trust holds real property. And she validly transferred an identifiable property interest (the land and $100,000 to the trust/trustees). If the trust purpose qualifies as a valid charitable purpose, Tippi has created a valid charitable trust.

Any function of a governmental or municipal nature, or any activity that is beneficial to the general community, is usually accepted as a "charitable" purpose. Because one of the traditional functions of government or of any organized society is to provide libraries for its citizens, Tippi's purpose is clearly charitable. The trust res consists of the land and the proceeds of Tippi's $100,000 check.

Who gets Tippi's stocks and bonds?
Who gets Tippi's stocks and bonds depends on whether they were "delivered" to the trust/trustee before she died. A trust instrument applies only to those assets that are transferred to the trust. Tippi's will leaves all of her assets to her daughter. The only claim the trust has to the stocks and bonds is that she transferred them to the trust *inter vivos*—before she died.

The trustees will claim that she transferred the assets to the trust when she created the trust. The facts state that the declaration of trust contained an "itemized list" of her stocks and bonds with a market value of $2 million. The trustees will argue that by itemizing the stocks and bonds in the document that declared her intent to create the trust, she was also declaring her intent to transfer the stocks and bonds to the trust. Because the stocks and bonds are intangible personal property, symbolic delivery is all that is necessary. The trustees will argue that by listing the property in the document creating the trust, the list constituted a symbolic delivery of the assets to the trust.

Absent other facts, listing personal property in the documents creating the trust is often sufficient to constitute delivery of the assets to the trust. The problem here is that the document expressing the intent to create the trust and listing the stocks and bonds goes on to expressly state that these "stocks and bonds *will be delivered*" to the trustees in installments in the future. Valid transfer of a property interest requires the intent to make a *present* transfer of the property interest and delivery. Betty, Tippi's only child and the beneficiary under her will, will argue that Tippi's statement that the stocks and bonds "*will be delivered*" constitutes merely a gratuitous promise to make a gift in the future — not a present transfer of the property interest. If the language is construed as constituting nothing more than a gratuitous promise to make a gift in the future, under traditional property principles, there is no transfer, and Betty is entitled to the stocks and bonds under the terms of the will.

The trustees have one final argument, however. The modern trend is to loosen the delivery requirements where there is clear and convincing evidence of the intent to make an *inter vivos* gift but the gift fails for want of delivery under traditional delivery standards. The modern trend is to uphold the gift despite the absence of traditional delivery.

In the end, who gets Tippi's stocks and bonds will probably turn on whether the court follows the traditional approach to delivery of gifts or adopts the modern trend. Most courts still follow the traditional approach.

Can the Board use the block of land as a public park and maintain it with the trust funds?

When a charitable trust is created for a particular purpose and the purpose cannot be accomplished, the trust is said to fail. A resulting trust in favor of the settlor is then imposed. Betty will contend that the trust purpose here (the construction and maintenance of a public library) has failed, and that a resulting trust should be imposed for the benefit of Tippi and her estate. On this theory, the Board should be ordered to transfer title to the trust res back to Tippi's estate.

However, the Board will argue that the *cy pres* doctrine should be applied to permit the use of the trust res for a public park. Under this doctrine, when the specific purpose for which a charitable trust has been created cannot be carried out, the court may permit the trust to continue for a *similar* purpose, provided this similar purpose fits within the testator's "general charitable intent." The court attempts to put itself into the testator's mind and decide whether the testator would prefer to support some reasonably comparable charitable purpose or to cause the assets to revert to his or her heirs.

Betty will contend that Tippi wanted to build only a library and would not have made any gift to the Board if she had known that it would not be used for this purpose. The Board will argue in rebuttal that the deed to the property was "in perpetuity," proving that Tippi intended the Board to keep the land even if some other good purpose had to be substituted.

Because courts ordinarily prefer to validate a charitable trust rather than destroy it, it is likely that the *cy pres* doctrine will be applied. Thus, the Board will likely be allowed to create and maintain the park with the land and funds given to the trust by Tippi, even if the Board doesn't get to use the proceeds of the stocks and bonds. (But the fact that the funds in the Board's possession are sufficient to maintain the land as a public park for only a little over ten years argues against bothering to create the park at all.)

Answer to Question 12

Important aspects: revocation on divorce, ademption, totten trusts and payable on death accounts, incorporation by reference, lists of tangible personal property, lapse and antilapse, stock dividends

What is the effect of the divorce upon the gift to Leonard?

Except as may otherwise be provided in a court order, another "governing instrument," or a contract providing for the division of the marital estate, a divorce has the effect of revoking a testamentary gift to the former spouse. Here, there is no property settlement agreement and no evidence of any court order, so Leonard would *not* be entitled to take anything from the estate. (UPC §2-804(b).) If Fay's estate is not disposed of by the other bequests, the residuary will be disposed of as if Fay had died intestate. If the other bequests exhaust all of Fay's assets, there will be no residue.

The UPC provides that, if a decedent dies leaving descendants (but no spouse), the estate passes to the descendants by representation. The estate is divided at the earliest level at which there are living descendants. (UPC §2-103(a)(1); UPC §2-106(b).) This means that, assuming both were alive, Linda and Michael would each receive one-half of the residuary estate. But because Michael is deceased, Roberta, his adopted daughter, would take his half of the residuary estate by representation.

How will the proceeds of the sale of the "business property" be disposed of?

Ademption:
At common law, a *specific* devise of property that was no longer in the testator's estate at his or her death was usually treated as "adeemed" —that is, canceled. A specific devise is a gift that is clearly identifiable as against all other assets of the estate. Because the Main Street property was disposed of by Fay many years before her death, ademption would appear to apply, wiping out the gift of this property to Linda.

However, the modern trend is to discourage ademption. Some states have statutes that create the presumption that the testator does not intend ademption if the proceeds of the specific bequest can be followed into other assets of the testator at his or her death. Some courts interpret the bequest as one of form only; a change in the form of a gift is not relevant if the testator intends one form to replace another.

The current version of UPC §2-606 adopts the presumption against ademption. It provides that even if the substituted assets are not clearly a replacement for the original bequest (in this case, one business property for another), a specific beneficiary is entitled to the value of any specific bequest, real or personal, to the extent that such property is not in the testator's estate at death, and to the extent that it is established that ademption would be inconsistent with the testator's manifested plan of disposition.

Here, however, there is strong evidence that ademption is *consistent* with the testator's plan of disposition. Following the sale of the business property, Fay put half of it in her commercial account and the other half in a savings account in the name of "Fay Woods, Trustee for Linda Woods." Based on Fay's actions, a strong argument can be made that Fay *did* intend for ademption to apply. Fay did not intend for Linda to get a pecuniary devise equal to the value of the business property as of its date of disposition ($20,000). Fay intended for Linda to get only $10,000 of the proceeds as evidenced by Fay putting only half of the sale proceeds in the savings account for Linda. Applying ademption therefore is more consistent with Fay's apparent manifested plan of disposition than not applying it. Ademption should apply to the business property (however, Linda should get the $10,000, but under a different doctrine—see below).

Is Linda entitled to the $10,000 in the savings account?
One of Fay's cash assets was the $10,000 deposited into a bank account designated "Fay Woods, Trustee for Linda Woods." Under traditional trust principles, this will probably be construed as a Totten trust (*i.e.*, the trust relationship is created by the designation upon the savings account). A Totten trust is in the nature of a revocable trust. The trust res is owned by the trustee during his or her lifetime and may be used or withdrawn by him or her, but passes to the beneficiary upon the death of the trustee. Thus, Linda should be entitled to the $10,000.

Under the modern trend, the money in the savings account can also be characterized as a payment-on-death account. While such accounts were invalid under common law, they are permitted under the UPC. (UPC §6-101.) Such payment-on-death designations are valid nonprobate transfers, and Linda would be entitled to it as such.

As for the half of the proceeds from the sale of the business property that Fay deposited in her commercial account, that money (along with the other $5,000 in the commercial account) would ordinarily fall to the residuary clause of her will. Because Fay and Leonard divorced, the residuary clause in favor of Leonard fails, and the property that otherwise would have passed under it falls to intestacy. Under intestacy Linda will receive one-half (or $7,500), and the other half that would have passed to Michael will pass to his adopted child, Roberta.

What disposition should be made of the jewelry described in the typed note?

The note designating the specific jewelry that would pass to Linda was not executed with the requisite testamentary formalities. The execution was not witnessed and therefore, the note does not qualify as a codicil. No part of the note except the signature and date was in the testator's handwriting, so it was not a valid holographic will. But Linda should still be able to convince the court to admit the list as part of the will.

First, under the doctrine of incorporation by reference, material extraneous to the will that was (1) in existence when the will was created; (2) referred to in the will in a way that shows the testator's intent to incorporate it; and (3) described sufficiently to permit its identification will become part of the will. (UPC §2-510.) Of course, the UPC does require that the extraneous writing be in existence when the will was executed, and it is not clear from these facts which document came first. However, because they are both dated on the same day and the will refers to jewelry "as is enumerated" on the list, the court will probably presume that the list preceded the will and should be incorporated.

Second, even if the list was not in existence at the time the will was created, it will probably still be incorporated under UPC §2-513. This provision states that a will may refer to an extraneous written list to dispose of specific items of tangible personal property provided that (1) the writing is signed by the testator; (2) the items and the devisee of the items are clearly identified; and (3) the items are "tangible personal property not otherwise specifically disposed of by the will, other than money." In addition, UPC §2-513 provides that "[t]he writing may be referred to as one to be in existence at the time of the testator's death; it may be prepared before or after the execution of the will; it may be altered by the testator after its preparation; and it may be a writing that has no significance apart from its effect on the dispositions made by the will." Because the note in question satisfies all of the requirements, it will be effective to constitute a gift to Linda of the jewelry mentioned in it.

How does Michael's death affect the gift of stock in the will?

Because Michael was a lineal descendant of Fay, the gift of stock to him (which would otherwise lapse because of his failure to survive Fay) will pass to Roberta, his descendant. (UPC §2-603(b).) Although adopted, Roberta is considered to be a child of both Wanda and Michael. (UPC §2-118.)

How does the stock dividend affect the testamentary gift to Michael?
Under the UPC, where the testator makes a gift of stock in the will, and the testator owns matching shares at the time the will is executed, the beneficiary gets all the additional shares of securities in the testator's estate as long as the additional shares were acquired as the result of action initiated by the corporate entity. (UPC §2-605.) This would include stock dividends. It doesn't matter that some of the securities included in the dividend are of a different class (*e.g.*, Class B) from those that were the direct subject of the bequest—so long as the issuing organization is the same. (UPC §2-605.) Thus, both the original stock and the stock dividends would pass to Roberta by reason of the antilapse provision.

In summary, Linda gets the $10,000 in the savings account and the jewelry listed in the note. Roberta gets all the XYZ stock. Linda and Roberta share equally the $15,000 in the commercial account.

Answer to Question 13

Important aspects: omitted spouse, holographic will, omitted child, revocation, revival, republication by codicil, dependant relative revocation, correction of testator's mistake

The impact of Tess's marriage on her 1998 will:
If Tess had not executed any other testamentary documents after she executed the will, her marriage to Hubert would have had a significant impact on her testamentary plans. Under the UPC, a surviving spouse who marries the testator *after* his or her will is executed is entitled under most circumstances to receive the value of his or her intestate share of all assets left by the testator, at least to the extent that the assets are not left to a child of the testator who was born before the marriage. (UPC §2-301.) Because it does not appear that Tess had a child before the marriage, Hubert would have been entitled to take his intestate share.

Effect of the 2000 "codicil":
When a testator labels a testamentary document a "codicil" rather than a "will," the normal assumption is that he or she intends only to alter, amend, or clarify a prior will. But when the document—although labeled a "codicil"—completely disposes of the testator's property, it will be strongly presumed that the testator intended a new will revoking all prior wills, not an amendment. See UPC §2-507(c). Under this rule of interpretation, the August 4, 2000, document will be presumed to represent a new and complete will, because it completely disposes of Tess's estate. The document satisfies the UPC's holographic will requirements (*i.e.*, a writing, with the material provisions in the testator's handwriting, signed by the testator, and which has testamentary intent). (UPC §2-502(b).) The so-called codicil became Tess's new will.

Effect of Sonny's birth:
If the 2000 document continued to control Tess's estate, Sonny would have the right to take his intestate share of her estate. Under UPC §2-302, if a testator has no child living at the time he or she executes the will, an omitted after-born child takes an intestate share, unless (1) it appears from the will that the omission was intentional; (2) the testator provided for the child outside the will and intended for that gift to be in lieu of the child taking under the will; or (3) the will devises all or substantially all the estate to the omitted child's other parent. Sonny qualifies as an omitted child relative to the 2000 will, and none of the exceptions apply (Hubert does not take "substantially" all of the estate). Sonny would have been entitled to an

intestate share. However, as we shall see, Tess's second codicil may have the effect of preventing Sonny from receiving his intestate share.

Did the second codicil revoke the first one?
On first reading, the second codicil appears to have revoked the August 4, 2000, document. The first sentence of the second codicil states, "I revoke my codicil of August 4, 2000."

If the codicil is construed as revoking the 2000 document, we are left with two options: Either (1) one-fourth of the estate goes to Harvale College, the rest to intestacy; or (2) the 1998 will is revived. There is no evidence to support the latter. As for the former, despite the clear statement in the codicil revoking the first codicil, one can argue that Tess merely wanted to abort the gift to State University. This is a tough call, but there is a good chance that the court will read both codicils in their entirety and conclude that Tess intended the second codicil to be merely an amendatory document (remember both codicils are *holographic* documents, a fact that should not be lost on the court). Extrinsic evidence is generally admissible to explain ambiguities in a will or codicil, and the fact that the second codicil resulted from Tess's dissatisfaction with professionalism in college athletics presumably can be proved. As a consequence of the strong desire by most courts to attempt to effectuate a testator's intent and to avoid intestacy, the second codicil will probably be deemed to have merely modified, *not* revoked, the August 4, 2000, document.

We have assumed in our discussion that the second codicil meets the formal requirements for a testamentary document under the UPC—even though it was unwitnessed, it is in the testator's handwriting and signed by her, so it is valid as a holographic testament. (UPC §2-502(b).)

Effect of the second codicil:
If we proceed under the assumption that the second codicil merely modified the first, it will have affected Tess's previous testamentary scheme in two ways.

First, a codicil is usually deemed to republish and reconfirm a prior will to the extent it does not change or modify the prior will. When Tess executed the second codicil, Sonny was already born. As a child in being, he would no longer qualify as a pretermitted child. Presumably, if Tess had intended otherwise, she would have made provision for Sonny in the second codicil. Because she chose not to, and because the second codicil is valid, Sonny will receive nothing from Tess's estate.

Second, the codicil probably effectively revoked the devise to State University. While Tess's statement, "Nothing to athletic factories like State University," does not specify that the gift is revoked, this conclusion is virtually inescapable, especially as Tess clearly expressed the terms of the alternative gift to Harvale. As we've discussed, extrinsic evidence is ordinarily admissible to explain ambiguities in a will or codicil, and proof that Tess was upset with professionalism in college athletics at the time the second codicil was made would be admissible. The second codicil revoked the devise to State University and substituted the Harvale academic scholarship fund for the earlier gift.

What is the effect of Tess's mistake?
State University will contend that under dependent relative revocation, in which there is a valid revocation based upon a mistake, and the testator would not have revoked but for the mistake, the revocation is not given effect—and the original gift is reinstated. State University will argue that although Tess validly revoked the gift to it in her second codicil, she acted under a mistaken fact (that the college was an athletic factory) and that had she known that the University had voted to discontinue all intercollegiate athletic programs, she would not have revoked the gift. (Where the revocation is by writing, invariably courts also require the mistake to be set forth in the revoking instrument—which is the case here.)

The problem with application of dependent relative revocation under these facts is that Tess made an express gift of the property in question to Harvale College. Dependent relative revocation typically applies where the requirements are otherwise satisfied and there is no valid express new gift. Here, the valid express new gift to a completely different university would make it extremely difficult, if not impossible, for the court to apply dependent relative revocation.

The general rule is that courts do not correct mistakes. Dependent relative revocation is a narrow exception to that general rule, which probably does not apply to these facts. The gift to State University is revoked.

Is the gift to Harvale College valid?
Historically, a gift to charity within the period—usually six months—immediately before the testator's death was invalid under statutes called mortmain statutes. Under such a statute, the gift to Harvale would be invalid. But no states still have mortmain statutes, and the Uniform Probate Code does not recognize the mortmain concept. The gift to Harvale is valid.

How should Tess's estate be distributed?
If we assume that the second codicil controls the disposition of Tess's estate, then Harvale College would receive one-fourth of Tess's estate, Hubert would receive one-half, and Martha one-fourth. This is the most likely result.

Answer to Question 14

Important aspects: holographic will, interested witness, partial revocation by physical act, lapse, secret trusts and semisecret trusts, determination of Nell's intestate heirs

1. Is the will valid?

Nelly's will should qualify as a holographic will. A holographic will is valid if it is signed by the testator and the material provisions are in her handwriting. Because Nelly's will is written in her own hand and signed by her, it should be probated. The fact that she signed at the bottom of page 1, instead of at the end of the document, should not invalidate the will; there is no requirement in most states, or under the UPC, that the signature be at the end of the document. See UPC §2-502, Official Comment. In any event, the two items that were written on page 2 (the date and Brad's signature) were not vital to the integrity of the document. The first page was sufficient to constitute a valid holographic will.

2. How should Nelly's estate be distributed?

Brad as interested witness:

Brad's signature as witness on the will probably will not invoke the common law interested witness doctrine to invalidate the will. True, he received a bequest under Nelly's will, but his signature was superfluous. No witness is required to support a holographic will. Brad's signature would ordinarily be ignored on the issue of the will's validity. In any case, under the UPC, the "signing of a will by an interested witness does not invalidate the will or any provision of it." (UPC §2-505(b).)

Was Ann's gift revoked by striking through her name?

Although not all states recognize partial revocation by act, the UPC permits revocation of any part or all of a will if the testator, or another in the testator's presence and at the testator's direction, performs the revocatory act on the will itself with the intent and purpose of revoking the will. (UPC §2-507.) The rule applies equally to a holographic will and a will that has been executed before witnesses. The revocatory act may consist of "burning, tearing, canceling, obliterating, or destroying" the will or any part of it. See UPC §2-507(a)(2).

There is no doubt that the lines through Ann's name constitute a revocatory act *if* performed by the testator with the intent to revoke or by another in the testator's presence and at her direction. The problem here is that it is impossible to tell who drew the lines through the gift to Ann. Brad is prepared to testify that, in his presence, he saw the testator draw the lines with the intent to revoke. The problem is that Brad is an interested witness with respect to this claimed act (he stands to take a share of the money in question if it falls to intestacy—see below). Moreover, the potential for fraud (maybe Brad drew the lines because he did not like Ann or just to increase the size of his share of the estate) is one of the primary reasons some states do not recognize partial revocation by act at all.

Brad could also invoke revocation by presumption. Where a will is last in the testator's possession and cannot be found following the testator's death, a presumption arises that the testator destroyed the will by act with the intent to revoke (at least where the testator had capacity until death). A variation on the presumption doctrine is where the will is found with revocatory marks on it. In this case the presumption arises that the testator made the marks with the intent to revoke. The presumption, however, is rebuttable if there is a more plausible explanation for why the will cannot be found (or why it has revocatory marks on it). Here, if there is evidence that Brad had access to the will either immediately before or immediately after Nelly died, Ann could argue that the more plausible explanation is that Brad drew the lines through the gift.

This is a close call and will depend on the credibility of the witnesses. Brad's credibility will be critical to this issue, but the facts look rather suspicious, particularly when coupled with his behavior and comments with respect to the gift of Nelly's stocks and bonds. Although it is a close call, it is more likely that the court will conclude that there is not enough evidence to establish that the gift to Ann was validly revoked.

Lapse of Charlie's share:
A devise is said to lapse when the beneficiary dies before the testator and the will fails to provide an alternative disposition of the property. Because Charlie predeceased Nelly, his $10,000 gift will lapse. Most states and the UPC have adopted antilapse provisions to protect certain devisees. If the devise is to a child of the testator who predeceases the testator, his or her surviving issue will take the devise in his or her place. (UPC §2-603.) Because Charlie had no descendants, there is no one to take his share under the antilapse provision. The failed gift will fall to the residuary clause, if there is one, otherwise to intestacy.

(The class gift doctrine does not apply here because the gift is not a single gift to a class—it is three separate bequests of $10,000 to three individuals.

The will made bequests of $10,000 to "*each* of my children." Any attempt to characterize the gift as a class gift would fail.)

The stocks and bonds:

A secret trust arises when a bequest in a will appears unconditional and unequivocal but was made upon the oral promise of the devisee to hold the devise in trust for someone else. No reference to the trust is made in the will. In a semisecret trust, the will makes reference to the existence of a trust but no beneficiary of the trust is specified. Presumably, the testator and the devisee have agreed orally who is to benefit from the trust. Here, because the language in Nelly's will directed Brad to use the stocks and bonds "as we have agreed," the arrangement would be viewed as a semisecret trust. The majority view under these facts is that the trust fails for lack of a designated beneficiary. Under these circumstances, the named trustee (*i.e.*, Brad) holds the stocks and bonds in a resulting trust for the benefit of the residuary beneficiaries. See Restatement 3d of Trusts, §8. If there is no residuary clause, they go to the testator's heirs as in intestacy. In a few jurisdictions, a constructive trust is imposed in favor of the intended beneficiary. See Restatement 2d of Trusts, §55, Comment h, applying the minority approach.

If the majority view is followed, the stocks and bonds here will pass by intestacy because there is no residuary clause. If the minority view is followed, the trust will be enforced according to its (secret) terms. Thus under the minority view, if Brad's testimony is believed, he will take outright (he is the remainderman after the life estate to Charlie), and if his testimony is *not* believed, the gift will fail and pass by intestacy. (Inasmuch as Brad is an interested witness who stands to benefit more if a constructive trust is imposed, the court may be suspicious of his self-serving testimony as to the terms of the semisecret trust and may favor a resulting trust so that Ann can share in the property.)

The house and Nelly's other personal effects:

When a testator fails to dispose of some of his or her property by an existing valid will, the property passes by intestacy. On these facts, the house and other personal effects would be shared equally by Brad and Ann. If the semisecret trust of Nelly's stock and bonds is deemed to fail (see above), then the stock and bonds will also pass to both by intestacy.

If we assume for the purpose of argument that Nelly herself struck through Ann's name and that the specific bequest to Ann was therefore invalid, does this also mean that Ann will be completely disinherited—that is, that she will not even receive her intestate share? Under the UPC, the testator may disinherit anyone, including a child, but he or she must do so "expressly." See UPC §2-101(b). It is unlikely that a court would find that by striking through Ann's name in a clause providing for a specific bequest of a limited amount, Nelly intended to disinherit Ann entirely. It's likely that Ann will be permitted to take her one-half intestate share along with Brad, whose testimony is likely to be discounted.

Answer to Question 15

Important aspects: testamentary capacity, interested witness, will execution, holographic wills, harmless error, revocation, dependent relative revocation, determining intestate heirs, ambiguity and extrinsic evidence

Was the document that Tate signed on December 2, 2007, a valid will?
Although the document prepared by Tate's lawyer in 2007 did not use or mention the word "will," it would appear to have been intended as Tate's will. This is evidenced by the following facts: (1) the document used the words, "I . . . dispose of all my estate as follows . . . ," and the words, ". . . I have intentionally omitted all my other heirs"; (2) it disposed of Tate's entire estate; (3) it was prepared at Tate's request by an attorney; and (4) Tate declared it to be his "will" when he withdrew it from his pocket during the party.

Tate's son, Art, will contend that Tate did not have the requisite testamentary capacity when he signed the document at the party. To be a valid will, the testator must be at least 18 years old and of sound mind at the time he or she executes the will. Sound mind generally requires that the testator have the ability to know (1) the natural objects of his or her bounty, (2) the nature and extent of his or her property, (3) the nature of the testamentary act he or she is performing, and (4) how all of these factors relate together to form an orderly disposition of the testator's property.

Here the facts indicate that Tate was "slightly intoxicated" when the will was executed. Sally will argue that Tate displayed the requisite testamentary capacity because (1) he characterized the document as his "will," (2) he had the presence of mind to have the document witnessed, and (3) he later referred to the document as his will when he tried to cancel it. Art will emphasize (1) that Tate had had "several drinks," (2) that Tate was "intoxicated" at the time he signed the document and asked the others to witness it, and (3) that as a matter of public policy individuals should be discouraged from executing wills while under the influence of alcohol. The mere fact that a testator has a drink before signing a will should not be enough to cause him or her to lose his or her testamentary capacity, but if a testator is drunk, it is unlikely that he or she has the requisite testamentary capacity. This is a close call under these facts and depends on how intoxicated Tate was (the facts are ambiguous on this issue — saying he was "intoxicated" but only "slightly"). This issue could go either way.

The fact that Sally was one of the witnesses to the will is not significant. Interested persons (*i.e.*, those receiving a bequest under the will) qualify as witnesses. (UPC §2-505(b).) Besides, because only two witnesses are needed under the UPC (UPC §2-502(a)(3)), Sally's signature as a third witness would be superfluous.

In summary, it is unclear whether the document Tate executed on December 2, 2007, is a valid will.

Was the typed document that Tate signed on January 20, 2008, a valid will?

Art and Sally will both contend that the document that Tate signed in his lawyer's office on January 20, 2008, was not intended to serve as a codicil to Tate's will, but only as a nonbinding memorandum that the lawyer would reduce to a more formal document that Tate would execute at a later date. There is no indication that the January 20, 2008, document was properly witnessed. Tate was in his lawyer's office when the memo was prepared and signed. If he had intended the memo to constitute his will, witnesses were available (the lawyer and his secretary were there). The memo did not satisfy the requirement of UPC §2-502 that two witnesses sign the will.

Nor could the January 20, 2008, memorandum be probated as a holographic will. The "material provisions" were not in Tate's handwriting. (UPC §2-502(b).)

An argument can be made that the January 20, 2008, memorandum should be treated as a valid will under UPC §2-503. This section allows a document not satisfying the formalities for a will to be treated as one, "if the proponent . . . establishes by clear and convincing evidence that the decedent intended the document . . . to constitute . . . the decedent's will. . . ." On these facts, CCF could argue that the handwritten statement written by Tate across the December 2007 will ("I have made a new will") shows that he intended the January 20, 2008, document to be his will. It is debatable whether this argument will be enough to meet the "clear and convincing evidence" standard of UPC §2-503.

It is unclear whether the January 20, 2008, document will qualify as a will. If it does, and if the December 2, 2007, will also qualified as a will, the latter will completely revoke the prior will by inconsistency. (UPC §2-507(a)(1).) If the January 20, 2008, document does not qualify as a will, whether Tate has a will depends on whether the December 2, 2007, document qualifies as a will.

Did Tate revoke the December 2007 will by the statement he wrote across it?

Assuming, *arguendo*, that the December 2007 document was validly executed, Art will contend that it was validly revoked by two independent means. First, he will argue that the words Tate wrote across the will constituted a valid holographic revocation that incorporated the will by reference. An express revocation can be accomplished by utilizing the steps necessary to make a valid holographic will—that is, the material terms must be in the testator's handwriting, and the document must be signed by the testator. Because the revocation was in Tate's handwriting and was initialed by him (the initials "TT" are sufficient to count as a "signature" —see UPC §2-502, Comment), these requirements were satisfied.

Art will also argue that the statement written on the will was a valid "revocatory act." UPC §2-507(a)(2) defines "revocatory act" to include a "canceling" of the will. Cancelation is effective "whether or not the ... cancellation touched any of the words on the will." The statement here qualifies under this section, and it serves to revoke the will.

Art's argument that the December 2007 will was validly revoked by the handwritten statements across it will probably succeed.

Should the December 2007 will still be probated under the doctrine of dependent relative revocation?

Under the doctrine of dependent relative revocation (DRR), where the testator validly revokes his or her will because of a mistake, and the testator would not have revoked the will but for the mistake, the doctrine of DRR authorizes the court to ignore the valid revocation and probate the will. Where the valid revocation is by act, invariably the courts also require proof of an alternative plan of disposition that fails. Where the valid revocation is by writing, invariably the courts require the writing to set forth the mistake and the mistake must be beyond the testator's knowledge. Sally will argue that if the court concludes that the December 2007 will was validly revoked but the January 2008 document is *not* a valid will, then the court should apply DRR to give effect to the December 2007 will.

Here, the December 2007 will was validly revoked. It appears that it was revoked because Tate assumed his January 20, 2008, document was a valid will. If that is not the case, Sally can successfully argue that the revocation was based upon a mistake. If the revocation is deemed to have been by act (see above discussion), the failed alternative testamentary scheme is the January 20, 2008, document. If the revocation is deemed to have been by writing (see above discussion), the writing sets forth the mistake ("I have made a new will") and the mistake is beyond the testator's knowledge. (Tate did not know that the January 20, 2008, document would not qualify as a valid will.) The only issue is whether Tate would have preferred that the revocation be ignored if he had known of the mistake—that is, if he had known that the January 20, 2008, document was not a valid will.

Because Art would be the sole recipient of Tate's estate if Tate were deemed to have died intestate, Art would contend that DRR should *not* be applied. There is no reason to believe that Tate would have wanted the initial will revived—the January 20, 2008, memorandum contained a completely different dispository scheme, and the facts do not show that Tate would have preferred his original scheme over intestacy.

Sally would argue in rebuttal that Tate would have preferred that his estate be distributed in accordance with the December 2007 will rather than according to an arbitrary state-drafted intestacy scheme. Sally will emphasize that as evidenced by both documents, the December 2007 document and the January 2008 document, Tate did not want his son to take a dime of his estate, and if the court were *not* to apply DRR, Tate's son would take *all* of his estate.

This is a close call. Although there is no affirmative evidence that Tate would have preferred the December 2007 will over intestacy, there is the argument that both documents evidence the intent that Tate's son not take any of Tate's estate. The court could go either way on this issue—but courts tend to favor decedents' family members, which would mean here that it is unlikely that the court would apply DRR.

The more probable result is that Tate will be deemed to have died intestate. His son Art will inherit Tate's entire estate. Section 2-103(a)(1) of the UPC gives the entire estate of one who dies without a spouse to the testator's "descendants"—and Art is Tate's only descendant.

Assume Tate's December 2007 will was probated under DRR. How would his estate be distributed?

For purposes of discussion, two questions arise if the December 2007 will is deemed revived. First question: Was Art alive when the will was made? If he was, then he would receive nothing. But if he was born after Tate made the December 2007 will, he would be considered an omitted child and he would receive his intestate share (the entire estate). (UPC §2-302.)

Second question: What was the consequence of Tate's mistake in describing his nephew as "Ron" instead of "Don"? Because (1) Tate has no nephew named "Ron," and (2) the description of the recipient in the will is otherwise ambiguous ("my favorite nephew"), we don't know on the face of the will which of his two nephews Tate preferred. In this instance, virtually all courts permit extrinsic evidence to prove the identity of the intended beneficiary. Under common law terminology, this is known as a latent ambiguity. Under the misdescription doctrine, extrinsic evidence would be admissible to establish the latent ambiguity. The court would strike the first letter of the nephew's name (the "R") and then decide whether the testator's intent is clear enough that it would feel comfortable giving the gift to Don (assuming that is what Tate intended—if he intended Zeke, the court probably would not be able to construe the will in favor of Zeke and the gift would be deemed to fail). Under the modern trend, courts are much more likely to admit extrinsic evidence to reform the will. In particular, under the scrivener's error doctrine, as long as there is clear and convincing evidence of the error and clear and convincing evidence of its effect upon testator's intent, the evidence is admitted to prove and correct the mistake (whether the favorite nephew is Don or Zeke).

If the gift to the "favorite nephew" cannot be saved, it will fail. Under the modern trend, the UPC approach, where part of a residuary gift fails, it goes to the other residuary takers. Here, particularly if the court applies the traditional common law approach, there is a good chance the gift may fail, in which event Sally would take all of Tate's estate. On the other hand, if the court applies the modern trend approach, it is likely that the court will reform the will and give half of the residuary estate to Tate's favorite nephew (whoever that may be) and the other half to Sally.

Answer to Question 16

Important aspects: holographic will, integration, incorporation by reference, holographic will (document #3), delivery requirements for deeds, harmless error, additional shares included in stock bequest, ambiguity and extrinsic evidence

Do any of the documents, either alone or together, constitute a valid will?

These facts require that we scrutinize all of the documents both separately and together. We will call the document found in Tawny's top desk drawer the "primary document."

Is the primary document, standing alone, a valid will?

For a holographic will to be valid, there must be a writing, with the material provisions in the testator's handwriting, signed by the testator, and the document must have testamentary intent. (UPC §2-502.) The primary document is in writing, and it is signed by the testator (first name is sufficient as long as the testator intended that to be her signature). There are, however, issues with respect to whether the document adequately expresses the "material provisions" and whether the document has "testamentary intent." With respect to testamentary intent (the party's intent that this document constitutes his or her will), some jurisdictions require the testamentary intent to be in the handwritten provisions of the document. Here, the word that arguably expresses that intent is "estate" —but there is precedent that "estate" is too ambiguous standing alone to constitute testamentary intent. Under the most recent version of the UPC, however, testamentary intent can be established by extrinsic evidence. If the court accepts Document #3 as the second page of the will, the express use of the word "will" and the overall intent as expressed by the two documents should be sufficient to establish testamentary intent. (One could also try to argue that Document #3 should be considered as page 2 of the will and that the two pages are one will under integration. Integration provides that all pieces of paper that were physically present at the time the will was executed and that the testator intended to be pages of the will constitute the pages of the will. The problem is that here there is no evidence as to which pieces of paper were physically present when Tawny signed the primary document.)

Even assuming, *arguendo*, that the primary document expresses testamentary intent, the problem is that the primary document, standing alone, still does not express the material provisions. The material provisions—that is, who gets what—are expressed in Document #1 and Document #2, found in the bottom drawer of the desk as described by the primary document. The primary document, standing alone, does not constitute a valid will.

Can the primary document be combined with Documents #1 and #2 to create a valid will?

The beneficiaries will attempt to argue that Documents #1 and #2 can be "combined" with the primary document to give the primary document its material provisions—thereby qualifying the primary document as a valid holographic will. There are two doctrines they can invoke. The first is integration (discussed above), but there is no evidence that Document #1 was physically present when the primary document was executed (and the language of the primary document implies just the opposite; the primary document expressly indicates that Documents #1 and #2 are elsewhere—in the bottom drawer of the testator's desk). It is unlikely that a court would give effect to either Document #1 or Document #2 under integration.

The second doctrine the beneficiaries will invoke to try to give effect to the material provisions in Documents #1 and #2 is incorporation by reference. Incorporation by reference permits a court to give effect to testamentary intent expressed in a document other than a will as long as the will expresses the intent to incorporate the document, the will describes the document with reasonable certainty, and the document was in existence when the will was executed. (UPC §2-510.) Here, the primary document makes reference to two pieces of paper that can be found in the bottom drawer. In fact, three pieces of paper were found. The first two read as if they are the documents to which the primary document was referring—they indicate to whom Tawny's property should be distributed. The third document, Document #3, reads like a codicil or page 2 of the primary document. As such, one can argue that when the primary document refers to "two pieces of paper" that will make known the testator's wishes for final distribution of her estate, the primary document (1) is expressing the intent to incorporate Documents #1 and #2 by reference, and (2) has described the documents being incorporated with reasonable certainty. The courts generally apply a low threshold to the first two requirements of incorporation by reference, so those elements are probably satisfied under these facts.

The problem is the third requirement. The party seeking to incorporate the documents must be able to prove that the documents being incorporated were in existence when the will was executed. Because the primary document is undated, this is a difficult task. The proponents of the holographic will, however, have two arguments. The first is based on the verb tense used in the primary document. The primary document says that the two pieces of paper "are in the bottom drawer" of my desk—not that they "will be" in the bottom drawer. The use of present tense arguably supports the position that Documents #1 and #2 were in existence at the time the primary document was executed. Second, the primary document expressly states that there are "two" pieces of paper in the bottom drawer. The primary document was able to give the exact number because the documents were already in existence. To the extent the court accepts these arguments as sufficient proof that the documents being incorporated were in existence at the time the will was created, the requirements to incorporate Documents #1 and #2 are satisfied.

Tawny's heirs will challenge the incorporation by reference arguments by arguing that (1) there is not sufficient evidence that Documents #1 and #2 are the documents to which the primary document is referring; (2) there is not sufficient evidence that Documents #1 and #2 were in existence when the primary document was executed; and (3) incorporation by reference permits a will to incorporate another document by reference, but the primary document does not qualify as a will unless the material provisions are incorporated by reference.

Incorporating the material provisions from Documents #1 and #2 into the primary document creates a document that arguably qualifies as a holographic will. It is, however, far from certain that a court would accept the incorporation by reference argument. Most courts take a strict approach to the requirement that the proponent must establish that the documents being incorporated were in existence at the time the will was executed. Here, that evidence is rather thin. If the court were to take the more traditional, strict approach, it is unlikely that the court would find a valid holographic will. The modern trend, however, focuses more on the testator's intent and takes a more lenient approach to the doctrine. If the court were to apply the modern approach, there is a good chance that the court would find a valid holographic will by incorporating the provisions of Documents #1 and #2.

Assuming the requirements for incorporation by reference are otherwise satisfied, Tawny's heirs might argue that it is inappropriate to incorporate the documents because the material provisions of both Documents #1 and #2 are typed, not handwritten. To the extent the documents are being incorporated into a holographic will, and one of the requirements of a holographic will is that the material provisions must be in the testator's handwriting, the heirs will argue that the material provisions of any document being incorporated by reference should have to be in the testator's handwriting as well. The courts, however, have rejected this argument. The material provision is the provision in the will that expresses the intent to incorporate the document. The document being incorporated into the holographic will does not have to be in the testator's handwriting. Incorporating typed material into a holographic will is permitted (but a testator cannot integrate typed material into a holographic will—another reason why integration is not helpful to the will proponents under these facts).

Can Document #3 be probated as a holographic codicil to the primary will?

Assuming that the primary document constitutes a valid will, the beneficiaries under Document #3 have a strong argument that it constitutes a holographic codicil to the primary document. Document #3 is in writing, it is signed by the testator, and it does a better job of expressing testamentary intent on its own (talks about the first page "of my will" and then calls this "Page 2"—thereby arguably establishing that the testator intended this document to be part of her will). This document also expresses some of the testator's material provisions ("everything else should be divided equally among Bob, Shirley, and Ann"). A strong argument can be made that this document qualifies as a valid holographic codicil to the primary document.

(To the extent a court might be reluctant to call the primary document a valid will, one might be able to give effect to the primary document through incorporation by reference. Here, the primary document makes reference to two pieces of paper that will be found in the bottom drawer. In fact, three pieces of paper were found. The first two read as the primary document indicated they would—they indicate to whom Tawny's property should be distributed. The third document, Document #3, reads like a codicil or page 2 of the primary document. As such, one can argue that when Document #3 refers to "my will" it is referring to the primary document. Most courts would hold that this reference adequately expresses the intent to incorporate the primary document and describes it with reasonable certainty. The question is whether there is sufficient evidence to establish that the primary document was in existence when Document #3 was created. There is only circumstantial evidence to support this claim. Because it is in the bottom drawer, and because it calls itself page 2, if the court concludes that page 1 is the primary document, there is sufficient evidence. That would permit the primary document to be incorporated by reference. Then the beneficiaries under Documents #1 and #2 would argue that the document being incorporated should be permitted to incorporate yet another set of documents per the arguments above to establish the material provisions.)

Summary:
A court could go either way on whether there is a valid will here, but a strong argument can be made that (1) the primary document, when combined with Documents #1 and #2, constitutes a valid holographic will; and (2) Document #3 constitutes a valid holographic codicil.

Is Document #1 (the deed) by itself a testamentary document?
Assuming, *arguendo*, that the court rejects the incorporation by reference argument and refuses to give effect to the primary document as a valid holographic will or Document #3 as a valid codicil, can Ann still successfully claim the house under Document #1—the deed? First, Ann cannot claim the house under the deed because the deed was not delivered *inter vivos*. A properly executed deed does not transfer the property interest until the deed is delivered. Delivery is an abstract concept, but it signifies the grantor's intent to relinquish all dominion and control over the property—to make a present transfer of the property interest in question. Where the grantor retains possession of the actual deed, the assumption is that the grantor has not delivered the deed. Because Tawny retained possession of the deed until she died, and because Tawny continued to live in the house and enjoy the benefits of the property, the deed was not delivered *inter vivos* and will not convey the house to Ann.

Ann may try to argue that the handwritten note attached to the deed constitutes a valid holographic will that incorporates the deed by reference and validly constitutes a testamentary transfer of the house. The note is in Tawny's handwriting, and Tawny validly signed it. But even if the case can be made that the note makes sufficient reference to the deed to permit incorporation by reference (a tough argument, but maybe because the documents are paper-clipped together and the use of the word "this"), there is no evidence of testamentary intent. Testamentary intent requires evidence that the testator intended the document to be taken down and probated as his or her will. There is nothing about Document #1, or the note attached to it, that expresses such intent. On the contrary, the reference to Document #1 in the primary document arguably indicates that Tawny intended the primary document to be the will and *not* Document #1 standing alone.

It is unlikely that Document #1 standing alone, or in conjunction with the handwritten note attached to it, can be given effect as a valid deed or can be probated as a valid will.

Assuming all the documents are read together as one integrated will, how should Tawny's estate be distributed?

The gift of "All my money—brother Bob":
There are several issues with respect to Tawny's gift to her brother Bob. First and foremost is the line through the gift and the handwritten interlineation "son Sam."

First, the handwritten interlineation does not qualify in its own right as a holographic will. There is not enough in the testator's handwriting to qualify as the material provisions, nor does the document, standing alone, have testamentary intent. The handwritten interlineation can be given effect only as part of the larger set of documents.

The problem is that when a document is incorporated by reference, it is incorporated as it exists on the day the will is executed. Subsequent amendments or modifications to the document cannot be given effect. Although the reference in the primary document is arguably sufficient to indicate that Document #2 was in existence when the primary document was executed, there is absolutely no way of knowing when the handwritten interlineation was made to Document #2. Sam cannot prove that the handwritten interlineation was on the document when the primary document was executed. Under a strict application of incorporation by reference, the handwritten interlineation should not be given effect. Moreover, assuming Document #3 qualifies as a valid codicil, and under republication by codicil, the codicil will re-execute, republish, and generally redate the underlying will, the same problem continues. Document #3, the codicil, is undated, so it is still impossible to prove that the handwritten interlineation was on Document #2 when the codicil was executed. Under strict application of incorporation by reference, the handwritten interlineation of the gift to "son Sam" cannot be given effect.

If, however, the jurisdiction has adopted the UPC's harmless error doctrine, Sam should be entitled to the money. Section 2-503 of the UPC validates a document or writing that doesn't meet testamentary formalities "if the proponent of the document or writing establishes by clear and convincing evidence that the decedent intended the . . . writing to constitute . . . (iii) an addition to or an alteration of the will . . . ." The comment to this section makes it clear that it is designed to cover the situation in which a testator crosses out some text and substitutes new text without a new signature and a new set of witnesses. The change from Bob to Sam probably satisfies this test, though there is no "clear and convincing" evidence that the change was made by Tawny herself rather than by someone else (say, Sam).

Assuming the jurisdiction has adopted UPC §2-503, there is a good chance Sam will take the money. Otherwise, the gift was validly revoked (assuming the jurisdiction recognizes partial revocation by act) and it will fall to the residuary where Ann, Bob, and Sam will share it equally.

The ABC stock:
The only issue with respect to the ABC stock is *when* the shares were acquired and *how* they were acquired. Because of the specific reference to ABC stock in Document #2, it is assumed that Tawny owned at least some shares of ABC stock at the time she executed the will. Under the UPC, where the testator makes a gift of stock in the will, and the testator owns matching shares at the time the will is executed, the beneficiary gets all the additional shares of securities in the testator's estate as long as the additional shares were acquired as the result of action initiated by the corporate entity. (UPC §2-605.) As long as Tawny either owned all $50,000 at the time Document #2 was executed, or any additional shares were acquired as a result of action initiated by ABC, Shirley will receive all of the ABC stock.

Jewelry:
There is a latent ambiguity in the gift. At the time of Tawny's death, she owned no jewelry, but she did own a jewelry box. The issue is whether the court will construe the entry in Document #2 "Jewelry—Ann" as referring to the jewelry box. Because of the ambiguity, extrinsic evidence will be admissible to help determine Tawny's intent (both under the common law approach, which only admits extrinsic evidence if the ambiguity is latent, and under the modern trend approach, which admits extrinsic evidence anytime there is an ambiguity). The key evidence will be the circumstances surrounding Tawny at the time the will was executed. Inasmuch as the date of the primary document is unknown, the court will focus on the date Document #2 was executed: June 1, 2008. If Tawny owned the jewelry box but not any jewelry on that date (or subsequently), Ann has a decent argument that Tawny was referring to the jewelry box. On the other hand, if Tawny owned jewelry on that date, Ann's argument that she is entitled to the jewelry box is weaker. (Though in that event, Ann might be able to convince the court that the gift should be construed as a specific gift and

that under the UPC she is entitled to the pecuniary value of the jewelry in question as of the date of its disposal.) If the court were to rule that Ann was not entitled to the jewelry box, it would fall to the residuary clause and be distributed equally to Ann, Bob, and Shirley.

Furniture:

Ann might argue that the devise of the house included the furniture within it. (How else could she enjoy the dwelling as much as Tawny?) But furniture in a home is usually considered personal property of the testator or testatrix and is not usually deemed part of the realty. There is no easy answer here, but because there is no clear indication that Tawny intended the furniture to go to Ann, it would probably be included in the residuary estate.

Summary:

This is a tough question with more uncertainty than certainty. At one end of the possibilities is that the court may rule that Tawny died intestate. Under that possible scenario, Ann and Sam would split all of her property equally. At the other end of the possibilities is that the court may rule that the combined documents constitute a holographic will and codicil. Under that scenario, Ann is likely to get the house; Sam is likely to get the money (as long as the jurisdiction has adopted the UPC's harmless error doctrine); Shirley is likely to get the ABC stock; Ann may or may not get the jewelry box (depending on the facts surrounding Tawny at the time the document was executed); and the furniture is likely to pass to Bob, Shirley, and Ann equally under the residuary clause in the codicil.

Answer to Question 17

Important aspects: omitted spouse, contractual wills, harmless error

Does the statute revoke the will in its entirety?

Under the plain language of the statute, because Andy's will did not mention his upcoming marriage to Patty, the will would be revoked, and Andy would die intestate. Patty could argue that because the will provides for Patty that the will provided for the possibility of future marriage, but that would be a difficult argument to make. Patty could also try to argue that the policy behind the statute, to protect new spouses, would in fact be defeated if the statute would be applied.

What effect would the revocation have on their contract?

If in fact the will was revoked by operation of the statute, then Andy would have breached the contract and Patty would be free to make any will she desired, presumably one that would not include Andy's sons as beneficiaries.

Could Patty argue scrivener's error?

Patty could argue that the will is valid under the doctrine of correction of mistakes. Under UPC §2-805, because the failure to reference the impending marriage was clearly a scrivener's error, the court could correct the error and nevertheless enforce the will. Correction of mistakes was not allowed under traditional common law, however, so in the absence of a statutory provision similar to the UPC or case law authorizing the court to correct mistakes, this argument would most likely fail.

Can Patty argue that the contract to make mutual wills overrides the operation of the statute?

Patty can also argue that the will is enforceable as a duly executed contract between Andy and her. Contracts to make wills are enforceable. The majority rule requires a writing to evidence such a contract (see UPC §2-514), but there is sufficient written documentation to establish the contract. Andy's sons could argue that Andy could breach the contract because he was the first to die, and Patty is therefore not harmed by the breach. However, Patty can argue that the contract was entered into for adequate consideration and is therefore enforceable. The court would be faced with competing claims: a revocation based on the plain language of a statute, intended to protect unanticipated spouses, and an otherwise enforceable contract to make a will. In other circumstances, courts have held that contractual wills must yield to the public policy of protecting new family members. However, in this case, the statute intended to protect Phyllis reduces the amount she would receive from Andy's estate, and in this unusual fact pattern the court may find that the contract between Andy and Patty takes precedence.

Answer to Question 18

Important aspects: will execution, holographic wills, antilapse, additions to stock bequests, ademption, interpretation of "personal effects," independent significance, determination of Tait's intestate heirs

1. Was the typewritten document dated September 17, 1995, a valid will?

The answer is "no." The document does not satisfy the formal requirements for a valid will. It was not signed by the testator. It was not acknowledged as a testamentary document before two witnesses. The testator's signature was not either witnessed by at least two subscribing witnesses or notarized.

2. Did the June 15, 2003, document create a valid holographic will?

The beneficiaries can make a very plausible argument that the June 15, 2003, document created a valid holographic will.

Hoby will contend that the June 15, 2003, document is *not* a valid holographic will because (1) it is not signed, but merely initialed; (2) it does not specifically incorporate by reference the distribution scheme set forth in the September 17, 1995, writing (and so contains no disposition of Tait's estate); (3) a subsequent document may not incorporate a prior document that is itself invalid as a testamentary document; and (4) even if the September 17, 1995, document were incorporated, there would still be no valid holographic will because the "material provisions" (*i.e.*, those describing the disposition of Tait's estate) are typewritten.

But the beneficiaries will reply as follows. First, the initials of the testator are ordinarily viewed as sufficient to satisfy the signature requirement in a will. Second, the word "adopt" should be construed to mean "incorporate by reference," because Tait obviously intended to give effect to the testamentary scheme in the September 17, 1995, writing. (It would not be helpful for the beneficiaries to argue that the word "adopt" should be read as "republish"; the majority view is that an invalid will *cannot* be republished.) The requirement that "material provisions" must be in the testator's handwriting is arguably satisfied by the words "I adopt" (*i.e.*, "I incorporate by reference") the typewritten draft. There is every reason to interpret the two documents together in this manner because they give effect to Tait's testamentary intentions instead of leaving her intestate. And lastly, the document adequately expresses testamentary intent. The opening reference to "sound mind" coupled with the later phrase "my last will" should be sufficient to indicate that Trisha intended the document to be her will. The case is even stronger when the language from the document being incorporated by reference is included in the analysis.

The beneficiaries should prevail. Therefore, the will (composed of the September 17, 1995, and June 15, 2003, documents together) is valid.

3. Assuming Tait had a valid will, how should her estate be distributed?

Minco stock:

Although Sal predeceased Tait, his daughter (Helen) would step into Sal's position under the antilapse provisions. (UPC §2-603(b).) Helen, although adopted, would be treated as Sal's issue. (UPC §§1-201(5), 2-118(a).)

The UPC provides that where a testator devises stock, and at the time the testator executed the will, the testator owned matching shares of stock, if thereafter the stock changes due to action initiated by the corporate entity, the beneficiary receives the benefit of the change—regardless of whether the language of the gift makes it look like a general or specific gift. (UPC §2-605(a)(1).) The facts are a bit ambiguous, but the natural inference from the language in the will is that Tait owned 150 shares of Minco stock when she executed her will. Moreover, the facts do not indicate how Tait acquired the additional shares. Assuming she acquired the additional shares as a result of action initiated by the company, Helen would take all of the additional shares. Therefore, Helen would receive all 300 shares of Minco stock unless Hoby was able to show that the additional shares of Minco stock were actually purchased by Tait from her general funds.

Zebco stock:

Hoby will contend that the gift of Oilco stock has been extinguished by ademption, and that, therefore, he is entitled to the Zebco stock via the residuary clause. When a testator devises a gift of *stock*, and he or she owned shares of stock at the time the will was executed that *match* the stock being devised in the will, the devisee is entitled to (1) any additional or other securities of the same entity owned by the testator at death by reason of action (such as a stock split or stock dividend) initiated by that entity, and (2) any securities *of another entity* owned by the testator as a result of a merger, consolidation, reorganization, or other similar action. (UPC §2-605.) Here, the facts are a bit ambiguous, but the natural inference from the language in the will is that Tait owned 500 shares of Oilco stock when she executed her will. As a result of the merger, she acquired 500 shares of Zebco. All 500 shares of Zebco stock in her estate appear to be the result of the merger. Unless Hoby can prove otherwise, Diane is entitled to all 500 shares of Zebco stock.

Abco stock:
Bill will contend that the Abco stock passes to him because it was found in the wall safe. But Hoby will argue—probably successfully—that stock is ordinarily not viewed as a "personal effect." The Abco stock should pass to Hoby under the residuary clause.

Jewelry:
Tait's personal jewelry will be considered a part of her "personal effects." Because it was found in the wall safe, Bill will argue that the jewelry passes to him. Hoby will assert that because she put her jewelry into the safe only after the will was made, Tait did not intend a specific testamentary act; in any event, the act did not comply with any of the necessary testamentary formalities. Thus, Hoby would contend, the gift to Bill should fail.

However, under the *acts of independent significance* doctrine, a will may dispose of property as a consequence of acts or events that have significance apart from their testamentary effect. (UPC §2-512.) Because placing items in a safe has a purpose that is nontestamentary in nature (*e.g.*, the testator may intend simply to prevent the articles from being misplaced or stolen), the fact that Tait's act also had a testamentary effect (effectuating the gift to Bill) would be irrelevant. Thus, Tait's jewelry should pass to Bill.

Bank account:
The bank account would pass to Hoby under the residuary clause of Tait's will.

4. If the will is not valid, how would Tait's estate be distributed?
Under intestacy principles, Hoby would receive the entire estate. The reasoning is as follows. All of Tait's surviving descendants are also Hoby's descendants and Hoby does not have other surviving descendants who are not descendants of Tait. (UPC §2-102(1)(ii).)

5. Result if Hoby had predeceased Tait, and the latter had then married John:
Hoby's interest would lapse, because he would not be considered a surviving spouse. John would be considered a pretermitted spouse and would take an intestate share. (UPC §2-301.) However, John would not get an intestate share of the whole estate—any devises to a child of the testator born before the testator married the surviving spouse (or to a descendant of that child, under UPC §2-603's antilapse provision) would be carved out first, and John would then get his intestate share of the balance. Thus, the Minco stock (which goes to Sal's daughter Helen), and the Zebco stock

(which goes to Tait's daughter Diane) would be removed from the computation. John would then get the first $150,000 plus one-half of the balance of the estate. (UPC §2-102(4).)

Other gifts would have to be abated to satisfy John's intestate share. The order in which items are abated is set forth in UPC §3-902: first, property not disposed of by will; then, residuary devises; then, general devises; finally, specific devises. Assuming there is no property passing to John outside of the will (the facts don't point to any), residuary devises, which include the Abco stock and the bank accounts (worth a total of $105,000), would be abated first. There are no general devises. The jewelry (the only asset not yet taken into account) is a specific devise; John would also take the value of this jewelry up to $45,000 to equal his $150,000, and one-half the value above that amount.

Answer to Question 19

Important aspects: holographic will, incorporation by reference, harmless error, independent significance, no residue of a residue rule

Was the September 20, 2005, document a valid will?
The September 20, 2005, document does not satisfy the UPC's requirements for a valid attested will. It is not acknowledged by two witnesses or notarized, and it is questionable whether it is properly signed. See UPC §2-502(a). However, the document may qualify for probate as a holographic will. To be a valid holographic will, a document need not be witnessed or notarized, but it must be in writing, signed by the testator; the "material provisions" must be in the testator's handwriting; and it must have testamentary intent. (UPC §2-502.)

Among the beneficiaries, Bessie is the one who would gain the most if Timothy is deemed to have died intestate. She will argue that the September 20, 2005, document was not a valid holographic will because (1) it was not signed by Timothy, and (2) it did not clearly and unambiguously dispose of Timothy's entire estate. The document refers to "one-half" of something, but it is not clear what that "something" is. Did Timothy mean one-half of the residue after subtracting the stock in the notebook he was keeping (although the facts don't tell us when he started to keep the notebook)? Or did he mean one-half of the entire estate? Or one-half of his stock only? We don't really know, and that strengthens Bessie's argument that the document should not be accepted because it does not contain a clear dispository scheme.

On the other hand, the Boys Club will assert the following: (1) by writing his own name in the body of the document, Timothy satisfied the signature requirement (UPC §2-502(b) does not say that the testator's signature must be at the foot of the document); and (2) a reasonable interpretation of the document is that Timothy wanted to divide his estate evenly between Bessie and the Boys Club because Timothy preceded the words "one-half" with the words "I . . . make this will." Given the usual desire of probate courts to effectuate the testator's wishes by accepting documents that display a testamentary intent, the September 20, 2005, document will probably be received as a valid holographic will.

If the September 20, 2005, document was not itself a valid will, was it republished, or otherwise made valid, by the June 30, 2008, document?
Although the June 30, 2008, document reads like a codicil, if the September 20, 2005, document is *not* a valid will, the later document cannot be a

codicil. A codicil is a subsequent will that merely amends or supplements a pre-existing valid will. But while the June 30, 2008, document cannot qualify as a codicil (thereby barring application of the republication by codicil to validate the September 20, 2005, document), the latter document may qualify as a valid holographic will, thereby permitting an argument under incorporation by reference to give effect to the testamentary intent expressed in the September 20, 2005, document.

The Boys Club will contend that the June 30, 2008, document was itself a complete and valid holographic will (rather than a codicil to an existing will) that incorporated the September 20, 2005, document by reason of the reference to "my former will." Although Timothy's language does not specifically incorporate the prior document, this argument will probably succeed. Because Timothy obviously believed that the first document was valid (as evidenced by his reference to his "previous will"), this result would effectuate his testamentary intent.

Finally, the Boys Club (as well as Dorothy) will argue that the two documents (September 20, 2005, and June 30, 2008) should be read together as a single will, enforceable under UPC §2-503's provision validating certain documents that don't meet all the testamentary formalities. Under that provision, noncompliance with the formalities is ignored "if the proponent of the document or writing establishes by clear and convincing evidence that the decedent intended the document or writing to constitute (i) the decedent's will [or] (iii) an addition to or an alteration of the will...." The September 20, 2005, document probably qualifies under (i) of this test, and the June 30, 2008, document probably qualifies under (iii).

Summary:
The court will probably accept the argument of the Boys Club (as well as of Dorothy) that the second document is a valid holographic will which incorporates the first by reference, and the court will dispose of Timothy's entire estate under the provisions of the two documents.

Does the black book become part of the testamentary scheme?
Because the black book does not on its face meet any of the testamentary formalities, it cannot by itself constitute either a will or a codicil. However, under the doctrine of incorporation by reference, a writing in existence when a will is executed may be incorporated into the will if the will's language manifests this intent and the will describes the writing sufficiently to identify it. Because (1) the June 30, 2008, document clearly refers to "stocks listed in my black book"; (2) the black book was found in the same

safe-deposit box as the 2008 document and contained a handwritten list of stock transactions; and (3) the black book existed on June 30, 2008, the requirements for incorporation by reference are met. Therefore, the black book becomes part of the testamentary scheme because the June 30, 2008, document is part of that scheme. (As to the effect of changes to the black book made after June 30, 2008, see the subsequent discussion.)

What is the effect of the June 30, 2008, document on Timothy's testamentary scheme?

If we conclude that the June 30, 2008, document is an integral part of Timothy's testamentary scheme, we need to determine just what the effect of that document is.

It is unclear from the June 30, 2008, document ("Bessie doesn't need all that") whether Timothy wanted to *revoke* the portion devised to Bessie in the September 20, 2005, document, or intended instead to *reduce* Bessie's one-half share of the entire estate by the value of the stocks listed in the black book.

If the June 30, 2008, document is interpreted as a mere reduction of Bessie's interest, Bessie would get half the estate ($70,000), less the value of the stocks ($40,000), or $30,000. If the document is interpreted as a revocation of Bessie's portion, then the distribution would be as follows: (1) the Boys Club would receive one-half of Timothy's estate ($70,000); (2) Bessie's child, Dorothy, would receive the stocks (value — $40,000). The issue then becomes what happens to the remainder of Timothy's estate ($30,000). Bessie will argue that because the will does not contain a residuary clause, the property in question falls to intestacy and as Timothy's closest heir, she takes the $30,000. (UPC §2-103(a)(3).) (Because Dorothy claims through Bessie, who is still alive, she would take nothing in intestacy.)

The Boys Club will argue, however, that the will should be read as containing only one clause, a residuary clause, and that under the UPC/modern-trend approach, if part of a residuary clause is revoked or fails, the revoked or failed gift passes to the other residuary clause takers.

A court could go either way on this, and many courts may favor Bessie as a family member over the Boys Club, but under the UPC the Boys Club has the stronger argument and should take the $30,000 if the June 30, 2008, document is construed as a revocation of Bessie's gift. But the better construction of the June 30, 2008, document is that it is merely a reduction ("she doesn't need *all* that" implies the testator is taking away part of it; if he had intended to take away all of it, the will would have simply read "she doesn't need that"), so Bessie would still take the $30,000 in question.

What is the effect of the stock transactions that occurred after June 30, 2008?

Bessie will contend that entries in the black notebook made after June 30, 2008 (the date of the second document), should be disallowed. She will argue that Timothy's act in making these entries should not be given testamentary effect because they did not comply with any of the necessary testamentary formalities. Accordingly, the XYZ stock should pass through intestacy.

Although the entries in the black notebook do not constitute a valid will in their own right, Dorothy has two arguments she can use to try to convince a court to give effect to the testamentary intent expressed in the black notebook. At first blush the most applicable argument is incorporation by reference. The clause in the 2008 will that "all stocks listed in my black book go to Bessie's child" meets the requirements for incorporation by reference. The black book was in existence at the time the will was executed, the express reference to it in the 2008 will evidences the intent to incorporate it, and the will describes it with reasonable certainty. The black notebook can be incorporated by reference into the 2008 will.

The problem with Dorothy's invoking incorporation by reference to claim the stocks listed in the black notebook is that strict application of incorporation by reference means that the notebook can be incorporated only as it existed on the day the will was executed. The entries made after June 30, 2008, could not be given effect. Dorothy would not be entitled to the 100 shares of XYZ stock purchased on July 7, 2008. As to the 100 shares of ABC stock that she sold on July 7, 2008, the first issue is whether the gift was originally a general gift or a specific gift. If construed as a general gift, the fact that the stocks were sold would not affect Dorothy's right to the gift. The personal representative would simply have to go out and purchase 100 shares of ABC stock. If the gift is construed as a specific gift, normally ademption would apply to the 100 shares that were sold. Under the UPC approach to ademption, however, the beneficiary of specifically devised property that is no longer in the estate has the right to a pecuniary devise equal to the value of the specifically devised property as of the date of its dispostion. Dorothy could argue that she is entitled to a pecuniary devise under this section. (Dorothy could not claim the XYZ stock under this UPC section as replacement property because the replacement property doctrine is limited to tangible personal property. Dorothy could, however, claim the XYZ stock under UPC §2-503 in that there is clear and convincing evidence that Timothy intended the writing to constitute an addition to his will.)

In the alternative, Dorothy could invoke the doctrine of acts of independent significance to claim the stocks listed in the black book. Under the doctrine of acts of independent significance, the will can make reference to acts outside the will, which can control either who takes under the will or how much a beneficiary takes as long as the referenced act has its own significance independent of its effect upon the testator's testamentary scheme. (UPC §2-512.) Here, Dorothy would claim that the will's reference to the stocks listed in the black book is the act outside the will that controls what she takes. Her argument is that the act of listing the stock in the black book was not just for testamentary purposes, it was also for general record-keeping purposes to help Timothy keep track of his stock purchases and sales. This argument is strengthened by the fact that almost all of the entries predate the creation of the will. Timothy created this black notebook not for testamentary purposes but for valid *inter vivos* purposes — to help him with his record keeping.

It is a close call whether a court would adopt the acts of independent significance argument. If it did, Dorothy would get all of the stocks listed in the black book — even the XYZ stock entered on July 7, 2008. Dorothy has a very strong argument under incorporation by reference, but her chances for the XYZ stock depend on whether the jurisdiction has adopted UPC §2-503 and whether the court would apply it to a document being incorporated into a will as opposed to the will directly. And whether Dorothy is entitled to the pecuniary value of the ABC stock that was sold depends on whether the gift is characterized as specific or general. The facts are ambiguous as to that issue.

Summary:
Based on the above analysis, The Boys Club will receive $70,000. Dorothy will receive the ABC stock that is still in the estate ($30,000). She has a decent chance of receiving the XYZ stock under acts of independent significance, and depending on whether the court characterizes the gift of all the stocks listed in "my" black notebook as a general or specific gift, she has an argument that she is entitled to a pecuniary devise equal to the ABC stock that was sold. If the language in the second document is construed as reducing Bessie's gift, the rest will go to Bessie; if it is construed as revoking Bessie's gift, the rest will probably go to the Boys Club.

Answer to Question 20

Important aspects: revocation, dependent relative revocation, incorporation by reference, harmless error, creation of trust, meaning of "heirs," determination of Thor's intestate heirs

1. Did Thor die testate or intestate?

Sandra (who would receive Thor's entire estate if Thor died intestate by virtue of being Thor's only surviving issue) will argue that Thor died intestate because: (1) Will #1 was expressly revoked by the note that was attached to it (*i.e.*, a will may be revoked by a subsequent writing that was executed with the necessary testamentary formalities, and the attached note qualifies as a holographic will); and (2) Will #2 is invalid because it was (a) not in Thor's handwriting (preventing it from qualifying as a holographic will), and (b) not either attested by two witnesses or notarized (preventing it from qualifying as an attested will).

The takers under the two wills (John, Gil, and Warren) will make the following three arguments that the court should find either Will #1 or Will #2 valid (either will would protect their interests equally).

Doctrine of dependent relative revocation (DRR):

Under DRR, where a testator validly revokes a will based upon a mistake, and the testator would not have revoked the will but for the mistake, the court is authorized to ignore the revocation and give effect to the validly revoked will. Where the revocation is by a subsequent will, the courts almost invariably require that the mistake be set forth in the writing and be beyond the knowledge of the testator. Here, Will #2 was not valid. But when Thor died, the handwritten note found stapled to Will #1 qualified as a valid holographic will that revoked Will #1. The revocation, however, was based upon the mistaken belief that Will #2 was valid. That arguably was the meaning of the reference "I have made a new will" (the note was dated the day after Thor executed what she thought was a valid Will #2). There seems little doubt that Thor revoked Will #1 on the mistaken belief that Will #2 was valid, that this mistake is set forth in the revoking instrument, and that this mistake was beyond Thor's knowledge. Lastly, inasmuch as Will #2 (what Thor really wanted) is nearly identical to Will #1 (for all practical purposes it is identical, now that Ethel is dead), there is no reason to doubt that if Thor had known of the mistake, she would not have revoked Will #1 (because it is closer to her desired testamentary scheme [Will #2] than it is to intestacy).

Incorporation by reference:
Alternatively, the heirs will stake their argument on the doctrine of incorporation by reference. Under this doctrine, a writing that is in existence when a will is made may be incorporated by reference, if the language of the will manifests this intent and describes the writing sufficiently to permit its identification. (UPC §2-510.) The heirs might argue that (1) the note that was attached to Will #1 was a valid holographic will because it was in the testator's handwriting and signed by her; and (2) the holographic will, by means of the statement "I have made another will," incorporated Will #2 into the terms of a valid holographic document.

Sandra will contend first that the validity of a holographic will should be judged by looking at the entire document, including the portions incorporated: Here, the requirement that a holographic will contain "material provisions" in the testator's handwriting is not met. On the contrary, Will #2, which contains all the material terms, was entirely typewritten. Second, Sandra will argue that the language that is asserted to be the language of incorporation ("I have made another will") does not evidence a clear intent to incorporate Will #2; it is merely a statement of past action that does not specifically refer to Will #2.

In response to Sandra's argument, the takers under Will #2 will argue that the holographic note adequately identifies and expresses the intent to incorporate Will #2 and that the material provisions are in Thor's handwriting. The material provision is the provision incorporating Will #2 by reference ("I have made a new will"). They will also emphasize that applying incorporation by reference is more consistent with Thor's clear intent.

Harmless error:
Under UPC §2-503, a document that was not properly executed with full wills act formalities may nevertheless be probated as the testator's will if there is clear and convincing evidence that the testator intended the document to be his or her will. Will #2 was a formal will, properly prepared, signed, and witnessed, except for the fact that there was only one subscribing witness, not two. There is little doubt that Thor intended this to be her will, as evidenced not only by the execution ceremony that she performed (signing the will and having it witnessed by one witness), but also by the fact that the next day she wrote a note revoking this first will because, as she herself wrote, "I have a new will." The reference is clearly to her second will, Will #2. There is clear and convincing evidence that Thor intended Will #2 to be her will.

Summary:
The takers under Thor's wills have several strong arguments. A court would probably apply DRR under these circumstances and probate Will #1. In the alternative, if the jurisdiction has adopted the UPC harmless error doctrine, there is little doubt that the doctrine would apply and the court would probate Will #2. Even the incorporation by reference argument, the weakest of the arguments made by the proponents of the wills, has a decent chance of success. Inasmuch as there is no practical difference between Will #1 and Will #2 (now that Ethel has died), it does not really matter which doctrine the court applies and which will the court probates. Sandra will lose on her argument that Thor died intestate.

2. Assuming Thor died testate, how should her estate be distributed?
If we assume that Thor died testate, we don't actually need to know whether the operative will is Will #1 or Will #2. Now that Ethel is dead, the two documents are functionally identical.

Was the $10,000 to Robert Rood an outright gift to him, or was it to be held in trust for Carrie?
Carrie will contend that because the $10,000 bequest to Robert Rood was "to be used" for her education, a trust for her benefit was created, and Robert has to spend the $10,000 as prescribed. Robert will argue that no trust was created because the language used was not clear enough. When Thor intended to create a trust, she used language that was clear and unequivocal, as evidenced by the terms "trustee" and "trust" in the second paragraph of both her wills. This is a close call. The language Thor used in the gift to Robert normally would be construed as imposing a legal obligation on him, not just a moral obligation, to use the money for the benefit of his daughter. That is enough to create a trust. But because of the more formal language used in the very next paragraph, there is the possibility that a court would conclude that the language in the gift to Robert was merely precatory. Ultimately this is a question of the decedent's intent, and under these facts it could go either way.

Would Sandra be entitled to receive anything?
Sandra would receive nothing. Ethel's interest under the trust was only a life estate. Ethel had no interest under the trust that she could devise under her will. The property under the trust passes pursuant to the express "gift over" clause that devises the property to Thor's heirs upon Ethel's death.

What shares would John, Gil, and Warren receive?
When a will provides that a decedent's property is to be distributed to his or her "heirs," distribution is usually made according to intestacy principles. Where there is no surviving parent and no descendants of the testator, distribution is made to the descendants of the decedent's parents, by representation. (UPC §2-103(a)(3).) The distribution is made "per capita at each generation," the division of the estate starting at the highest level at which there are living members. (UPC §2-106.) The highest level at which there are living members is that shared by John and Gil and by Warren's deceased parent, the child of Thor's deceased sister Bessie. Therefore, the estate is split into thirds. John and Gil take one-third each. Warren takes his parent's one-third by representation. Thus, John, Gil, and Warren would each receive one-third of Thor's remaining estate (after the $10,000 gift to Rood).

3. Assuming Thor died intestate, how should her estate be distributed?

An heir does not have to survive until the close of distribution of an intestate decedent's estate to be entitled to take his or her share. An heir need only survive the decedent by 120 hours (as established by clear and convincing evidence). (UPC §2-104.) Here, Ethel, Thor's only descendant, survived Thor by 120 hours and therefore is entitled to take all of Thor's estate as her only surviving descendant. (UPC §2-103(a).) Ethel's interest in Thor's estate vested before Ethel died, making her interest devisable and inheritable. Ethel validly devised her interest to Sandra, her friend. When Thor's estate is finally distributed, Sandra will be entitled to all of it under the terms of Ethel's will.

Answer to Question 21

Important aspects: issue, enforceability of excluding adopted children, failure of trust, determination of trustor's heirs

Can the remainder of the trust be distributed to Gladys's child and grandchildren as "issue"?

The trust specifically excludes adopted persons, so Gladys's child and grandchildren would not be eligible beneficiaries under the trust. If the clause excluding adopted persons is struck for some reason, then the surviving child would receive one-half of the remainder, and the two grandchildren would each receive one-fourth, under all systems of multi-generational division.

What does the trust provide regarding distribution of the remainder if Gladys dies without issue?

The trust provides for distribution of a trust remainder if a child of the testator dies before age 45, but that does not apply because Gladys lived to age 96. Even if a court attempted to reform the trust by following the scheme of distribution if a beneficiary died before age 45, that disposition would also fail because there are no living siblings or issue of siblings of Gladys.

How is the remainder to be distributed because the trust language failed to direct distribution?

Upon failure of a trust to be fully distributed pursuant to its terms, the remaining trust property returns to the trustor, in this case the testator. Because the residuary beneficiary of the testator's will was the trust, the trust principal will be distributed to the testator's intestate heirs. Gladys's brother's wife is not an intestate heir of the testator, but Gladys's adopted daughter and grandchildren are intestate heirs because intestacy statutes include adopted persons. The remainder of the trust will therefore be distributed one-half to the surviving child of Gladys and one-fourth to each grandchild.

Answer to Question 22

Important aspects: simultaneous death, independent significance, ambiguity, dependent relative revocation, antilapse, class gifts

1. Disposition of Betty's estate:
We will assume that Betty's will was executed with the requisite testamentary formalities (the facts are silent as to this point).

Effect of simultaneous death:
Under UPC §2-702, a beneficiary is not deemed to have "survived" the testator unless the beneficiary lives at least 120 hours following the testator's death. Therefore, for purposes of Betty's will, Wilma did not "survive" Betty. Consequently, the $100,000 goes to "the natural persons who are beneficiaries of Wilma's last will and testament. . . ."

Acts of independent significance:
Inasmuch as the provisions of Wilma's last will, not Betty's will, will control who takes Betty's gift of $100,000, the use of Wilma's will to dispose of Betty's probate property must be validated. At first blush, because Betty is referring to the provisions of another document, incorporation by reference might appear to be the most logical doctrine to use. But because Wilma executed a new will in 2002, two years after Betty executed her will, Wilma's 2002 will cannot be incorporated into Betty's will because it was not in existence at the time Betty executed her will. The beneficiaries under Wilma's will have to invoke events of independent significance.

Under the doctrine of acts of independent significance, the will can make reference to acts outside the will, which can control either who takes under the will or how much a beneficiary takes as long as the referenced act has its own significance independent of its effect upon the testator's testamentary scheme. (UPC §2-512.) Here, the referenced act in Betty's will that will control who takes the $100,000 is Wilma's act of executing her last will and testament. That act has its own significance apart from its effect on Betty's will—Wilma's will also controls who takes Wilma's estate. Thus, the referenced act has its own significance independent of its effect on Betty's will. Acts of independent significance can be used to validate the provision in Betty's will letting Wilma's will control who takes the $100,000.

Takers under Wilma's will:
Although Wilma's will *may* exclude Bill (based on the codicil), Bill has several arguments to support his claim that he should be permitted to participate in the distribution under Wilma's will. First, Bill could point out

that he was one of the three beneficiaries of Wilma's will *as that will was constituted when Betty's will was made* in 2000. Thus, Bill would claim that he is entitled to one-half of the $100,000 gift made by Betty.

Mary would argue, however, that the language in Betty's will should be read literally. Thus, Wilma's "last will and testament" (*i.e.*, the will as it stood at Wilma's death) designated only Mary as a "natural person" beneficiary.

Second, Bill can also argue that where there is an ambiguity in a will, the vague provision will ordinarily be construed in a manner that would effectuate the testator's probable intent. The term "last will and testament" could mean Wilma's will as it existed (1) in 2000 (when Betty's will was made), or (2) when Wilma died. However, Betty obviously wanted to bestow an additional gift upon those particular persons who were the objects of Wilma's bounty. Because Wilma finally decided to reward only Mary, not Bill, Betty would presumably have preferred to do the same.

Lastly, Bill can claim that Wilma's codicil should be ignored under dependent relative revocation (discussed below). Whether Bill will prevail on this argument depends on the evidence.

State University is not a natural person, and therefore would not share in the gift.

In summary, whether Bill is included as a beneficiary under Wilma's will depends on his dependent relative revocation argument. If he is successful, he and Mary will split Betty's gift of $100,000. If he is unsuccessful, Mary would receive the $100,000 bequest.

How should the balance of Betty's estate be distributed?
The balance of Betty's estate is left "to my children, share and share alike." Because both "children" predeceased Betty, the following issues arise: (1) does the gift fail completely, and (2) if not, how should the residue be distributed among Betty's descendants?

Does the gift fail?
The gift does not fail—it will be saved either by the antilapse provision, UPC §2-603(b), or by the Uniform Probate Code provision covering class gifts to family members where the form of distribution is not specified, UPC §2-708.

Alice will argue that the gift should be saved by the antilapse provision. There are two different provisions of the UPC antilapse doctrine that may apply, but the result here is the same under both provisions. First, assuming that the gift to Betty's "children" qualifies as a class gift (the gift is described in the aggregate; the beneficiaries are not named individually but collectively; the beneficiaries share a common characteristic and no one else with that characteristic is excluded; and it appears that her overall testamentary scheme was to treat her children equally), the applicable provision is §2-603(b)(2), which states: "Each deceased devisee's surviving descendants who are substituted for the deceased devisee take by representation the share to which the deceased devisee would have been entitled had the deceased devisee survived the testator." Notice that under this language, the first division is made at the level of the deceased devisee (because of the last clause, "had the deceased devisee survived the testator"). Applying that provision to the facts here, Betty's children, Charles and Jane, would have split the residue of her estate 50-50 ($200,000 each). Therefore, Charles's 50 percent would be split equally by his surviving descendants, George and Fred (so each would take 25 percent of Betty's residue or $100,000 each). Jane's 50 percent would pass to her surviving descendant, Alice, who would take the whole share (50 percent of Betty's residue, or $200,000).

In the alternative, there is a slight chance (but not a good chance) that a court might construe the gift to Betty's "children" not as a class gift but rather as a nonclass gift to a group of individuals: Betty's children. Under that construction, UPC §2-603(b)(1) would apply. It provides in pertinent part that if "the deceased devisee leaves surviving descendants, a substituted gift is created in the devisee's surviving descendants. They take by representation the property to which the devisee would have been entitled had the devisee survived the testator." Notice again that under this language, the first division is made at the level of the deceased devisee (because of the last clause "had the deceased devisee survived the testator"). Betty's children, Charles and Jane, would have split the residue of her estate 50-50 ($200,000 each). Charles's 50 percent would be split equally by George and Fred ($100,000 each), and Jane's 50 percent would pass to her surviving descendant, Alice (all $200,000). The result here is the same as under the class gift provision above.

George and Fred will argue, however, that UPC §2-708 should apply. Section 2-603(b)(2) of the UPC expressly excludes class gifts to "'issue,' 'descendants,' 'heirs of the body,' 'next of kin,' 'relatives,' or 'family,' or a class described by language of similar import." Class gifts of such nature are excluded from antilapse protection because they already express the idea of representation under which a deceased class member's descendants are already substituted for him or her pursuant to UPC §§2-708, 2-709, and

2-711. Under such provisions, if all of the class members are deceased, the property is distributed in the same manner as if the testator had died intestate. (UPC §2-708.) Although the property passes to the surviving descendants of the deceased devisees, the first division of the property would be at the first generation where there is a living descendant. (UPC §2-709(b).) Under this approach, George, Fred, and Alice would each take one-third of the residue ($133,333.33 each). George and Fred are better off under this approach.

Alice's argument, however, should prevail. The antilapse provisions of the UPC apply to class gifts unless the class is composed of family members of the testator and the express language describing the class implicitly includes reference to multiple generations. Here, Betty's use of the word "children," while constituting a class of family members, does not constitute a reference that implicitly contains multiple generations. The antilapse provisions should apply (UPC §2-603(2) most likely), and Alice should take $200,000, George and Fred $100,000.

[There is a small chance that a court might construe the language "share and share alike" in Betty's devise to her "children" to mean that in the event the children should predecease Betty (and the antilapse doctrine should come into play), that Betty wanted the grandchildren to also "share and share alike." While this argument is plausible, the language is not clear enough to overcome the statutory scheme created by the express provisions of the UPC. It is unlikely that a court would find that the phrase "share and share alike" here is express enough to constitute the testator's intent to apply a different distribution scheme than the default scheme applied by the UPC provisions.]

2. Disposition of Wilma's estate:
We will assume that Wilma's will and codicil were executed with the requisite testamentary formalities (the facts are silent as to these points).

A factual mistake that induces a testator to make a particular disposition is ordinarily ***not*** a basis for invalidating a will. However, some states may deny probate of a will if (1) the mistake appears upon the face of the document, *and* (2) the alternative disposition that the testator would have desired is inferable from the will. Generally and historically, extrinsic evidence of an error is not admissible. Because the mistake here does not appear on the face of the will, the codicil deleting Bill because of his "ingratitude" is valid.

Dependent Relative Revocation (DRR):

Bill will argue dependent relative revocation. Under the doctrine of dependent relative revocation (DRR), where the testator validly revokes his or her will because of a mistake, and the testator would not have revoked the will but for the mistake, the doctrine of DRR authorizes the court to ignore the valid revocation and probate the will. Where the valid revocation is by writing, invariably the courts require the writing to set forth the mistake and the mistake must be beyond the testator's knowledge. Here, Wilma validly revoked her will in writing when she executed the valid codicil. The revocation was based upon a mistake—she thought her son was being ungrateful. The codicil expressly recites the mistake, the mistake clearly caused Wilma to revoke the gift to Bill, and the mistake was beyond Wilma's personal knowledge. There appears little doubt that if Wilma had known of the mistake, she would not have revoked the gift to Bill. The key is if Bill can prove to the court's satisfaction that the revocation was based upon a mistake. If the "thank you" letter can be found, there is a good chance that Bill will be successful under DRR and the codicil will be ignored. On the other hand, if the claimed "thank you" letter cannot be found, the court may conclude that Bill's self-serving testimony that he wrote and mailed a "thank you" letter is insufficient to overcome the express terms of the codicil.

[If Bill is successful on his DRR claim, Betty's gift of $100,000 to the natural persons who are beneficiaries of Wilma's last will and testament would be split 50-50 between Mary and Bill.]

Was Wilma's gift to her children a class gift?

It is a bit unclear whether Wilma's gift to her children was (1) a class gift, or (2) a gift to each of her children, individually. If it was an individual gift to each child, then the codicil would simply cancel the gift to Bill. Assuming the clause in Wilma's will devising her estate between her children and State University were construed to constitute a residuary clause, under the modern trend and UPC approach the revoked gift would not fall to intestacy but rather would be distributed pro rata to the other beneficiaries in the residuary clause. Mary would take half of the gift to Bill, and State University would take the other half. (If the jurisdiction still followed the traditional common law "no residue of a residue" approach, Bill's one-fourth would fall to intestacy where he and Mary would split it (Bill would end up with one-eighth of Wilma's residuary estate in that event).) This "individual gifts" interpretation is at least weakly buttressed by the codicil's statement, "I delete the gift to my son, Bill" (as opposed to, say, "I modify the gift to my children to include only Mary . . . .").

If, however, "my children" was intended to set up a class gift (with the class being Wilma's children), Mary would take the entire one-half of the estate.

Unfortunately for Bill, the term "children" is ordinarily viewed as denoting a class gift (*i.e.*, Wilma did *not* state something like, to "Bill and Mary, my children"). This ordinary construction probably outweighs the small countervailing weight to be given to the "I delete the gift to my son Bill" language. Thus, if the court does not apply DRR, Mary and State University will probably share Wilma's estate equally; if the court does apply DRR, Mary and Bill will split 50 percent of Wilma's estate and State University will take the other 50 percent.

Answer to Question 23

Important aspects: revocability of *inter vivos* trust, spendthrift trusts, trust termination, and material purpose

1. Was the trust effectively terminated by Ball during his lifetime?

Under the traditional, and still majority, rule, an *inter vivos* trust is ordinarily irrevocable unless the settlor expressly reserves the power to revoke the trust. The modern trend, as evidenced by the Uniform Trust Code (UTC), is to reverse the default rule and to presume that an *inter vivos* trust is revocable unless the trust expressly provides that it is irrevocable. (UTC §602(a).) Here, Ball expressly reserved the power to revoke the trust, so the *inter vivos* trust is revocable under either approach.

Thus, the question becomes whether that power was effectively exercised? Although the trust provided that this power was to be exercised only by a writing that was (1) signed by Ball, and (2) delivered to the trustee, Sam will argue that Ball's oral communication to the trustee was sufficient to accomplish a revocation. However, a power to revoke is ordinarily narrowly construed—it can be exercised only in strict accordance with its terms. See Restatement 2d of Trusts, §330 and Comment j thereto. Therefore, Ball's phone call probably was not effective to revoke the trust during his lifetime.

[The modern trend, as evidenced by the UTC and the Restatement (Third) of Trusts, is to make it easier for a settlor to revoke a revocable trust. The UTC and the Restatement (Third) of Trusts permit revocation even if the settlor only "substantially complied" with the method provided for in the will (UTC §602(c)(1); Restatement 3d of Trusts, §63, Comment i.) And they provide that if the method in the trust is not expressly made exclusive, as long as there is clear and convincing evidence that the settlor intended to revoke the trust, the trust is revoked. (UTC §602(c)(2); Restatement 3d of Trusts, §63, Comment h.) The facts here are unclear as to whether the trust "expressly" made the method of revocation exclusive. Assuming it did, the argument can be made that Ball's oral statement was substantial compliance. This is a tough argument to make, however, because substantial compliance in the wills context has been construed as requiring not only clear and convincing evidence of the person's intent but also as requiring sufficient steps to be taken toward the requirements that one could conclude that the actor has "substantially complied" with the requirements. Here, a mere telephone call arguably is not enough—but the equities of the facts (he died unexpectedly the very next day before being able to write the letter) may be enough for a court under the modern, intent-based approach.

The rest of the analysis of this question will assume that the trust was *not* validly revoked.]

2. Is the trustee obligated to pay Pearl past or future alimony out of the income and, to the extent necessary, the principal of the trust?

A spendthrift trust is one in which, by statute or the terms of the trust, the beneficiary is unable to voluntarily or involuntarily transfer his or her interest in the trust. Spendthrift trusts are valid in almost all jurisdictions, and bar creditors of a beneficiary from reaching his or her interest in the trust to satisfy a claim. However, in many states (and under the Restatement (Second) of Trusts) an ex-spouse or child of a trust beneficiary can override the spendthrift clause for the purpose of securing support. See Restatement 2d of Trusts, §157(a); see also UTC §503. In other states, there are statutes that protect the interest of beneficiaries in a spendthrift trust, but only to the extent necessary to secure their proper care, maintenance, and support.

Therefore, the trustee would probably be obliged to pay Pearl for past and future alimony out of the trust's income. Because Sam has only an *income interest* in the trust, and because even those states allowing the beneficiary's children or ex-spouse to reach the trust limit the invasion to the beneficiary's interest, the trustee cannot be compelled to pay Pearl out of the principal.

3. Do Sam and Pearl have the legal power to terminate the trust?

The interests in the trust are an equitable life estate in Sam and a contingent remainder in Carol, subject to open for other children who may be born to Sam. The contingency is that Carol must survive Sam (*i.e.*, Carol's interest does not vest until Sam's death).

The majority rule is that beneficiaries may compel termination of a trust if (1) all of the beneficiaries are legally competent and join in the request to terminate, and (2) termination will not defeat a material purpose of the settlor in creating the trust. See Restatement 3d of Trusts, §65; see also UTC §411.

The first problem is that all beneficiaries must not only consent but have legal capacity to consent. While Sam is competent, Carol is a minor and, therefore, incompetent. A guardian *ad litem* might be appointed to represent Carol's interests. Neither Sam nor Pearl, however, can be appointed as guardian *ad litem* because they have interests that are adverse to Carol (*i.e.*, to the extent Sam or Pearl receive income from the trust, the trust res, which would ultimately be distributed to Carol, is diminished). Assuming that a guardian other than Sam or Pearl was appointed, valid consent could be given by all three present beneficiaries.

The second, bigger problem is the requirement that *all* beneficiaries consent. The class of Sam's children is open until Sam dies. Thus, the interests of potential, unborn children cannot be determined or adequately represented at this time. Therefore, the "consent by all beneficiaries" requirement probably cannot be satisfied at this time, and the trustee probably cannot be compelled to terminate the trust.

There is a last, probably fatal (depending on whether the court takes the traditional approach or the modern approach), difficulty: Termination of the trust would violate a material purpose of the settlor in creating the trust. The choice of a spendthrift trust by Ball evidences his intention to provide a lifetime income interest to Sam, free from Sam's improvidence. This purpose would be defeated if the trust was revoked. See Restatement 2d of Trusts, §337, Comment l. (The Uniform Trust Code offers an *optional* provision that the presence of a spendthrift clause is not presumed to constitute a material purpose. Section 411(c) of the UTC and Comment e of the Restatement (Third) of Trusts, §65, say that a spendthrift clause is not enough, by itself, to automatically conclude that termination of the trust would defeat a material purpose.)

Answer to Question 24

Important aspects: holographic will, incorporation by reference, ademption, additions to stock bequests general versus specific gifts, lapse and antilapse, intestacy, and express disinheritance

Which, if any, of the documents found in Taylor's safe-deposit box may be admitted to probate?

Because the typewritten document bears no signature and is not witnessed, it lacks the requisite testamentary formalities. Thus, this document, standing alone, is *not* a valid will and, therefore, may not be admitted to probate. The handwritten document, however, is signed and evidences a testamentary intent (*i.e.*, it states, "This is the way I want my property to go"). It would therefore arguably qualify as a holographic will.

The beneficiaries could then argue that the doctrine of *incorporation by reference* should be applied to provide the necessary material provisions (the "who gets what"). Under this doctrine, a writing that was in existence when a will was made and that is incorporated by the will becomes part of the will (even though the separate writing was not created with the requisite testamentary formalities). (UPC §2-510.) Here, the typewritten document obviously preceded the handwritten one (because the latter makes reference to the former), and the handwritten one clearly refers to the typewritten one (by the language, "The attached is the way I want my property to go . . ."). Therefore, the typewritten document should be incorporated into the valid holographic writing.

In response to this argument, Doris (who would prefer Taylor to have died intestate) could contend that the incorporation by reference doctrine should not be applied here, because to do so would nullify the requirements for a valid holographic will. To be valid as a holographic will, a document must be signed by the testator, and contain "material provisions" in the testator's handwriting. (UPC §2-502(b).) Doris would argue that because the bulk of the provisions of the two documents taken together are typewritten, and the only one in handwriting is the residuary clause, the "material portions in the testator's handwriting" requirement is not satisfied if incorporation by reference is used.

However, the residuary clause is certainly a material provision, as is the clause incorporating the typewritten document into the holographic will. Therefore the material provisions arguably *are* in the testator's handwriting. Thus, the court will probably hold that the handwritten note was a valid holographic will that successfully incorporated the typewriting.

Alternatively, the two documents together could be validated under UPC §2-503's "harmless error" provision, by which a document that is shown by "clear and convincing evidence" to have been intended by the decedent as his or her will can be admitted to probate even though it does not meet testamentary formalities.

In summary, the two documents found in Taylor's safe-deposit box probably together constitute her will.

What is the effect of the destruction of the home on the gift to Aunt Marie?

The devise of the home to Aunt Marie is a "specific" devise. Under the Uniform Probate Code, where the subject of a specific devise is no longer in the testator's probate estate, the specific devisee has the right to "any proceeds *unpaid* at death on fire or casualty insurance" on the specific devise. (UPC §2-606(a)(3).) This clause does not help Marie, however, because here the proceeds had already been paid to Taylor prior to her death.

Aunt Marie might be able to benefit from UPC §2-606(a)(6), which provides that "unless the facts and circumstances indicate that ademption of the devise was intended by the testator or ademption of the devise is consistent with the testator's manifested plan of distribution, [the specific devisee has the right to] the value of the specifically devised property to the extent the specifically devised property is not in the testator's estate at death and its value or replacement is not covered by [other paragraphs of §2-606(a)]." Because Taylor never conveyed the house to anyone else (which would have weakened Marie's case that Taylor wanted her to have the house's value), and because the house was "transformed" into insurance proceeds only very recently, through no voluntary act by Taylor, Marie will probably convince the court that, under UPC §2-606(a)(6), ademption should not apply and she should get the insurance proceeds (plus any other money needed to make up the value of the house before destruction).

What is the effect of the stock split upon the gift to Al of XYZ stock?

Under the UPC, a beneficiary of a gift of securities under a will is entitled to any accretion of that stock resulting from action initiated by the corporation as long as the testator owned matching shares of the stock at the time he or she executed the will. (UPC §2-605(a)(1).) Here, although the facts are a bit ambiguous, the natural inference is that Theresa owned 200 shares of XYZ stock when she executed the will. Assuming that is the case, Al would receive all 400 shares of XYZ stock.

What is the effect of the bequest of 20 shares of IBM to Frank?

A gift of stock when no such shares are owned by the testator is usually held to be a general bequest. This is especially true where, as here, the form of the gift is "100 shares of XYZ" rather than "*my* 100 shares of XYZ." Where the gift is found to be a general one, the executor is normally required to use the estate's cash to buy the specified property and pay it to the beneficiary. Thus, Taylor's executor must purchase 20 shares of IBM stock from the residuary portion of the estate and give those shares to Frank.

What is the effect of Sarah's death prior to Taylor?

A gift to a beneficiary who predeceases the testator ordinarily lapses. However, under the UPC's antilapse statute, if the beneficiary is the testator's grandparent, or a lineal descendant of the testator's grandparent, who died leaving descendants, the descendants take in place of the beneficiary as long as the testator does not express a contrary intent. (UPC §2-603(b)(1).) Although Sarah was a lineal descendant of Taylor's grandparents, she had no issue. Thus, the gift to Sarah will lapse. Where the lapsed gift is a gift of the complete residuary, the property involved passes by intestate succession.

Who takes the property passing by intestate succession?

Under the UPC, where the decedent is not survived by a spouse, the intestate succession is to the deceased's descendants. In this case, that would be Doris, Taylor's daughter. See UPC §2-103(a)(1). The question is whether the language "to my daughter Doris — NOTHING" affects the intestate distribution.

At common law, a testator could not use words in the will to prevent a person from taking her intestate share of property not covered by the will — the only way to disinherit someone was to bequeath all property to others under the will. But UPC §2-101(b) changes this result: "A decedent by will may expressly exclude or limit the right of an individual or class to succeed to property of the decedent passing by intestate succession." The Comments to this provision make it clear that testamentary language stating that X gets nothing suffices, even if the language does not expressly mention intestacy. Thus the language "to my daughter Doris — NOTHING" is sufficient to disinherit Doris. Instead, the residuary will go by intestate succession to the next in line, Taylor's brother Ben. See UPC §2-103(a)(3).

Answer to Question 25

Important aspects: revocation on divorce and nonprobate assets, interested witness, legal malpractice and privity, lapse and antilapse, *cy pres*, omitted spouse

Who is entitled to the life insurance proceeds?

First, Wisteria is still named as the beneficiary of the life insurance policy. However, under UPC §2-804, designation of a spouse as beneficiary of a life insurance policy is automatically revoked upon dissolution of the marriage with the spouse. Wisteria is therefore not entitled to the insurance proceeds unless there was a contrary provision in the divorce settlement or court order. The provision in the will giving the insurance proceeds to Sylvia is also problematic. The general rule is that a provision in a will cannot change the beneficiary designation of a life insurance policy or similar nonprobate transfer, even if at the time of making the will the testator had power to change the beneficiary. Life insurance policies are contracts between the insured/owner of the policy and the insurance company, and changes are governed by the contract. The gift to Sylvia in the will would therefore be ineffective to change the beneficiary from Wisteria to Sylvia, but because the designation of Wisteria was revoked by divorce, the insurance proceeds are now most likely payable to Herman's probate estate, unless he named an alternate beneficiary or the insurance contract provides otherwise. Paying the insurance proceeds into the estate means the proceeds may be subject to disposition under the terms of the will, and Sylvia could make an argument that she should receive the proceeds through the estate. Her rights to the proceeds will be subject to the claims of Abigail, however (see below).

In some jurisdictions, Sylvia's rights to the insurance proceeds may also be affected by the fact that she acted as a witness to the will. However, UPC §2-505 provides that an interested witness does not affect the validity of the will or the bequest to the interested witness.

If Sylvia fails to collect the insurance proceeds, she may think about suing Ava the lawyer for malpractice. Ava should have advised Herman that the proper way to give Sylvia the insurance proceeds was to change the beneficiary designation with the insurance company rather than to make a bequest in the will. Depending on the law of the state, however, Ava may be able to argue that Sylvia was not her client and that Sylvia does not have privity of contract with her and cannot sue her for malpractice.

How is the bequest to Carla distributed?

Carla predeceased Herman so the bequest to her lapsed. Carla was a descendant of a grandparent of Herman, so the antilapse statute, UPC §2-605, is triggered. However, Carla did not leave any descendants, and her husband is not eligible to take her share under the antilapse statute, so the gift lapses.

How will the bequest to the church be distributed?

Herman's church no longer operates the homeless shelter, so his intentions cannot be carried out. The probate court may apply the *cy pres* doctrine, however, to save the charitable gift. Under this doctrine, if a donor has a general charitable intent but the gift is impossible or impracticable to carry out, the court can alter the terms of the gift to carry out the donor's intent as closely as possible. Here, if the court finds that Herman had a general charitable intent, the court would have to determine whether Herman was more concerned about supporting his church's charitable activities or more concerned with the homeless shelter, and fashion a remedy accordingly (such as giving the funds to the church for the elderly program or giving the funds to another homeless shelter). If the court decides that Herman intended only to benefit that particular shelter and did not have general charitable intent, the gift would lapse and fall into the residue. It should be noted that if the Uniform Trust Code is in effect in the jurisdiction, then the court has more freedom to apply *cy pres* and does not have to find a general charitable intent. (UTC §413.) The gift to the church is subject to claims of Abigail, however, as discussed below.

How will the remainder of Herman's estate be distributed?

Herman's will gives the remainder of his estate to Wisteria. However, because they were divorced, the gift to Wisteria is revoked. (UPC §2-804.) The residue of Herman's estate will therefore be distributed under the intestacy statutes. His surviving spouse, Abigail, will be entitled to the entire residue. (UPC §2-102(1).) Brad is not entitled to a share because if there is a surviving spouse and no descendants, only the decedent's parents are entitled to a share of the estate under the UPC.

Abigail has a claim to more than just the residue, however. Herman and Abigail were married after his will was executed, so she can claim as an omitted spouse under UPC §2-301. Unless Herman had made other provision for Abigail that indicated such provision was in lieu of a testamentary provision, she will be entitled to her intestate share of his entire estate. The issue will be whether the retirement plan benefits which are now payable to Abigail will be considered such "other provision" that would disqualify Abigail as an omitted spouse. The fact that Herman named her because he was required to do so indicates that he lacked the requisite intent. However, the amount of the retirement benefits will also be a factor; if they are considerable in light of Herman's remaining assets, particularly considering that Abigail is already receiving the bulk of Herman's assets, then it is likely a court would find that Abigail is not an omitted spouse within the terms of the statute. If she qualifies as an omitted spouse, she receives the entire estate (including the insurance proceeds). If she does not qualify, she will receive the retirement benefits and the residue of Herman's estate, less the gift to the church (assuming the court applies *cy pres*) and less the gift of the insurance proceeds to Sylvia.

Answer to Question 26

Important aspects: ascertainable beneficiaries, powers of appointment, ademption, requirement of delivery for valid lifetime gift, testamentary intent, undue influence, vested remainder

Can the gift to business advisors and travel companion be enforced?
In order for this to be considered a valid trust, the beneficiaries must be ascertainable. Arguably, Roger will be able to identify who was serving as Roger's broker, accountant, lawyer, and the like at the time of his death, and who was accompanying him on his trips to puzzle conventions. However, the fact that Roger, as personal representative of the estate, can choose the recipients who will share in the funds may give him too much discretion to impose the fiduciary obligations required of a trustee. This should not be an obstacle, since frequently discretion to determine distributions among beneficiaries is granted to trustees. However, if a court considers either that the beneficiaries are too indefinite or that there is insufficient limitation on Roger's control to classify this as a valid trust, then the eligible recipients can argue that this is a limited power of appointment granted to Roger. A power of appointment is not a fiduciary relationship. A limited power of appointment typically identifies a group of persons among which the power holder can select to benefit from the subject property.

How will the puzzle library be distributed?
Melinda will argue that the library is still in Tobey's estate and she therefore is entitled to it under the terms of the will. The Museum has several available theories to claim ownership of the library, however. First, the Museum can argue that the gift to Melinda adeemed because Tobey made a valid gift of the library to the Museum during his life. Melinda will counter this with the argument that the library was never delivered, and a valid gift requires delivery. At most, Tobey expressed an intention to give the library to the Museum but died before it was carried out. Although the Museum did not yet have physical possession of the library at the time of Tobey's death, it can argue symbolic delivery or constructive delivery. Constructive delivery is giving the donee access to the property. Symbolic delivery is used when actual delivery is impractical, so the donor gives a symbolic item, such as a document. The Museum can argue that Tobey gave the library to the Museum when he first began discussions, and that actual physical delivery was delayed because the room was being constructed. His gift was confirmed by his attendance at the dinner announcing the gift, which could be considered the symbolic delivery. Melinda can counter that Tobey's gift

was conditional and he was waiting to see that the room was prepared properly before he effectuated the gift.

If the Museum loses on the delivery argument, it may try to argue that Tobey created a trust of the library for the benefit of the Museum. In other words, Tobey's attendance at the dinner confirmed that although he still had possession of the library, he had placed the library in trust, with himself as trustee, for the benefit of the Museum. The terms of the trust were that upon the completion of the dedicated room, the library would be transferred out of the trust to the Museum. Melinda could answer this theory with the response that Tobey made no indication that he had imposed fiduciary duties upon himself with regard to the library, and had not used any language to indicate a trust was intended.

Finally, the Museum could argue detrimental reliance on Tobey's promise to give the library.

Was the handwritten crossword puzzle a valid codicil to the will?

The crossword puzzle was all in Tobey's handwriting and signed and dated by Tobey, so it would be valid as a codicil if it is found that Tobey intended it to be such. The other beneficiaries would argue that this was just a draft of a crossword puzzle and not intended as a codicil. Maria could argue, however, that the fact that he signed and dated it indicates he intended it as a codicil, and given Tobey's fondness for crossword puzzles, it is not surprising that he would put a codicil in that form. The other beneficiaries may also argue that Maria exerted undue influence over Tobey. She was in a confidential relationship with him, as his caregiver, which in some jurisdictions would create a presumption of undue influence if other "suspicious" circumstances were present. (Restatement 3d of Property: Wills and Other Donative Transfers, §8.3, Comment h.)

Will the pending dissolution of Little College affect the disposition of the residuary trust set up for Aunt Belinda upon Aunt Belinda's death?

The gift to Little College is a vested remainder. The College was in existence at the time of Tobey's death and available to take the interest. The vested remainder is therefore an asset that will be part of the sale to Big University. There was no condition in the will that the College still be operating at the time of Aunt Belinda's death in order to take.

One argument that could be made against Little College is UPC §2-707, which is a departure from the common law and requires that a remainderman survive to date of distribution in order to take, even if the instrument does not condition the interest on survival. The section is written to apply to human beneficiaries rather than entities, however, so this would have to be an argument by analogy. That may be difficult since this rule is such a radical change from the common law. Also, if Little College does not take the remainder, there do not appear to be any other heirs of Tobey with standing to make the argument, because the facts stated that Aunt Belinda was his only living relative. Only the state would be in line to take, under the principle of escheat.

Answer to Question 27

Important aspects: trustee powers, duty to diversity, duty of prudence, duty of loyalty, duty to account

Did Gary violate his fiduciary duties with respect to the sale of the house?

Generally, unless the trust instrument provides otherwise, the trustee has the power to sell trust assets. Gary may have been required to inform Jan before selling the house, however. (UTC §813, Comment.) The house was an irreplaceable asset, with special meaning to Jan because of its history, and that status may require advance notice to Jan before sale.

Arguably, the sale of the house was proper because the trust was illiquid and not diversified. Under the modern portfolio theory, a trustee has a duty to diversify. However, selling a home with such an unusual value that quickly does not appear to be prudent. Gary has a duty to get the highest price possible. The assessed value is not necessarily the highest value of the property, particularly for a home that has a special history that may increase the value on the open market. Gary should have had the property appraised for its actual market value. Also, the actual selling price was somewhat less than $2 million, because the purchase price was to be paid over time and Alfred did not have to pay interest. Therefore, the actual selling price was $2 million less the interest that could be earned on $2 million over an 18-month period. Gary clearly violated his duty to manage the trust assets prudently by selling the home at such a low price without investigating the actual market value of the home.

In addition to the problems with the price, Gary took an unsecured promissory note as payment. The promissory note could conceivably be worthless. There was no reason to take on this kind of risk. Risky investments may be justifiable if the potential reward is great, but here, there was no reward other than getting the face value of the note paid. Also, this was too large a percentage of the total trust to risk, even if there was potential for a significant gain. Alfred in particular seemed like a poor risk because he was going through a divorce and worked in a volatile industry. Accepting the unsecured promissory note was another breach of Gary's duty of prudence.

There may also be a violation of Gary's duty to loyalty. Gary was hoping to get a personal benefit from selling the house to Gary. Self-dealing is prohibited; Gary could not sell the home to himself or to someone closely affiliated with him. (UTC §802.) A transaction that is affected by a conflict between the trustee's fiduciary and personal interests is presumed to be voidable by the beneficiaries. There was clearly a conflict between Gary's fiduciary duty to get the best deal possible for the trust and Gary's personal desire to please Alfred to further his own musical career. According to the UTC, the presumption of voidability may be rebutted by evidence that the transaction was not affected by the conflict (including evidence that a fair price was paid). It does not appear from the facts that Gary could rebut that presumption, however.

Did Gary violate his fiduciary duties in the way that he handled the business interest held by the trust?

Gary was in a difficult position with respect to the business because he owned one-half of the business and held the other one-half as trustee for Jan. The potential for conflict of interest was obvious, but presumably Tommy understood those conflicts when he named Gary as trustee. Conflicts of interest are waivable by the grantor of the trust, and it could be argued that Tommy implicitly waived the conflict present in this situation.

Gary still has problems with the way that he has handled the business interest, however. First, Jan was asking questions about how the business was doing and Gary did not give her details but just gave general reassurances. It appears that Gary was violating his duty to account to Jan. This is a critical duty because without an accounting Jan cannot know whether Gary is fulfilling his fiduciary duties. It also appears that Gary's failure to sell to the competitor was foolish. Gary can argue that his refusal was consistent with Tommy's intent, because Tommy would prefer bankruptcy to selling out to this competitor, and he named Gary as trustee because he knew Gary would understand that. However, Gary also has a duty to administer the trust for the benefit of Jan, and Tommy cannot relieve Gary of all fiduciary duties even though he could set them as low as possible. Tommy's dislike of a certain person should not relieve Gary of the duty to protect the value of the trust assets. Even though it might have been reasonable to refuse the offer from the competitor, retaining the business might have violated Gary's duty to diversify.

Summary:

Gary violated numerous fiduciary duties. First, he sold the house for less than fair market value in a transaction in which he had a conflict of interest. Jan's claim against Gary for the breach of the duty of loyalty should subject Gary to a higher claim for damages than duty of care breach. For a breach of a duty of care, Gary would have to compensate the trust for the difference between the actual sales price and the fair market value of the home at the time of the sale. For a breach of the duty of loyalty, Jan has the power to void the sale or demand that Gary compensate for the value of the home as of the current time—in essence, providing the trust with the means to re-acquire the home.

With respect to the business interest, Gary had inherent conflicts of interest that may have been waived by Tommy. However, he failed to account properly to Jan, and held on to the business longer than he should have, ultimately losing the entire value of the trust's interest.

Answer to Question 28

Important aspects: trust creation, constructive trust, duty to inform, duty to carry out trust purposes, duty to segregate and earmark trust assets, duty of loyalty, statutes of limitations for breach of trust, damages for breach of trust

Did Don create a trust when he transferred the drugstore to Hally?
A valid trust is created when a person transfers property to another person as trustee for a third party. It need not be in writing unless the nature of the property triggers the Statute of Frauds (*e.g.*, a transfer of real property). When Don transferred the drugstore business to Hally, he did not use the terms "trust" or "trustee," but he made clear to her that she was to operate the business and use the profits for the benefit of Kevin's education and then distribute the business to Kevin when he became a licensed pharmacist. The business did not contain any real property interest, unless in the jurisdiction a lessee's interest in a lease is considered real property. Because the trust property consisted of personal property, and Don made clear to Hally that the business was to be operated by her for the benefit of Kevin, this is a valid express trust.

Kevin may also argue that if the court does not find an express trust was created, that the court should hold that there is a constructive trust. A constructive trust is imposed when property is held by a party who obtained the property through unjust enrichment, fraud, or other misconduct. The person holding the property is declared to be "trustee" for the person who is rightfully entitled to the property and the property is then ordered to be transferred to the "beneficiary" of the constructive trust. Here, the court should hold that there has been an express trust created, albeit through informal means. However, if the court declines to do so, it may find that there is a constructive trust because Hally accepted the property from Don with an acknowledgment of his conditions and then proceeded to ignore those conditions. It also appears from the facts that in the initial years, while Don was alive, Hally observed the conditions and only broke her agreement after his death.

Was Hally required to inform Kevin about the trust arrangement?
A trustee has a duty to inform the beneficiaries of the existence of the trust and to keep the beneficiaries informed of any information necessary for the beneficiaries to be able to protect their interests. (UTC §813.) By not informing Kevin of the trust, Hally was able to treat the property as her own and breach her fiduciary duties to carry out the terms of the trust, without interference from Kevin.

What other fiduciary duties did Hally breach?

The terms of the trust were for Hally to use net profits of the business for Kevin's educational expenses while he was getting his pharmacology degree, and to transfer the business to Kevin when he was out of school. She complied with the term requiring her to remit net profits for Kevin's education only while Don was alive, and ceased complying with that term upon his death. This was a breach of the duty to carry out the trust purposes. (UTC §801.) It was also a breach of her duty of loyalty, because it appears she kept the funds for her own use. In addition, by changing the drugstore business to a spa services business, and selling the business, she further violated another purpose of the trust, which was to preserve and then transfer to Kevin the drugstore business that was started by his father. Hally may argue that it was necessary for her to change the focus of the business in order to maintain the financial value of the trust. She would have to prove that the drugstore business as established by Don had ceased to be viable, and that it would have been imprudent of her to maintain that business model. However, it appears that Don's purpose for setting up the trust was to keep the drugstore business going in order to pass it on to Kevin as a family legacy. Unless Hally could show that the business would have failed regardless of how well it was being run, she would not succeed with this argument. Merely enhancing the value of the trust assets would not be sufficient justification because Don was less concerned with the bottom line than with passing on the business to his grandson.

It appears that Hally has also failed to keep the trust assets segregated from her own assets and to earmark trust assets as belonging to the trust, which are necessary duties of a trustee. Otherwise, the trust assets and their increases or decreases in value are difficult to distinguish from her own and may become subject to her personal creditors.

Finally, it appears that Hally is attempting to misappropriate the assets for herself, breaching her duty of loyalty to Kevin.

Can Kevin now bring an action against Hally for breach of her fiduciary duties?

Hally may try to argue that it is too late for Kevin to bring an action against her, because it has been more than five years since Don delivered the business to her. However, the general rule is that the statute of limitations does not begin to run against an aggrieved beneficiary's claim until either the beneficiary knew or should have known of the breach or until the trust terminates. Kevin was unaware of the existence of the trust, as a result of Hally's violation of her duty to inform him of the trust. In addition, she cannot claim that the trust has terminated, because Kevin has just obtained his pharmacy degree. Either the trust has just terminated or will terminate shortly, as soon as Kevin obtains his pharmacist license. That was the time specified by Don for Hally to distribute the drugstore to Kevin and terminate the trust. Under UTC §1005, a beneficiary has five years after termination of a trust to bring an action.

What damages can Kevin and Tamara claim?
Kevin can claim damages sufficient to restore his father's drugstore business to him (which may be impossible) or may claim Hally's profits from the sale of the trust property to the spa chain, if greater. (UTC §1002.) In addition, Kevin (and perhaps Tamara, if she was paying for Kevin's educational expenses) may request reimbursement for his educational expenses that should have been paid from the profits of the business.

Answer to Question 29

Important aspects: alternate distribution, flexibility, noncharitable trusts, enforceability of will provisions and public policy

What are the practical problems presented by the client's plan?
First, she wants to condition the bequest to the one named person on his ability to find three more bearing that last name, but she does not provide for any alternative disposition if the named person fails. Second, she also does not provide for the possibility that the searching beneficiary finds more than three. For example, he could find two, and then find one more who turns out to be a twin. Does only one twin get to share? Understandably she wants to provide an incentive for the known person to search because otherwise he would have an incentive not to find any more persons with that name so he could keep a larger share of the estate. It would be preferable to set up a trust, the beneficiaries of which would be persons meeting her criteria, and appoint a professional trustee to administer the trust and oversee the search for additional beneficiaries. Another practical problem is that the known person or any person found subsequently would have an incentive to have children or adopt so that the children could participate. She would need to set limits on descendants of persons already included. She also has to consider how the money will be managed while the search is on for others with her last name.

Would this be a valid trust?
A noncharitable trust generally requires ascertainable beneficiaries, although the UTC allows certain noncharitable purpose trusts. See UTC §409. However, this trust would have ascertainable beneficiaries. There is at least one person who fits the requirements, and the trustee can be directed to search for others for a specified period of time. If the trust is created in a jurisdiction that has not abolished the Rule Against Perpetuities, the trust will have to be drafted with certain deadlines. Even if the Rule was not a concern, as a practical matter a deadline would have to be placed on the search. Note that her original idea, to require the one known person to locate three others, would not have violated the Rule against Perpetuities because the persons would have to be found during the lifetime of the known person.

Would the gift conditions be enforceable?
Courts will refuse to enforce provisions in wills and trust that violate public policy. This does not seem to violate public policy, but there may be a problem with the required promise to name children. If she wants to

ensure that the name is passed on, she could include new generations as trust beneficiaries, but she would run into the practical problems mentioned above.

Sample provision:
I give the residue of my estate to Bank, as trustee, to hold, administer and distribute the property as follows. The beneficiaries of the trust are Uma UnusualName and all other persons located by the trustee within ten years of establishment of this trust who meet the following requirements:

- His or her legal last name is UnusualName.
- His or her last name at birth was UnusualName.
- He or she can trace five generations of family members whose legal last name was UnusualName [is this requirement too onerous?].
- No ancestor of such person is currently or has previously been a beneficiary of this trust.

The trustee is directed to engage professional search firms to aid in locating eligible beneficiaries and is authorized to pay all reasonable fees charged by such firms and to expend any other reasonable amounts in the attempt to locate eligible trust beneficiaries. During the term of the trust, the trustee shall pay all of the income, at least annually, in equal shares to the then living beneficiaries of the trust as determined on December 31 of the prior calendar year. Upon the tenth anniversary of the establishment of the trust, the trust shall terminate, and all assets remaining in the trust shall be distributed in equal shares to the then living beneficiaries of the trust as determined on such tenth anniversary.

Answer to Question 30

Important aspects: hotchpot, equalizing bequests, incorporation by reference, independent significance

The hotchpot approach is a calculation method whereby the value of the lifetime transfers are added to the value of the estate, the shares are calculated based on this larger sum, and then each recipient's share is reduced by the lifetime transfers received by them. In equalizing gifts to beneficiaries in a will, the drafter has to consider what gifts are to be taken into account in making the determination of shares. There should either be a de minimus value to the gift to avoid arguments that every birthday gift should be included or a provision that only gifts on a schedule prepared by the testator would be considered in the calculation. There may be issues of compliance with the incorporation by reference doctrine if the schedule needs to be updated after the will is signed. Other documentation, required for the gift, can serve as evidence of applicable gifts under the doctrine of independent significance. Some testators limit the adjustment to gifts for which a gift tax return is required (so gifts under the annual exclusion amount would not be included in the calculation) because those gifts are easy to identify. Also, the calculation usually does not take into account the time value of money; for example, if Mom bought Sue a house in 1990 for $100,000 and it is now worth $200,000, and Mom bought Jim a house in 2010 for $200,000, and it is still worth $200,000, should Jim's share be reduced by $200,000 and Sue's share reduced by $100,000, or should they both get equal reductions? Another drafting issue is whether the share of a deceased child that is to pass to that child's descendants shall be reduced by lifetime gifts.

Sample provision:
The residue of my estate shall be distributed in equal shares to my three children, after adjustment for lifetime transfers to them as provided in this paragraph. The executor shall calculate the children's shares as follows: first, the executor shall add to the value of the net estate available to be distributed to my children at my death, all gifts given by me to any of my children listed on the schedule of gifts predating this will now held my accountant, which is incorporated herein by this reference, and all gifts from me to any of my children that were in excess of $5,000 and for which written evidence of such gift was delivered to my accountant. Gifts after the date of this will shall be included in the calculation only to the extent they exceed $5,000.00. The resulting sum shall be divided into equal shares, one share for each of my children then living and one share for each child of

mine that predeceases me leaving descendants then living. Each such share shall be reduced by the value of any gifts from me to such child that was included in the initial calculation required in this paragraph. The resulting amount shall be the share of such child, and shall be distributed as provided below.

Multiple-Choice Questions

1. On July 1, Jim Williams died intestate from injuries received in an automobile accident. His wife Wanda died the next day from injuries received in the same accident. Jim and Wanda were survived by one child, Bob, and two grandchildren, who are the children of the deceased daughter of Jim and Wanda. Jim's net estate available for distribution is $200,000. How should Jim's estate be distributed?

   A. $125,000 to Wanda's estate; $37,500 to Bob; and $18,750 each to the two grandchildren.

   B. $125,000 to Wanda's estate; $25,000 each to Bob and the two grandchildren.

   C. Nothing to Wanda's estate; $100,000 to Bob; $50,000 each to the two grandchildren.

   D. Nothing to Wanda's estate; $66,666 each to Bob and the two grandchildren.

2. Leonard and Evelyn were married ten years ago. They had no issue. Five years ago, Leonard executed a will leaving everything to Evelyn, if she survived him; if she failed to survive him, the estate was to go to Leonard's mother and father in equal shares. Leonard's sister Sue and his brother-in-law Ken witnessed this will. Last year, Leonard and Evelyn were divorced. Leonard died recently without ever expressly revoking his will. He was survived by Evelyn, his sister Sue, and a brother, Ted. Both of Leonard's parents died in an automobile accident three months before his death. How should Leonard's estate be distributed?

   A. All to Evelyn.

   B. Half to Sue and half to Ted.

   C. All to Ted.

   D. All to Sue.

3. One year ago, Dan, an unmarried 19-year-old who was illiterate and without issue, asked his friend to write the following:

   > I, Dan Smith, do hereby declare that this is my will. I want everything I have to go to my mother. My brother, Les, is not to get anything I own.
   >
   > X
   >
   > Witnessed:
   >
   > Ben Jones . . . Thorp Curry

   The mark "X" that appeared at the bottom of the will was made by Dan in the presence of Ben Jones and Thorp Curry, who signed as witnesses.

Dan died, survived only by his brother, Les, and by his grandmother, Ann Smith. Dan's mother predeceased him by one week. How should Dan's estate be distributed?

A. All to the estate of Dan's mother.

B. All to Dan's grandmother, Ann Smith.

C. Half to Dan's grandmother, Ann Smith; half to Dan's brother, Les.

D. All to Les.

4. Ellen Morris recently died intestate. Her husband Ed had predeceased her. Ellen and Ed adopted a daughter, Lisa, and they also had a biological son, Tom. One year ago, Ellen gave Tom $10,000 to invest in a fast-food franchise, telling him orally that it would be deducted from his share of her estate, unless it was repaid prior to her death. A friend of Ellen was present when the conversation with Tom took place and is prepared to testify as to Ellen's statement. Ellen's net estate available for distribution is separate property of $150,000. How should her estate be distributed?

A. $75,000 each to Lisa and Tom.

B. $80,000 to Lisa; $70,000 to Tom.

C. $150,000 to Tom; nothing to Lisa.

D. $150,000 to Lisa; nothing to Tom.

5. John created an *inter vivos* trust naming his children as income beneficiaries and his grandchildren as beneficiaries of the corpus. John's sister Ann then executed a valid will that contained the following bequest:

I leave the sum of $100,000 to those persons who are the income beneficiaries, at the date of my death, under an *inter vivos* trust created by my brother, John.

At Ann's death, John had two children, Adrian and Kimberly. Ann was survived by her mother Rita, by her brother John, and by a sister, Lisa. How should Ann's bequest be distributed?

A. To Adrian and Kimberly, in equal shares.

B. To the trustee of the trust created by John with the income to be paid to Adrian and Kimberly and, at their death, the $100,000 to be paid to John's grandchildren.

C. To Rita.

D. One-half to Rita; one-fourth each to John and Lisa.

Multiple-Choice Questions

6. Bill executed a valid will that contained the following bequest:

    I leave the sum of $500,000 to those persons who are the residuary legatees under my mother's last will and testament.

    At the time Bill executed his will, his mother had executed a valid will that left her residuary estate to Bill's uncles, Tom and Tim. Thereafter, she revoked that will and executed a new one, naming State University as her residuary legatee.

    When Bill's mother died, her residuary estate was paid to State University. When Bill died, he was survived by his wife Ann, and by one child, Emily, both of whom were provided for in his will. Bill's residuary estate was left to the American Red Cross. To whom should the $500,000 bequest be paid?

    A. To Tim and Tom, in equal shares.

    B. To State University.

    C. To the American Red Cross.

    D. To Ann as intestate property.

7. Carly executed a valid will devising her condominium to her brother Tom, and the residue of her estate to Lighthouse University, her alma mater. Several years later, Carly bought a house and entered into an installment land sales contract with Buyer for the sale of the condominium.

    Carly placed the $10,000 initially paid by Buyer as a down payment on the condominium in a separate savings account entitled "Condominium Proceeds Account." All subsequent payments have also been deposited in that account.

    At Carly's death, the account contained $15,000; the unpaid balance under the contract of sale was $100,000. Carly was survived by her parents and her brother Tom.

    Assuming that neither the will nor the surrounding circumstances indicate anything further about how Carly would have wanted the account and the unpaid balance of the installment sales contract to be distributed, how should these two items be distributed?

    A. The account to Lighthouse University and the balance of the installment sales contract to Tom.

    B. The account and the balance of the installment sales contract to Tom.

    C. The account to Carly's parents and the balance of the installment sales contract to Tom.

    D. The account and the installment sales contract to Lighthouse University.

8. Larry, a widower, executed a valid will that included the following three bequests:

   1. I give, devise, and bequeath my home to my son Ron.
   2. I give, devise, and bequeath the sum of $100,000 to my daughter Carolyn.
   3. I give, devise, and bequeath my residuary estate, in equal shares, to my son Ron and my daughter Carolyn.

   At the time that Larry executed his will, he owned a home worth approximately $100,000. One year later, he conveyed this home to his son Ron by a simple quitclaim deed that made no reference to the will. At the same time, he made a gift of $50,000 in cash to his daughter Carolyn. Shortly before his death, Larry purchased a home for $200,000, which he paid in cash. Larry recently died. His estate consists of $100,000 in cash and his home. He is survived only by Ron and Carolyn. How should his estate be distributed?

   A. To Ron and Carolyn equally.
   B. The home to Ron; the cash to Carolyn.
   C. The home to Ron and Carolyn, equally; $100,000 in cash to Carolyn.
   D. The home to Ron; $75,000 in cash to Carolyn; $25,000 in cash to Ron.

9. Bert died on July 1 from multiple gunshot wounds received in the course of a family dispute. His wife, Sofia, was convicted of murdering Bert. The conviction was affirmed on appeal. Bert left a will disposing of all of his property to Sofia, if she survived him. His estate consists of $100,000 in cash, a life insurance policy payable to Sofia as the primary beneficiary (with Bert's issue as secondary beneficiaries), and a home held in the name of Bert and Sofia as joint tenants with right of survivorship. Bert was survived by Sofia and three grandchildren. How should Bert's estate be distributed?

   A. The cash should be distributed to Sofia pursuant to the will. The insurance proceeds should be payable to Sofia pursuant to the beneficiary designation, and the joint tenancy is extinguished leaving title in Sofia alone.
   B. The cash should be distributed to the three grandchildren equally. The insurance proceeds should be payable to Sofia pursuant to the beneficiary designation, and the joint tenancy is extinguished leaving title in Sofia alone.

C. The cash should be distributed to the three grandchildren equally. The insurance proceeds should be payable to Sofia pursuant to the beneficiary designation, and the joint tenancy is severed with the half owned by Bert passing to the three grandchildren equally.

D. The cash and insurance proceeds should be distributed to the three grandchildren equally. The joint tenancy is severed and the half owned by Bert should pass to the three grandchildren equally.

10. Jamir executed a valid will disposing of his entire estate to his father. One year later, Jamir executed a second will that revoked the first will and disposed of his entire estate to his mother. Six months later, Jamir tore up the second will, stating to his friend Steve, who was present at the time, "This will take care of my estate so that my father gets it under the other will that I executed." At Jamir's death, the first will was found among his papers. He was survived by his parents and two sisters. How should Jamir's estate be distributed?

    A. To his father under the first will.
    B. To his mother under the second will.
    C. Equally, to his mother and father by intestate succession.
    D. Equally, to his sisters by intestate succession.

11. Suppose that, under the facts in question 10, (1) Jamir's second will had provided that $1,000 was to go to his mother, with the remainder of his estate to go to his father, and (2) at the time he tore up the second will, Jamir said only, "Wills are for wimps." How should Jamir's estate be distributed?

    A. To his father under the first will.
    B. $1,000 to his mother and the remainder to his father under the second will.
    C. Equally, to his mother and father by intestate succession.
    D. Equally, to his sisters by intestate succession.

12. Edgar validly executed Will #1, which disposed of his entire estate to his brother Tom. One year later, Edgar validly executed Will #2, which disposed of his entire estate to his sister Wilma. Will #2 did not contain a revocation clause. Six months later, Edgar validly executed Will #3, which expressly revoked Will #2 and left Edgar's estate to the American Red Cross. Will #3 made no reference to Will #1. One year later, Edgar revoked Will #3 by physical act. At Edgar's death, Will #1 was found among his important papers with an unsigned and undated note on it

which read, "This is my will." Edgar was survived only by his brother Tom and his sister Wilma. How should Edgar's estate be distributed?

A. To Tom under the terms of Will #1.

B. To Wilma under the terms of Will #2.

C. To the American Red Cross under the terms of Will #3.

D. To Tom and Wilma by intestate succession.

13. Kristin executed a valid holographic will that contained the following provision:

> Within the next few days, I will prepare a list of some personal items that I wish to be given to the persons named thereon.

Several days later Kristin prepared and signed the following handwritten list:

> Mother's diamond ring—Laura
>
> Dad's diamond stickpin—Larry
>
> My ruby ring—Samantha

Kristin died and was survived by her children, Rusty and Rosa. Under the will, the residue of her estate, after providing for Rusty and Rosa, was given to the American Red Cross. Laura, Larry, and Samantha are friends of Kristin. How should the rings and stickpin be distributed?

A. To Laura, Larry, and Samantha.

B. To the American Red Cross as part of the residuary.

C. To Rusty and Rosa, as part of their bequests under the will.

D. To Rusty and Rosa under intestate principles.

14. Cary executed a valid will that made, among others, the following bequest:

I give, devise, and bequeath my grand piano to my sister Roberta, with the hope that she will realize her dream of becoming a concert pianist.

The residue clause of Cary's will reads as follows:

> I give, devise, and bequeath the remainder of my estate to my brothers and sisters, share and share alike.

At the time he executed the will, Cary had one brother, Ted, and three sisters, Roberta, Edwina, and Judy. Ted predeceased Cary and was survived by his wife and one child. Roberta predeceased Cary and was survived only by her parents. Edwina and Judy survived Cary. How should Cary's estate be distributed?

- **A.** The piano and one-fourth of the residuary to Roberta's parents. One-fourth of the residuary each to Edwina, Judy, and Ted's child.
- **B.** One-third of the estate each to Edwina, Judy, and Ted's child.
- **C.** One-half of the estate each to Edwina and Judy.
- **D.** One-sixth of the estate each to Ted's wife and child. One-third of the estate each to Edwina and Judy.

15. Tim executed a valid will disposing of his real estate to "my nephew Albert" and devising the remainder of his estate "to my brothers and sisters, share and share alike." Tim specifically disinherited his own children. When he died, Tim was survived by Albert, two brothers, one sister, and his (Tim's) three children. Albert has one child, a son. After Tim's death, Albert filed a valid, written statement renouncing his interest in Tim's estate. How should Tim's estate be distributed?

- **A.** Real estate to Albert; residue to Tim's brothers and sister.
- **B.** The entire estate to Tim's brothers and sister.
- **C.** The entire estate to Tim's children.
- **D.** The real estate to Albert's son; residue to Tim's two brothers and sister.

16. Tom executed a valid will disposing of "all my real estate to my sister Joan" and "the rest, residue, and remainder of my estate to my brother Bill." The will also contained a provision stating, "My executor is hereby directed to pay all of my just debts." At the time Tom executed his will, he owned Blackacre, which was worth $100,000, and stock worth $100,000. One year before his death, Tom borrowed $90,000 from ABC Bank and gave the bank a mortgage on Blackacre to secure payment of the debt. He then lost all of the borrowed money gambling in Las Vegas. Blackacre is now worth $125,000 and the unpaid mortgage is still $90,000. The stock is worth $300,000. How should Tom's estate be distributed?

- **A.** Blackacre, encumbered by the mortgage, should be distributed to Joan; the stock should be distributed to Bill.
- **B.** Blackacre should be distributed to Joan free and clear of the debt; the stock remaining after payment of the debt should be distributed to Bill.

C. Blackacre and $90,000 worth of stock should be distributed to Joan; the remainder of the stock should be distributed to Bill.

D. Because Tom's testamentary scheme was to treat Joan and Bill equally, Blackacre and the stock should be sold, the debt to ABC Bank paid, and the remainder distributed equally to Joan and Bill.

17. John and Betty met in Hawaii, where both were vacationing. They spent much of their time together. After they returned to their homes, Betty discovered that she was pregnant. After her child, Jennifer, was born, Betty, who had never married John, sued John to establish paternity. Although John denied that Jennifer was his child, the jury found by clear and convincing evidence that John was the father. The court entered judgment accordingly. Thereafter, John refused to acknowledge Jennifer as his child or to spend any time with her, but did pay the support ordered by the court. When John died, his will (executed prior to the birth of Jennifer) left his entire estate to ABC Charity. John was survived by Betty, Jennifer, and his parents. How should his estate be distributed?

    A. To Jennifer.

    B. To ABC Charity.

    C. Half to Jennifer, and the remainder to ABC Charity.

    D. Half to Jennifer, and the remainder to John's parents, in equal shares.

18. Jane had two children, Will and Mark, by her first marriage. After the death of her first husband, she remarried and had one child, Kane, by her second husband, Steve. Jane then died. One year later, Mark died intestate. Mark was survived only by Will and Kane. Steve is still alive. How should Mark's estate be distributed?

    A. To Will.

    B. To Will and Kane, in equal shares.

    C. One-third each to Steve, Will, and Kane.

    D. One-half to Steve; one-fourth each to Will and Kane.

19. Tanesha owned a company that designed and produced puzzles, bookmarks, and other gift items. Tanesha's will provided that if she still owned the company at her death, $10,000 would be distributed to each of those persons working at the company at the time of her death. This provision is an example of what doctrine of will construction?

    A. Integration.

    B. Independent Significance.

C. Incorporation by Reference.

D. Republication by Codicil.

20. When Lisa was seven years old, her parents were killed in an automobile accident. The night of the accident, her aunt and uncle, Harvey and Ann, arrived and told Lisa that she was going to go live with them and "be our little girl." Several years later, they told Lisa, "You're going to court with us so that you can be our little girl forever." Harvey and Ann held Lisa out as their daughter. She participated in every way as a member of their family. Harvey had a son, Bob, from a previous marriage. When Harvey died intestate, Ann claimed his entire estate. After consulting an attorney, Lisa found out that, while Harvey and Ann had obtained legal custody of her, there had been no formal adoption. Harvey was survived by Ann, Lisa, Bob, and Harvey's parents. How should his estate be distributed?

A. The first $300,000, plus three-quarters of the balance of the estate to Ann; the remaining one-quarter of the estate to Harvey's parents.

B. The first $150,000, plus one-half of the balance of the intestate estate to Ann; the remaining one-half to be divided between Bob and Lisa, equally.

C. One-half of the intestate estate to Ann; the remaining one-half to be divided between Bob and Lisa, equally.

D. The entire intestate estate to Ann.

21. Patricia was preparing for a trip to the Caribbean. She wrote the following and signed it in her own handwriting:

> I am getting ready to take a cruise. If I don't return from the cruise, I want my entire estate to go to the County Art Museum.
>
> /s/ Patricia

Patricia took the cruise and returned. One month later, she died. She was survived by her mother and a brother. How should her estate be distributed?

A. To her mother, because the holographic will was not dated.

B. To her mother and brother, equally.

C. To the County Art Museum.

D. One-half each to the County Art Museum and her mother.

22. Arnold and his father, Clay, orally agreed that Clay could live in Arnold's house, that Arnold would provide Clay with food and clothing, and that Clay would make a will leaving his entire estate to Arnold

at Clay's death. When Clay died, he left a valid will that (1) made no reference to the agreement with Arnold, and (2) disposed of his entire estate to Anne. How should Clay's estate be distributed, assuming that (1) Clay was survived by Arnold and Arnold's brother, Tom, and (2) Anne also wishes to take the estate?

A. Anne.

B. Arnold.

C. Arnold and Tom, equally.

D. One-half to Anne and one-half to Arnold and Tom, equally.

23. Suppose that, in question 22, Arnold and Clay had put their agreement in writing and that Clay moved into Arnold's home and has lived there until the present. (For this question only, assume that Clay is still alive.) Several years ago, after signing the agreement, Clay transferred one-half of his assets to Tom. What remedy, if any, can Arnold obtain against Clay or Tom while Clay is still alive?

A. Specific performance to require Tom to transfer the assets to Arnold.

B. Anticipatory breach of the agreement, with damages paid to Arnold.

C. An injunction preventing Clay from transferring his assets and requiring Tom to reconvey the assets to Clay.

D. Anticipatory breach of the agreement, with a constructive trust being imposed upon the assets transferred to Tom.

24. Two years before her death, Toni, a widow, executed and took home with her a valid will in which she gave her entire estate to her church, First Baptist. At her death, the will could not be found. Her attorney, Agnes, has a conformed copy of the will and can testify that she had a conversation with Toni the week before her death in which Toni affirmed that her will, as executed, still represented her testamentary wishes. Toni was survived by her two children, Rob and Adam, both of whom were born prior to the making of the will, and her parents. To whom is it likely that the estate will be distributed?

A. To the First Baptist Church.

B. Half of the estate to the First Baptist Church; half to Rob and Adam, equally.

C. To Rob and Adam.

D. Half of the estate to Toni's parents; half to Rob and Adam, equally.

Multiple-Choice Questions

25. Parker, a widower, executed a valid will that disposed of his entire estate to "the children of my best friend, Sam Riley." At the time the will was executed and at Parker's death, Sam Riley had no children. After Parker's death, Sam had three children, Bob, Sally, and Ellen. Parker was survived by his sister, Ann, and his parents. To whom should Parker's estate be distributed?

    A. To Bob, as Sam's first-born child.
    B. To Bob, Sally, and Ellen, at Sam's death.
    C. To Ann.
    D. To Parker's parents.

26. Suppose that, in question 25, the gift was "to the children of my best friend, Sam Riley" and that at the time Parker died, (1) Bob, Sam's eldest child, was already alive, and (2) Sally and Ellen were born after Parker's death. To whom should Parker's estate be distributed?

    A. To Bob.
    B. To Bob, Sally, and Ellen.
    C. To Ann.
    D. To Parker's parents.

27. Suppose that, in question 25, the gift was "to the children of my best friend, Sam Riley, who reach the age of 25." When Parker died, Bob, the eldest child, was 15. Prior to Bob's reaching age 25, Ellen was born. Sally was born after Bob reached age 25. How should Parker's estate be distributed?

    A. To Bob.
    B. One-half each to be held for Bob and Ellen until they reach age 25, and then paid to them; but if either dies before reaching age 25, remainder to the one who survives.
    C. One-third to Bob; remainder to be held until Ellen and Sally reach age 25, and then distributed to them equally. If they fail to reach age 25, the remainder to be split among the other members of the class who reach age 25.
    D. One-third to Bob, Ellen, and Sally, immediately.

28. Suppose that, in question 25, the only gift was "$10,000 each to the children of my best friend, Sam Riley" and that at the time Parker died, Sam Riley had no children. Bob, Sally, and Ellen were born after Parker's death. To whom should Parker's estate be distributed (assuming that the will made no other gifts)?

A. $10,000 to Bob; one-half of the remainder to Ann; the balance to Parker's parents.

B. $10,000 each to Bob, Sally, and Ellen; the balance to Parker's parents.

C. To Parker's parents.

D. To Ann, entirely.

29. At a meeting at their lawyer's office, Edward and Mary both validly executed reciprocal wills in which each disposed of his or her property to the survivor; upon the death of the survivor, all property was to go to their children. Mary died, her will was probated, and her property was distributed to Edward. Thereafter, Edward executed another valid will, leaving all of his property to his friend, Ann. When Edward died, he was survived by one child, Tim, and by two grandchildren who were the issue of Lisa, the predeceased daughter of Edward and Mary. How should Edward's estate be distributed?

A. One-half to Tim, and one-fourth each to the grandchildren pursuant to Edward's original will.

B. One-half to Tim, and one-fourth each to the grandchildren by intestate succession.

C. All to Tim by intestate succession.

D. All to Ann.

30. Bill executed a last will and testament. It made two bequests, as follows:

1. $10,000 to my son, Jim.
2. All the rest, residue, and remainder of my estate to my daughter, Elizabeth.

The will also explicitly revoked a prior valid will that had expressly disinherited Jim and left everything to Elizabeth. Bill was survived by his two children (Jim and Elizabeth) and his parents. It is admitted by all parties that Bill's first will was valid. Assuming that there are grounds for opposing the probate of Bill's second will, who may contest probate of the will?

A. Jim only.

B. Jim or Elizabeth.

C. Jim or Elizabeth or Bill's parents.

D. Elizabeth only.

31. John and Beth Askew were married for many years. During the course of their marriage, a son, Clay, was born. Clay was the only child John ever had. Although he had no rational basis for his suspicions, John believed that Clay was conceived as the result of a relationship between Beth and another man. Although Beth denied this, John persisted in his belief. John refused to participate in a DNA test, but Clay had John's blue eyes and coloring and shared a rare blood type with John. Beth died when Clay was four. When Clay was six, John executed a holographic will (the only will he ever made), reading as follows:

> My wife has betrayed me. She gave birth to a child by another man. The child is not mine, although I have provided a home for him. I therefore disinherit Clay. I leave everything to my aunt, Matilda Askew.
>
> /s/ John Askew

John died without changing his belief or the will. Should the will be admitted to probate?

   A. No, if John was suffering from an insane delusion.

   B. Yes, if the will was validly executed.

   C. No, because John had been unduly influenced in his beliefs.

   D. Yes, because John has the absolute right to disinherit his son.

32. Assume the same facts described in question 31, except that (1) there was a rational basis for John's belief that Clay was the product of an illicit relationship, and (2) the final sentence of John's holographic will (leaving everything to Aunt Matilda) was omitted. John died without changing (1) his belief that Clay was the product of an illicit relationship, or (2) the purported will. Should the document be admitted to probate?

   A. No, because the purported will is not a valid testamentary document.

   B. No, because a natural father cannot disinherit his son.

   C. Yes, because the writing constitutes a valid holographic will.

   D. No, because John's belief about Clay's parentage was mistaken, although rational.

33. When Ashley was married to Bob, she named him as beneficiary of the life insurance provided by her employer (an airplane manufacturer) as part of her compensation package. She and Bob divorced, and she married Hector. She signed a will naming Hector as the sole

beneficiary and stated in the will that Hector was to receive the proceeds from the life insurance. She did not take Bob's name off of the insurance as beneficiary, however. She has now died. Who receives the life insurance proceeds?

A. Hector, because she changed the beneficiary in her Will.

B. Hector, because she and Bob had divorced.

C. Bob, because he was named as the beneficiary.

D. Bob, because federal law governs.

34. Fred Jones, an attorney, had represented Ellen Morris for many years. Ellen requested that Jones prepare a will for her and that a bequest of $10,000 to Jones be included in the will. Jones, sensing that it would be improper for him to draw a will in which he was a legatee, asked his associate Michael Fox to prepare the will. Fox did so and returned the will to Jones for execution by Ellen. When Ellen died, Jones filed an application to probate the will. Assuming that Ellen's son, Thad, who received the residue of the estate, wishes to contest the will, upon what basis is he most likely to be successful?

A. Undue influence.

B. Fraud.

C. Lack of testamentary capacity.

D. Violation of the Rules of Professional Conduct applicable to lawyers.

35. Fernanda's Will provided "I give my car to my godson Billy" and gave the residue of her estate to her daughter Celeste. At the time of the Will Fernanda had a new Volvo station wagon. Fernanda had included Celeste in all appointments with the lawyer when doing her estate planning. Fernanda also signed a power of attorney appointing Celeste as her attorney in fact if she became incapacitated. Celeste was given copies of the will and the power of attorney by Fernanda. Fernanda became incapacitated, and Celeste took over Fernanda's affairs under the power of attorney. Celeste sold the Volvo, even though Fernanda did not need cash, because Fernanda was not driving and Celeste thought the insurance and license fees on the car were an unnecessary expense. Fernanda has now died. What does Billy receive?

A. Nothing, because "my car" is too vague.

B. Nothing, because Celeste sold the only car owned by Fernanda.

C. The value of the Volvo.

D. Nothing from the estate, but he can sue Celeste.

36. Robin Thomas was married to Hal Thomas. One month after they agreed to a "trial" separation, Robin met Craig Jones (a very wealthy businessman) at a bar in another city. When Craig proposed to Robin two months later, Robin accepted. When Robin and Craig applied for a marriage license, Robin represented that she was single. One week after they were married, Craig signed a valid will that left one-half of his estate to "My beloved wife, Robin," and one-half to his Aunt Martha. In his will, Craig explicitly stated that although he had two children from a previous marriage, he wanted them to receive nothing (because they had sided with his previous wife). Aunt Martha, however, had stood by him.

    Craig died one month later, survived by Robin, Aunt Martha, and his two children. His children requested that the will be denied probate. What action is the court likely to take?

    A. Admit the will to probate, because Craig can leave his estate to whomever he wishes.

    B. Admit the will to probate, but impose a constructive trust upon Robin's share in favor of Aunt Martha.

    C. Deny the will to probate, because it was procured by fraud.

    D. Deny the will to probate, because Craig was mistaken as to Robin's marital status.

37. John executed a will giving his friend, Ted, a power of appointment over the residue of John's estate. The residuary clause reads as follows:

    > I give, devise, and bequeath the rest, residue, and remainder of my estate to such person or persons as my friend, Ted, may appoint either by deed during Ted's lifetime or by his will; if my friend, Ted, does not exercise this power of appointment, at Ted's death the residue of my estate shall be distributed to my heirs.

    The power of appointment given to Ted is classified as a:

    A. General power presently exercisable.

    B. Special power presently exercisable.

    C. General testamentary power.

    D. Special testamentary power.

38. Suppose that, in question 37, Ted fails to exercise the power during his life, but executes a will that disposes of his property as follows:

    > I give $10,000 to my only son, Bill. All the rest, residue, and remainder of my estate, I give to my wife, Ann.

How should the property over which Ted was given a power of appointment under John's will be distributed?

A. To Ann.

B. The first $50,000, plus one-half of the balance to Ann; the remainder to Bill.

C. To John's heirs.

D. To Ted's heirs.

39. Suppose that, in question 37, at the time he executed his will, John had three children, Art, Bob, and Charles. Art died before John without a spouse or issue. Art left a will devising all his property to the American Red Cross. At John's death, Bob and Charles were living; however, both predeceased Ted. Bob left no issue, but was survived by his wife, Sally, to whom he left his entire estate by will. Charles was survived by his wife, Marcy, to whom he left his entire estate by will, and by one child, Ned.

Assuming that Ted failed to exercise the power of appointment (during his lifetime or by his will), how should the property be distributed?

A. One-third to the American Red Cross; one-third to Sally; one-third to Marcy.

B. One-half to Sally; one-half to Marcy.

C. One-half to Marcy; one-half to Ned.

D. All to Ned.

40. Suppose that, in question 37, Ted exercised the power of appointment by his will, and that the main provision read as follows:

> I give, devise, and bequeath all of my property, including any property over which I hold a power of appointment, as follows:
>
> 1. The property over which I hold a power of appointment to John's children, Art, Bob, and Charles, in equal shares; and
> 2. The rest, residue, and remainder of my property I give to my wife, Ann.

Suppose further that (1) all of John's children predeceased Ted, and (2) none of them left surviving spouses or issue. Ted was survived by Ann and Bill, his son by reason of a previous marriage. John's only living heirs were his two brothers. How should the property that was subject to Ted's power be distributed?

A. To John's brothers, in equal shares.

B. To Ann.

C. The first $150,000, plus one-half of the balance, to Ann; the remainder to Bill.

D. To Bill.

Questions 41-44 are based on the following fact situation:

Ten years ago, T purchased 300 shares of the stock of Rex, Inc., a family corporation. Nine years ago, T executed a valid will, which provided as follows:

1. I give 300 shares of Rex, Inc., stock and $1,000 to my brother-in-law Ben.
2. I give the sum of $15,000 to my son Mike.
3. I give the residue of my estate to my wife Doris.

Liz, T's second child (by Doris), was born after T executed his will and on the very day T was seriously injured in a heated altercation with his brother-in-law, Ben. T subsequently sold his Rex stock for $15,000 and invested the proceeds in municipal bonds.

Doris obtained a valid final judgment of divorce from T nine months ago. T married Kay six months ago.

One week ago, T died as a result of the injuries he received in the altercation with Ben. Ben was arrested for voluntary manslaughter, tried, and convicted.

T died without revising his will. T's estate, entirely his separate property, consisted of the municipal bonds now worth $20,000 and cash of $160,000 on deposit at City Bank. T is survived by Ben, Mike, Liz, Kay, and Doris.

41. How much of T's estate will Doris receive?

    A. One-half.

    B. The entire estate, less the gifts to Mike and Ben.

    C. Nothing.

    D. None of the above.

42. How much of T's estate will Kay receive?

    A. One-half.

    B. The entire estate, less the gifts to Mike and Ben.

    C. Nothing.

    D. None of the above.

43. How much of T's estate will Liz receive?

    A. One-fourth.

    B. One-third.

    C. Nothing.

    D. None of the above.

44. How much of T's estate will Ben receive?

   A. Nothing, because the gifts to Ben were adeemed by extinction.

   B. Nothing, because he killed T.

   c. The value of the stock when it was sold, plus $1,000.

   D. $21,000 (the value of the bonds at T's death, plus $1,000).

45. Tallulah's will left her home to her nephew Aiden, her diamond bracelet to her sister Brenda, her Picasso print hanging in her bedroom to her friend Calista, her Mercedes to her friend Daniel, and the residue of her estate to her daughter Edna. After signing the will, Tallulah gave the bracelet to Brenda. Tallulah died instantly in a car accident that totaled the Mercedes. Aiden and Calista both predeceased Tallulah. Aiden left a daughter surviving him, Augusta, and Calista left a son surviving her, Calvin. How is her estate distributed?

   A. The entire estate goes to Edna.

   B. The home goes to Augusta, the insurance proceeds for the totaled Mercedes goes to Daniel, and the residue goes to Edna.

   C. The home goes to Augusta, the Picasso goes to Calvin, the value of the bracelet goes to Brenda, and the residue goes to Edna.

   D. The home goes to Augusta, the Picasso goes to Calvin, the insurance proceeds for the totaled Mercedes go to Daniel, and the residue goes to Edna.

46. Ralph devised property to Sam in trust to pay the income to Linda for life, and on Linda's death to distribute the principal to such of Linda's issue as Linda should appoint by will. If Linda did not exercise the power of appointment, at Linda's death Sam was to distribute the principal to Linda's then-living issue, the issue to take per stirpes.

Prior to Linda's death, she delivered a written letter to Sam stating that she released all rights that she might have as donee of the power of appointment that Ralph had given to her. Thereafter, Linda executed a will that disposed of all the property she owned, including any property "over which I hold a power of appointment," to her son Adam. When Linda died, she was survived by two children, Adam and Ron, and by a grandchild, Martha, the issue of a predeceased daughter, Karen. How should Sam distribute that part of Ralph's property subject to appointment?

   A. To Adam, Ron, and Martha, in equal shares.

   B. To Adam.

C. To Adam and Ron, in equal shares.

D. To Ralph's heirs.

47. Suppose that, in question 46, Linda did not release the power of appointment. Prior to Linda's death, she entered into a contract with Adam, one of her children. The terms of the agreement were that, in exchange for the payment of $10,000 to Linda by Adam, Linda agreed to exercise the power of appointment in favor of Adam. Adam paid the $10,000. However, at Linda's death, her will provided for exercise of the power in favor of Adam, Ron, and Martha, equally. How should the court distribute the property?

    A. To Adam, pursuant to the contract.

    B. To Adam and Ron, equally, as Linda's children.

    C. To Adam, Ron, and Martha, pursuant to the exercise of the power.

    D. To Adam, Ron, and Martha, as takers in default of the power.

48. Alice transferred $1 million to her brother Jim; the transfer was carried out without any statement of conditions by Alice. Two weeks later, Alice told Jim, "That $1 million I gave you is to be held by you for the benefit of all of my children. If you don't agree, I want it all back." Jim responded by telling Alice, "You gave me that money, I'll use it the way you want me to." Alice later heard that Jim had told other people that he wasn't going to give Alice's children a penny. Alice filed suit against Jim to recover the money, but died before the case came to trial. Assume that:

    (1) Alice died survived by two children, Bill and Penny, and

    (2) Alice's will left everything to Bill and Penny.

    How should the court order distribution of the money?

    A. To Jim, outright.

    B. To Penny, outright.

    C. To Jim in trust for Bill and Penny.

    D. To Bill and Penny, outright.

49. Stephanie executed a will that gave all her property to her son Rick. Thereafter, she wrote and delivered to her brother, Sam, a letter that read as follows:

    > Dear Sam: As you know, I am leaving for Europe in two weeks. When I return, it is my intent that my farm, on which you now reside, shall be placed in trust for the benefit of your children. I have given the rest of my estate to Rick. All my love, Stephanie.

Stephanie died while on her European trip. She was survived by Sam, Sam's daughter Tina, Stephanie's mother Ann, and Rick. How should the court dispose of the farm?

- **A.** Because a valid trust was created upon delivery of the letter to Sam, the farm should be distributed to Sam as trustee for Tina.
- **B.** No valid trust was created, and so the farm should be distributed to Rick pursuant to the will.
- **C.** Although no valid trust was created at the time of delivery of the letter, a trust came into being upon Stephanie's death, and so the property should be distributed to Sam as trustee for Tina.
- **D.** No valid trust was created, and so the farm should be distributed to Rick under intestacy principles.

50. Christina executed a valid will that made the following bequest:

    > I give, devise, and bequeath to my friend John, as trustee, the sum of $15,000. I direct that he invest this money and, once each year, use the income therefrom to throw a party for the persons who are my three best friends at the time of my death.

    At Christina's death, John advised the court that he was willing to carry out the terms of the trust. He also stated that it was unclear who Christina's three best friends were at the time of her death, but that if he had to guess, he'd say that they were Ann, Barbara, and Cary. The residue of Christina's estate was bequeathed to her mother. How should the court distribute Christina's estate?

    - **A.** $15,000 to John, as trustee to be used for the purpose stated in the will; remainder of the estate to Christina's mother.
    - **B.** $15,000 to John, as trustee of a trust for *all* of Christina's friends; remainder of the estate to Christina's mother.
    - **C.** $5,000 each to Ann, Barbara, and Cary; remainder of the estate to Christina's mother.
    - **D.** All to Christina's mother.

51. T was feeling very weak. After T signed her typed will in front of X and Y, Y left the room to obtain a glass of water for T. While Y was away, X signed the will as a witness. When Y returned, she signed the will in front of X and T. Which of the following statements is correct?

    - **A.** T has a valid holographic will.
    - **B.** T has a valid formal will.

C. T's will is invalid, because the witnesses did not sign in each other's presence.

D. T's will is invalid, if the will was undated.

52. T was in a hospital, feeling increasingly weak. T announced to X and Y that the document that he was about to ask them to witness was a will. After T signed the typewritten will, he began to cough continuously. Dr. Debbie rushed into T's hospital room and asked X and Y to leave. They left the room and signed T's will as witnesses in the hospital lobby. Which of the following statements is correct?

    A. T has a valid holographic will.

    B. T has a valid formal will.

    C. T's will is not valid, because the witnesses did not sign in his presence.

    D. T's will is not valid, if X and Y did not actually read the document.

53. Bruce made the following bequest in his will:

    > I give, devise, and bequeath the sum of $10,000 to my friend, Selma, as trustee, the income and such portion of the corpus as may be necessary to be used by her to provide care and shelter for my dog, Rusty.

    The remainder of Bruce's property was bequeathed to the Humane Society in the city where Bruce lived. At Bruce's death, Selma declared that she was willing to carry out the terms of Bruce's trust. How would Bruce's estate be distributed under traditional trust principles?

    A. $10,000 to Selma to be held in trust for Rusty; the remainder to the Humane Society.

    B. $10,000 to Selma free of trust; the remainder to the Humane Society.

    C. All to the Humane Society.

    D. None of the above.

54. Elaine made the following bequest in her will:

    > I give, devise, and bequeath the sum of $1 million to my husband Will, if he survives me, as trustee, the income from such trust to be paid to my husband so long as he remains unmarried. In the event that my husband shall remarry, or upon his death, whichever shall first occur, I appoint my brother Tom, as successor trustee, to pay the income to my children, so long as they remain unmarried. In the event they marry, or upon their deaths, whichever first occurs, to pay all accrued income and principal to my alma mater, State College.

Elaine was survived by her husband Will, her brother Tom, and her children, Bob and Ellen. Will, Bob, and Ellen have petitioned the court to strike the conditions that they not marry and distribute the property in other respects in accordance with the trust. How should the court distribute Elaine's estate?

- **A.** The court should strike the conditions as to all beneficiaries and distribute $1 million to Will, as trustee.
- **B.** The court should strike the conditions as to Will, but not as to Bob and Ellen and distribute $1 million to Will, as trustee.
- **C.** The court should strike the conditions as to Bob and Ellen, but not as to Will, and distribute $1 million to Will as trustee.
- **D.** The court should declare the trust invalid and distribute the property pursuant to the residuary clause of the will, or by intestate succession, whichever is appropriate.

55. Judith made an unconditional bequest of $200,000 in her will to her brother Earl. The bequest was preceded by a conversation between Judith and Earl, in which Earl agreed to hold the property in trust for Judith's friend Grace. The residue of Judith's estate was bequeathed to her "brothers and sisters, in equal shares." At Judith's death, Earl advised Grace, as well as his brothers and sisters, that the $200,000 was his, outright. Judith was survived by Grace, Earl, one other brother, and two sisters. What of the following should guide the court in regard to the bequest to Earl?

    - **A.** The oral agreement to hold the funds in trust is enforceable by Grace as an express trust.
    - **B.** The oral agreement to hold the funds in trust is unenforceable as an express trust, but the court will impose a constructive trust in favor of Grace.
    - **C.** The oral agreement to hold the funds in trust is unenforceable as an express trust, but the court will impose a resulting trust, and the property will pass under the residuary clause to Judith's brothers and sisters.
    - **D.** The bequest passes to Earl alone.

56. Suppose that, in question 55, the bequest by Judith in her will was to "my brother, Earl, in trust for someone mentioned to him during my lifetime." If Earl refuses to perform the trust, what action should the court take in regard to the bequest to Earl?

A. The oral agreement to hold the property in trust may be enforced as an express trust by Grace.

B. The oral agreement to hold the property in trust may be enforced as a constructive trust by Grace.

C. The oral agreement to hold the property in trust may be enforced as a resulting trust by Judith's brothers and sisters.

D. The bequest passes to Earl, outright.

57. Amy Jones deposited $10,000 in a bank account at First Bank. The account was created as "Amy Jones, Trustee for Karen Smith." Karen Smith is Amy's friend. Amy used this account as her checking account, depositing her monthly paychecks into the account and paying her bills from it. Karen Smith had no knowledge of the account. After creating this account, Amy executed a will in which she left all of her property to her brother, Ed Jones. Amy recently died and was survived by her parents, her friend Karen, and her brothers, Ed and Warren Jones. The balance in the account at Amy's death was $35,000. How should the bank account be distributed?

A. To Karen Smith.

B. To Ed Jones.

C. To Karen, Ed, and Warren, in equal shares.

D. To Amy's parents, in equal shares.

58. Suppose that, in question 57, Karen Smith predeceased Amy Jones, and that (1) Amy never changed the designation on the bank account, and (2) Karen was survived by her daughter, LeeAnn, and her husband Mike Smith. Suppose further that Karen, after the birth of LeeAnn, executed a valid will disposing of all of her property to her husband Mike. How should the bank account be distributed?

A. To Mike Smith.

B. To LeeAnn.

C. To Ed Jones.

D. To Amy's parents, in equal shares.

59. Able created a revocable *inter vivos* trust with Blackacre (a farm) as the trust res, Baker as the trustee, and Carl as the beneficiary. Baker, as trustee, was directed to pay the income from the trust (*i.e.*, profits from operation of the farm) to Carl, until Carl reached age 45, and then to deed Blackacre to Carl in fee simple absolute. The trust contained no statement regarding Carl's right to alienate his interest in the trust.

Carl, in order to satisfy a debt he owed to Sam, made a written assignment of "all my right, title, and interest in Blackacre" to Sam. Under these circumstances:

A. Sam acquires no interest in Blackacre.

B. Sam acquires a right to the income interest only.

C. Sam may require the trust to terminate, and Baker to convey Blackacre to him (because Carl no longer owns any interest in the property).

D. Sam may require the trustee to pay the income to him until Carl reaches age 45, and then to deed Blackacre to him when Carl reaches age 45.

60. Suppose that, in question 59, subsequent to the assignment to Sam, (1) Carl assigned his interest in the trust to Ted, and (2) Ted was the first to notify Baker of the assignment. Between Sam and Ted, who has the greater right?

A. Sam, because the first assignment has priority.

B. Sam, but only if Sam gave present consideration in exchange for the transfer.

C. Ted, because the first assignee to notify the trustee of his assignment prevails.

D. Ted, if he gave present consideration for the transfer.

61. Alice created a trust in her will that provides that the income shall be paid to her children during their lifetimes, and upon the death of her last child, the principal shall be divided among her grandchildren. The trust contains the following clause:

> My children shall not, by way of present or future anticipation, assign their interest in this trust under any circumstances. The income interest of my children shall not be subject to the claims of their creditors, whether by voluntary or involuntary transfer.

After Alice's death, one of her children, Beatrix, directed that her income installments be paid to her sister, Karen, in satisfaction of a debt that Beatrix owed to Karen. Under these circumstances:

A. The transfer of Beatrix's income interest is void.

B. The transfer of Beatrix's income interest is valid, and the trustee must pay Beatrix's income interest to Karen.

C. The transfer of Beatrix's income interest is valid to the extent (1) the trustee decides to honor the purported transfer, and (2) Beatrix, the beneficiary, does not revoke the transfer.

D. Although the transfer of Beatrix's income is void, the debt owed to Karen by Beatrix is deemed to be satisfied, because Karen knew the transfer was void.

62. Suppose that, in question 61, the United States obtained a judgment against Beatrix for unpaid income taxes. Under these circumstances:

A. The judgment of the United States takes priority over a spendthrift clause, and the trustee must pay the income to the United States.

B. The judgment of the United States takes priority over a spendthrift clause, and the trustee must deliver principal sufficient to satisfy Beatrix's income tax delinquency to the United States.

C. The spendthrift clause is valid against the judgment of the United States, but the trustee may pay the income to the United States until Beatrix objects.

D. The spendthrift clause is valid against the judgment of the United States, and so the trustee may not pay any of Beatrix's income to the United States.

63. In her will, Kathy created a trust by transferring stocks and bonds worth $1 million to National Bank as trustee, for the following purpose:

> The trustee shall distribute to my grandchildren such amounts of income as it, in its sole and complete discretion, deems appropriate for their comfortable support and maintenance. At the death of the last of my children to die, the trustee shall distribute all unpaid income and the principal of this trust to my grandchildren then living, per capita.

After Kathy's death (but before the death of her children) one of Kathy's grandchildren (Larry) incurred a debt that he could not pay. The creditor obtained a judgment against Larry. Under these circumstances:

A. The creditor may levy against Larry's income interest in the hands of the trustee.

B. The creditor may obtain a lien against (but not a sale of) Larry's remainder interests in the hands of the trustee.

C. The creditor may levy against Larry's income and remainder interests in the hands of the trustee.

D. The creditor may not levy against Larry's income or remainder interests in the hands of the trustee.

64. Caleb died owing $2 million to his college friend Svetlana. He left the following assets: $1 million in a stock account, a $500,000 life insurance policy payable to his wife, $750,000 in a 401(k) plan through his employer also payable to his wife, and a home with $100,000 in equity. Which assets are available to pay Svetlana?

    A. All assets listed in the question are available to Svetlana.

    B. None of the assets listed in the question are available to Svetlana.

    C. All of the listed assets except for the life insurance are available to Svetlana.

    D. The stock account and the equity in the house in excess of the homestead exemption are available to Svetlana.

65. Ted created an *inter vivos* trust by transferring $500,000 to First National Bank, as trustee. The declaration of trust provided that the income of the trust was to be paid to Ted during his lifetime. At his death, the principal was to be distributed to Ted's daughter, Mae. The trust provides as follows:

    > No beneficiary of this trust may, by way of present or future anticipation, assign his or her interest in this trust, under any circumstance. The income interest of any beneficiary shall not be subject to the claims of creditors, whether by way of voluntary or involuntary transfer.

    Several years after this trust was created, Ron obtained a judgment against Ted in the sum of $400,000. This obligation arose after the trust was created. Under these circumstances:

    A. The income interest of Ted is exempt from his creditors.

    B. Ron may not levy on Ted's interest in the hands of the trustee, but may levy on any income actually received by Ted.

    C. Ron may levy on Ted's income interest, but not on the remainder interest.

    D. Ron may levy on both the income and remainder interests.

66. Leslie created a trust of $250,000, with the First Bank as trustee, for the following purpose:

    > The principal of this trust, together with all accrued income therefrom, shall be paid over to the person who discovers a cure for cancer.

    This trust is:

    A. Valid, because its purpose is to promote medical research.

    B. Invalid, because it will benefit a limited number of persons.

C. Invalid, because it is not certain to vest within the allowable period of the Rule Against Perpetuities.

D. Invalid, because it is not certain ever to vest.

67. Suppose that, in question 66, the trust had the following purpose:

> The principal of this trust, together with all accrued income therefrom, shall be used for charitable purposes.

This trust is:

A. Invalid, because the beneficiaries are unascertainable.

B. Invalid, because the trust violates the Rule Against Perpetuities.

C. Valid, with the trustee authorized to pay over the proceeds to any charity that the trustor had supported during his lifetime.

D. Valid, with the trustee authorized to use the trust funds to support any recognized charity.

68. Terry created a testamentary trust that provides as follows:

> I give, devise, and bequeath the sum of $500,000 to my alma mater, Normal University, the income therefrom to be used to provide scholarships for worthy students from the state of Arizona.

Terry was a graduate of Normal University. After Terry's will was executed, Normal University ceased to operate as a university. Its facilities were sold to Welcome University, a privately owned, profit-making school. Terry devised the remainder of her estate to her parents. Terry died recently. Under these circumstances:

A. The charitable gift should be distributed to Welcome University.

B. The charitable gift should be distributed to another nonprofit university chosen by the court.

C. The charitable gift should fail and be distributed to Terry's parents.

D. The charitable gift should fail and be distributed to Terry's heirs.

69. Settlor made a testamentary, charitable gift of $1 million to Delphi University for the following purposes:

The income from this gift shall be used to provide scholarships for the education of white, male students at Delphi University who regularly attend their respective churches, temples, or synagogues. Women and minority students probably receive sufficient aid already. I do not wish to spend my money on atheists.

Delphi is a nonprofit, nonsectarian, coeducational institution. It has prided itself on educating disadvantaged persons, regardless of race or creed. It desperately needs money to provide additional scholarships for its students. However, Delphi is prohibited by its charter from accepting a gift with racial restrictions. Settlor recently died. Under these circumstances a court would probably:

A. Strike all of the restrictions, and sustain the entire gift to Delphi.

B. Substitute another institution that can adhere to the restrictions.

C. Strike the racial restriction only and sustain the gift to Delphi with the other restrictions attached.

D. Void the gift and distribute the funds to the residuary legatees or trustor's heirs.

70. Edward is the trustee of an *inter vivos* trust created by his father. The trust res consists of an office building that produces revenue that is equivalent to a 2 percent return on investment. In order to increase income resulting from the trust, Edward personally purchased the office building from the trust for $200,000 and caused the trust to invest the proceeds in higher-yield assets. The trust instrument made no mention of a power to sell or mortgage trust assets. Under these circumstances, the most likely result under traditional trust principles is:

A. Edward violated his fiduciary duty by selling the trust asset.

B. Edward violated his fiduciary duty in purchasing the trust asset for himself, regardless of whether he paid the fair market value for the property.

C. Edward violated his fiduciary duty in purchasing the trust asset for himself, but only if he paid less than the fair market value for this asset.

D. Edward did not violate his fiduciary duty.

71. Suppose that, in question 70, Edward had, in his capacity as trustee, elected to borrow funds, using the office building as security for the debt, and had then invested the borrowed funds in higher-income-yielding assets. Under these circumstances, the most likely result under traditional trust principles is:

A. Edward breached his fiduciary duty.

B. Edward breached his fiduciary duty, if the net income of the trust is reduced by his actions.

C. Edward breached his fiduciary duty by borrowing funds, if he has the power to sell the asset.

D. Edward did not breach his fiduciary duty.

72. Blunder Bank was trustee of a trust set up by Gigi in her will, which provided that the income was to be paid to Gigi's children for life, then upon the death of all of Gigi's children, to their children for life, and then when all of the children's children had died, to the then living descendants of Gigi's children. The trust provided that it would terminate earlier if the applicable perpetuities period expired, with all assets being distributed to the then living descendants of Gigi's children. The original assets in the trust were 3 office buildings in downtown Blunderville. It is now 50 years after the trust was established. All of Gigi's children are dead, and the income beneficiaries are Gigi's children's children. There are four income beneficiaries, all in their seventies, and there are 10 living great-grandchildren of Gigi who would be remainder beneficiaries if the trust ended immediately. The Bank has held onto the 3 buildings and pays the rent to the income beneficiaries. Downtown Blunderville has been hit with hard times, and the buildings are worth much less than they were at the start of the trust. In addition, the Bank has invested very little of the rent into maintenance of the buildings, just doing what was necessary to keep them habitable, so they are now very run down and outdated. Which of the Bank's fiduciary duties have been violated?

A. Duty to diversify, duty to be impartial, duty to segregate trust assets, duty to protect trust assets.

B. Duty to diversify, duty to be impartial, duty to protect trust assets, duty to invest prudently.

C. Duty to diversify, duty to be impartial, duty to protect trust assets, duty to delegate responsibly.

D. Duty to diversify, duty to be impartial, duty to segregate trust assets, duty to protect trust assets, duty not to delegate.

73. Claire created a testamentary trust as follows:

> The trustee shall pay so much of the income as she shall, in her sole, absolute, and uncontrolled discretion, determine is necessary for the care, maintenance, and support of my children, until my youngest child shall reach the age of 25 years, at which time all accrued income and principal shall be distributed to my children, share and share alike.

At Claire's death all of her three children were minors. The trustee thereafter paid all of the income annually to the oldest child. When the youngest child reached the age of 25, the two youngest children sued the trustee, claiming that the trustee had breached her fiduciary duty by not previously paying any of the income to them. Under these circumstances:

A. The court has no power to review the "sole, absolute, and uncontrolled" discretionary decisions of the trustee.

B. Although the court has the power to review discretionary decisions of the trustee, the trustee will be presumed to have acted reasonably under these circumstances.

C. The court has the power to review the discretionary decisions of the trustee and to impose liability for those decisions made arbitrarily or in bad faith.

D. The court has the power to review the discretionary decisions of the trustee and to impose liability for those decisions the court believes were not sound.

74. Ted is the trustee of an *inter vivos* trust. The trust res is composed of $300,000 in cash. The beneficiaries are Ted's nephews and nieces. Ted recently located a parcel of unimproved property that is available for sale. The price of the property is $300,000, and Ted projects that the property will increase in value to $500,000 within two years. Under these circumstances, the best statement of Ted's rights and duties is that he may:

A. Invest in this property, if a prudent investor would do so.

B. Invest in this property, if he obtains an appraisal showing that the value of the property is now at least $300,000.

C. Not invest in this property, regardless of what the trust instrument authorizes.

D. Not invest in this property, unless the trust instrument specifically authorizes real estate investments.

75. Karl, a college professor, is the trustee of a trust created by his father-in-law for the benefit of Karl's children. Karl accepted a visiting professorship at Cambridge University for an academic year. Because he was going to be out of the country, Karl retained Edward, a stockbroker, to act as the substitute trustee for that year. Karl executed a document authorizing Edward to "exercise all powers and fulfill all duties that I now possess as trustee." Under these circumstances:

A. Karl is effectively relieved of his duties as trustee during the year, and is not liable for any breach of fiduciary duties that might occur.

B. Karl is not relieved of liability for any breach of fiduciary duties, but properly delegated the powers of the trustee to Edward.

C. Karl is not relieved of liability for any breach of fiduciary duties, but Edward may exercise all discretionary powers of the trustee under the trust.

D. Karl has breached his fiduciary duty and is liable for all damages resulting from Edward's acts or omissions.

76. Suppose that, in question 75, Edward was employed by Karl to make investment decisions pertaining to trust assets. Karl unquestioningly adhered to Edward's suggestions, which were based upon Edward's judgment alone. One of the securities purchased for the trust at Edward's suggestion dropped in value, causing a significant loss to the trust estate. Under these circumstances, the most likely result under traditional trust principles is:

A. Karl is liable to the trust, if (and only if) a prudent investor would not have purchased the stock.

B. Karl is liable to the trust, without regard to whether a prudent investor would have purchased the stock.

C. Karl is liable to the trust only if Edward failed to act as a competent stockbroker.

D. To determine if Karl is liable to the trust it is necessary to determine if he utilized reasonable care in selecting Edward to make investment decisions.

77. Suppose that, in question 75, Karl loaned trust funds to himself at a higher rate of interest than the prevailing market rate for similar loans. Karl used the loan to invest in several new stocks, which he later sold at a substantial profit. Upon selling the stocks, Karl repaid the loans to the trust, together with all accrued interest. Under these circumstances, Karl:

A. Breached his fiduciary duty to the trust, but no damage has occurred.

B. Breached his fiduciary duty to the trust, and must remit the profits he made on the sale of the stock to the trust.

C. Has not breached his fiduciary duty to the trust, but would have been liable for any losses that the trust might have suffered in this type of transaction.

D. Has not breached any duty to the trust, because he had promised to pay and did pay a higher rate of interest than the market rate.

78. When Selena was in her twenties and engaged to marry a penniless artist, her parents were worried about her future and set up a trust for her with the express purpose of providing for her support under the assumption that her husband would not be able to support them. The trustee was directed to distribute so much of the income and principal of the trust as the trustee deemed appropriate for her support, taking into account her other resources, and at her death the remainder of the trust was to be distributed to her then living children. Selena is now in her seventies and married, her parents are dead, she and her husband are billionaires, and she has three grown, successful children. The value of the trust is now $3 million. The trustee of Selena's trust, a bank, has not distributed funds to Selena in years because she does not need the money. She and her children have contacted the bank and requested that the trust be terminated. Selena and the children told the bank that Selena and her husband can get a better return on the trust funds if invested with their other assets. The bank refuses, claiming that there is still a trust purpose to carry out. Selena sues. What is the likely result?

A. Because the trustors are dead, the trust cannot be terminated earlier than dictated by the trustors.

B. Because all of the beneficiaries agree, the trust can be terminated.

C. Because there is no longer a purpose of the trust to be accomplished, and the beneficiaries all agree, the trust can be terminated.

D. Because the trustee does not consent to the termination, the trust cannot be terminated.

79. Amy is the trustee of a testamentary trust that consists of $300,000 in cash. The trust instrument provides that Amy is entitled to receive trust income that is "necessary to her proper support, maintenance, and education." The principal passes to Amy's children upon her death. Amy recently purchased a business for the trust for $100,000. However, because she failed to research the new business carefully, she subsequently learned that there were several lawsuits pending against it. As a consequence, the business was actually worth only $25,000. The trust document has a provision that states: "The trustee shall not be

liable for negligence in administering the trust assets, or any activity undertaken on behalf of the trust." Under these circumstances:

A. Amy would not be liable for any losses that occurred, under any circumstances.

B. Amy is liable for the loss incurred by the trust corpus, but not for any loss of income.

C. Amy is liable for the loss of trust income, but not the loss of corpus.

D. Amy would not be liable for the losses, unless her actions amounted to gross negligence.

80. Laura is the trustee of an *inter vivos* trust, the ABC Trust. She signed a contract with Xavier whereby Xavier was to perform certain accounting services for the trust. (Laura signed the contract, "Laura, as trustee for the ABC Trust.") A bona fide dispute arose concerning whether Xavier had adequately performed the services. Laura refused to pay (or have the trust pay) for the services. Xavier sued Laura personally on the contract. Under traditional trust principles, if Xavier prevails on the merits:

A. Laura will be personally liable for breach of contract, but may indemnify herself from trust assets (assuming she acted in good faith).

B. Laura will not be personally liable for breach of contract, because she may be sued only in her capacity as trustee.

C. Laura will be personally liable for breach of contract, and may not be indemnified from trust assets.

D. Laura will be personally liable for breach of contract, and may not be indemnified from trust assets unless the trust instrument specifically contains an exculpatory clause.

81. Bill, the trustee of an *inter vivos* trust having a trust res of $500,000, negligently struck Phyllis while driving his car. At the time, he was on his way to a meeting with the trust's investment adviser. Phyllis sued Bill, individually and as trustee of the trust, for her damages ($300,000). Under traditional trust principles, under these circumstances:

A. Bill is personally liable for any judgment, but may indemnify himself from the trust's assets.

B. Bill is not personally liable for any judgment, but may be sued in his capacity as trustee of the trust.

C. Bill is personally liable for any judgment and may *not* be indemnified from trust assets.

D. Bill is personally liable for any judgment and may not be indemnified from trust assets, unless the trust instrument specifically contains an exculpatory clause.

82. Suppose that, in question 81, (1) the tort was committed by an employee of the trust who was hired by Bill, while on trust business, and (2) the damages sustained by Phyllis were $600,000. Under traditional trust principles, under these circumstances:

A. Bill is personally liable for the damages, but may seek indemnity from the trust and, to the extent not satisfied therefrom, may seek indemnity from the beneficiaries.

B. Bill is personally liable for the damages, and may seek indemnity from the trust, but only to the extent of the trust assets.

C. Bill is not personally liable for the damages, but must pay such damages from the trust assets.

D. Neither Bill nor the trust assets are liable for the woman's damages, but she can recover from Bill's employee.

83. Ben created a testamentary trust by bequeathing 300 shares of Bloomfield, Inc., common stock to Adams National Bank, as trustee. The trustee was instructed to pay the income to Ben's children for life, and the remainder to his grandchildren at the death of the last survivor of his children. Bloomfield has a net profit for the current year. However, due to plans to expand its facilities, it does not wish to declare cash dividends. It has decided to declare a stock dividend of one share for each four shares of stock currently owned by shareholders. The trust created by Ben will receive 75 shares of Bloomfield, Inc., common stock. Under traditional trust principles, under these circumstances:

A. Add the stock dividend shares to the corpus of the trust.

B. Distribute the stock dividend shares to the income beneficiaries.

C. Distribute half of the stock dividend to the income beneficiaries, and the other half to the corpus of the trust.

D. Distribute stock equal in value to the cash dividend that would have been declared but for the expansion plans to the income beneficiaries, and add the remainder of the stock to the trust corpus.

84. Taft Trust company is the trustee of a trust created by Marlon Cando. Marlon transferred certain real estate to the trust with instructions to

use the income therefrom "for the relief of the poverty of American Indians." After 20 years, the trust corpus is to be paid to the Animal Welfare League. Taft has determined that, of the three properties conveyed to it as trustee, two are unproductive, in that they produce no current income. Under these circumstances, the most likely result under the modern trend is:

A. Taft is not obligated to sell the two properties; but if it does so, all proceeds are allocated to the corpus of the trust.

B. Taft is not obligated to sell the two properties; but if it does, the trustee must apportion the proceeds between the income beneficiaries and the principal.

C. Taft is obligated to sell the two properties, and all proceeds must be allocated to corpus.

D. Taft is obligated to sell the two properties; and when the sale is made, the trustee must apportion the proceeds between the income beneficiaries and the principal.

85. Louise is the trustee of a trust created by her mother. The income beneficiaries of the trust are Louise and her two brothers. The remaindermen are Louise's two sisters. The corpus of the trust consists of two income-producing properties. During the course of each year, the trust must pay for maintenance, real estate taxes, and insurance on the properties. Under traditional trust principles, under these circumstances:

A. Maintenance is charged to the income beneficiaries; but taxes and insurance are chargeable against the corpus of the trust.

B. Maintenance and taxes are charged to the income beneficiaries; but insurance is chargeable against the corpus of the trust.

C. Taxes and insurance are chargeable against the income beneficiaries; but maintenance is chargeable against the corpus of the trust.

D. Maintenance, taxes, and insurance are chargeable to the income beneficiaries, exclusively.

86. Ellen created an *inter vivos* trust by transferring $100,000 in trust to First National Bank, as trustee, for the benefit of her children for life, with the remainder to her grandchildren. The trust document did not state whether Ellen retained the power to revoke or modify the trust. After the creation of the trust, Ellen delivered a letter to the trustee, advising it that she wished to revoke the remainder gift to the grandchildren and to substitute her nephews as remaindermen. The trustee rejected Ellen's modification of the trust. Angered by the trustee's

response, Ellen delivered a second letter to the trustee, revoking the trust in its entirety. The trustee rejected this letter also. Under traditional trust principles, under these circumstances Ellen is entitled to:

A. Modify the trust by revoking the gift to the remaindermen and substituting her nephews, but cannot revoke the trust in its entirety.

B. Revoke the trust in its entirety, but cannot modify it.

C. Modify and revoke the trust.

D. Neither revoke nor modify the trust.

87. Mom died intestate. She had two daughters, Debbie and Ashley. Debbie predeceased Mom, leaving two sons surviving her, Drew and Derek. Ashley has two daughters, Pam and Patty, and two sons, Paul and Peter. At Mom's death, everyone else is alive except Debbie. Ashley disclaims her interest in Mom's estate. How is Mom's estate to be distributed?

    A. In equal shares to Drew, Derek, and Ashley.

    B. 50 percent to Ashley and 25 percent each to Derek and Drew.

    C. 25 percent each to Derek and Drew, and 12.5 percent each to Pam, Patty, Paul, and Peter.

    D. In equal shares to Drew, Derek, Pam, Patty, Paul, and Peter.

88. Andrew died with a will leaving his ranch to his daughter Naomi for life, remainder to Naomi's children, and the rest of his estate to the Home for Retired Celebrities Who Went through Rehab at Least Twice. At the time of Andrew's death, Naomi had no children. Who are the parties who hold an interest in the ranch at Andrew's death, and what type of interest does each of them hold?

    A. Naomi has a life estate and Naomi's children have a vested remainder subject to open.

    B. Naomi has a life estate, Naomi's children have a vested remainder subject to open, and the Home has an executory interest.

    C. Naomi has a life estate, Naomi's children have a vested remainder subject to open and subject to divestment, and Andrew has a reversion.

    D. Naomi has a life estate, Naomi's children have a contingent remainder, and Andrew has a reversion, which passes to the Home under the residuary clause.

89. T had possession of his original will. T made statements to several people that he tore up his will. When he died, his will was not found, but a different document was found. This document was typewritten and

titled "Last Will of T," and it was signed by T and dated two years after T had told people he had torn up his will, but it was not witnessed. What happens to T's estate, and why?

A. T's estate is distributed under the intestacy statutes.

B. The second document can be probated as a holographic will.

C. The second document can be probated under the harmless error doctrine.

D. The first document (which had been torn up) can be probated under the doctrine of dependent relative revocation.

90. Olive devised Blackacre to Agnes for life, then to Boyd for life, then to Charlotte. Charlotte went out drinking with Agnes and Boyd, things got ugly, and Charlotte ended up running down Agnes and Boyd with her car in the tavern parking lot, killing both Agnes and Boyd. What happens to Blackacre?

    A. Charlotte now has fee simple title to Blackacre because the life estates have been terminated.

    B. Blackacre is distributed in equal shares to the heirs of Agnes and Boyd.

    C. Blackacre is held for the benefit of Agnes's heirs for the remainder of her actuarial life expectancy, then for Boyd's heirs for the remainder of his actuarial life expectancy, and then to Charlotte.

    D. Blackacre is distributed to the heirs of Olive.

91. Terry's will leaves her entire estate to "my cousin Arnold and my friend Beatrice, in equal shares." Both Arnold and Beatrice predecease Terry. Arnold leaves one daughter, Gina, surviving him, and Beatrice leaves one son, Kevin, surviving her. Terry's sister Sheila survived Terry but was left nothing under the will. Who takes Terry's estate?

    A. Sheila.

    B. Gina.

    C. Gina and Kevin, in equal shares.

    D. Gina and Sheila, in equal shares.

92. Abigail and Uriah were a childless couple who owned a ranch jointly. As they got older, they needed help running the ranch, so Uriah's nephew Neil agreed to move with his family to the ranch and help them run it, gradually taking over operations, while still providing them with all the profits less a modest salary for himself until the death of the survivor of them. In return, they agreed in writing to leave the farm to him

at their deaths. When Abigail died, her will provided that her share of the ranch would be held in trust for Uriah, and on Uriah's death it would pass to Neil. Then Neil died, leaving his entire estate to his wife. His wife and children remained on the ranch and continued to run the ranch. Because Neil had died, Uriah decided to write a new will, leaving his share of the ranch to his new girlfriend from the Senior Center. When Uriah died, Neil's wife and children contested his will. How much of the ranch will Neil's family receive?

   A. All of the ranch to Neil's wife.
   B. An undivided one-half interest in the ranch to Neil's wife.
   C. One-half the ranch to Neil's wife and one-half to Neil's children.
   D. None of the ranch.

93. A cycling club collected $150,000 from its members and gave the money to Bank as trustee. The purpose of the trust was to cover expenses of a private investigator to look into the unsolved murder of a member of the club, with the remainder to be held in trust as a reward for any person providing information that would lead to an arrest. The president of the club was given authority to review the Bank's actions and enforce the terms of the trust. Which of the following statements is most accurate?

   A. The trust is unenforceable because it violates the Rule Against Perpetuities.
   B. The trust is unenforceable because it has no ascertainable beneficiaries.
   C. The trust is enforceable for up to 21 years.
   D. The trust is enforceable as a charitable trust.

94. At Mom's request, Sarah brings a stack of insurance documents that Mom needs to sign. Unbeknownst to Mom, Sarah slips in the signature page of a will that leaves Mom's entire estate to Sarah. Sarah tells Mom to sign "wherever there's a sticky note." Mom does as she's told, not knowing one of the pages was a will. Which of the following is the most accurate theory to use to challenge the will?

   A. Fraud in the inducement.
   B. Fraud in the execution.
   C. Undue influence.
   D. Lack of testamentary capacity.

Multiple-Choice Questions

95. Tess has died, leaving an estate of $1 million, two Swedish cousins as her only living relatives, and a typewritten document titled "Memorandum" that states only "I intend that all of my assets are to be held for my use during life and then distributed to the Tiny Tim Foundation, a charity that helps seriously ill and impoverished children, upon my death." The memorandum is dated and signed by her but not witnessed. What arguments could be made successfully on behalf of the Tiny Tim Foundation?

    A. None; the document is not a valid will.
    B. The memorandum set up a valid trust for Tess for life, remainder to the Foundation.
    C. The memorandum was a gift with symbolic delivery.
    D. B and C.

96. Selma went to her lawyer to create a trust for her granddaughter Bertha. Selma asked the lawyer to serve as trustee, and he accepted. The trust agreement contained a provision that "The trustee of the trust incurs no liability to the beneficiaries of the trust for any loss except those due to the trustee's willful misconduct." The lawyer did not discuss this clause with Selma. The trust was funded with stock in a very successful local biotech company. The lawyer set up the trust but never got around to diversifying the assets. The local biotech company was sued because one of its products turned out to be dangerous, and the company went bankrupt. Bertha has sued the lawyer/trustee because her trust is now worthless. Which of the following is true?

    A. Bertha will lose because it is not a breach of fiduciary duty to keep the original trust assets.
    B. Bertha will lose because the exculpatory clause relieves the trustee of liability.
    C. Bertha will win because the trustee's conduct amounted to "willful misconduct."
    D. Bertha will win because the exculpatory clause is unenforceable.

97. George was an elderly man facing eye surgery, and needed assistance with his day-to-day financial matters. He went to the bank and requested that his oldest son Tom be added to his bank account so that Tom could sign checks and pay his bills while George was recuperating. The bank gave George a form to convert the account to a joint account of George and Tom with right of survivorship. George completed the form and informed Tom, who then took over responsibility

for paying George's bills. George died without changing the account. His will, executed after the account was set up, gives his entire estate to his three children, Tom, Dana, and Harry, in equal shares. How should the account be distributed?

    A. All to Tom, because the account was joint with right of survivorship.

    B. In equal shares to Tom, Dana, and Harry, because the later will overrides the bank account designation.

    C. In equal shares to Tom, Dana, and Harry, because George did not intend the account to be joint with right of survivorship.

    D. To Dana and Harry equally, because Tom exerted undue influence over George.

98. Sally owned and operated a small farm. Her niece Alberta moved onto the farm and began helping Sally. Alberta was offered a lucrative job with a neighbor, so to entice her to stay, Sally and Alberta orally agreed that if Alberta stayed Sally would leave her the farm on her death. Sally then executed a quitclaim deed, giving the farm to Alberta, and put the deed in her safe deposit box, inside a sealed envelope that said, "to be given to Alberta upon my death. Signed, Sally." Sally has now died intestate, leaving Alberta and Alberta's five siblings surviving her. How will the farm be distributed?

    A. To Alberta, because the deed is a valid transfer to her.

    B. To Alberta, because the deed is valid as a nonprobate transfer under the Uniform Probate Code.

    C. To Alberta, because of her contract with Sally.

    D. Equally to Alberta and her five siblings.

99. Tabitha executed a will in 2002, leaving her house to her niece Judy and the remainder of her estate to her next-door neighbor Andy. In 2005, she executed a codicil, leaving her house to her nephew Dan, and otherwise confirming the terms of the 2002 will. In 2007, she tore up the codicil because she had fought with Dan, and she put the pieces in the drawer with the original will. In 2008, she and Dan resolved their differences, so she went into the drawer and taped the pieces back together. Now Tabitha has died. How will her estate be distributed?

A. She died intestate because tearing up the codicil revoked the underlying will also.

B. Taping the codicil together revived the codicil, so Dan gets the house and Andy gets everything else.

C. The codicil revoked the gift in the will to Judy, but the codicil's gift to Dan was revoked, so Andy takes everything.

D. When the codicil was revoked, the gift to Judy was revived, so Judy gets the house and Andy gets the residue.

100. Mom's Will left $500,000 each to her two daughters, Delia and Doris, and left the remainder of her estate ($5,000,000) in trust for her disabled son, Steve. On Steve's death, the remainder of the trust is to go to Delia and Doris. Delia was named the trustee of the trust. Delia used $2 million of the trust funds to purchase a beautiful lakefront home with extensive gardens for Steve to use as a residence. Steve used $2 million of the him from going anywhere in the home other than a part of the first floor, although he is taken through the gardens in his wheelchair daily, weather permitting. Delia hired herself as primary caretaker for Steve and moved into the residence. She pays herself a six figure salary from the trust and hired round-the-clock attendants to see to Steve's care. She kept $1 million of the trust funds in money market funds (the equivalent of savings accounts) to have available cash in the case of emergencies and invested the remainder of the trust funds with a stockbroker friend of hers, although she isn't really sure how those funds are invested because she cannot understand the statements that the brokerage house sends. Doris is worried about what is happening to the money and has been pressing Delia for an accounting, but Delia refuses, saying that Doris does not have a right to see the trust books. What fiduciary duties are being violated by Delia?

A. Duty of loyalty, duty to delegate responsibly, duty to diversify, and duty to keep beneficiaries informed.

B. Duty to keep beneficiaries informed, duty to diversify, and duty to delegate responsibly.

C. Duty to delegate responsibly, duty to keep beneficiaries informed, duty to invest prudently and duty to diversify.

D. Duty to delegate responsibly, duty to keep beneficiaries informed, duty to invest prudently, and duty of loyalty.

101. Rebecca deeded Blackacre to Margaret for life, remainder to Viola's heirs. Viola was alive at the time of the deed and had no spouse but had three children. What interest do Viola's children have at the time of the deed?

   A. Contingent remainder.

   B. Vested remainder subject to open.

   C. Vested remainder subject to divestment.

   D. Executory interest.

Multiple-Choice Answers

Multiple-Choice Answers

1. **C** An heir who does not survive the decedent by *120 hours* is deemed to have predeceased the decedent. (UPC §2-104.) Because Wanda is deemed to have predeceased Jim, her estate takes nothing. The deceased daughter's grandchildren are entitled to take their parent's share of the estate by right of representation. (UPC §2-103(1).) Thus, the estate is split into two shares of $100,000 each. Bob takes one share and the grandchildren split the other share. Choices **A** and **B** are incorrect, because they assume that Wanda is entitled to take a share of the estate. Choice **D** is incorrect, because it assumes that Bob and the grandchildren take *per capita* instead of by representation.

2. **B** If after executing a will, the testator is *divorced*, the divorce *revokes any testamentary disposition* to the former spouse, unless the will provides otherwise. (UPC §2-804(b).) Because Leonard and Evelyn were divorced, her gift was revoked (even though she survived him). The gift over to Leonard's mother and father fails because they did not survive him. Leonard's sister and brother take in place of Leonard's parents pursuant to the antilapse statute, because they are descendants of a beneficiary related to the testator. (UPC §2-603(b).) Although Sue was a witness to the will, the will is valid and the gift to her is also valid so long as there is no showing of undue influence by her. (UPC §2-505.) Choice **A** is incorrect because it presumes the gift to Evelyn was not revoked by the divorce. Choice **C** is incorrect because it assumes Sue cannot take because she was an interested witness. Choice **D** is incorrect; there is no basis for precluding Ted from inheriting.

3. **B** This is an unusually tricky question, so follow closely. Any person 18 or older who is of sound mind may make a will. Every nonholographic will must be in writing signed by the testator and by two other persons each of whom witnessed either the signing or the testator's acknowledgment of either (a) the signature or (b) that the document is a will. A mark made by the testator suffices as a signature. The will was valid because Dan was 19, he signed the document with a mark, and the execution of the will was witnessed by two witnesses. Because Dan's mother predeceased him, the gift to her fails.

   Under the antilapse statute, Les would normally take his mother's share, as her sole descendant—but this would happen as a "substitute gift," not by having Dan's property pass through the mother's estate. (UPC §2-603.) However, the antilapse doctrine applies only "[i]n the absence of a finding of a contrary intention . . . ." (UPC §2-601.) A court would probably conclude that the language in the will disinheriting Les manifests Dan's intent not to have the antilapse provision apply. If so, the estate would pass by intestacy because all bequests would have failed. Here, too, Les would ordinarily take, under UPC §2-103(a)(3). But again, the UPC honors the testator's wishes: UPC §2-101(b) protects a decedent's choice to "expressly exclude or limit the right of an individual . . . to succeed to property of the decedent passing by intestate succession." The disinheritance language here would certainly meet this test. Consequently, the estate would go to the next in line—the decedent's grandmother. (UPC §2-103(a)(4).)

Choice **A** is incorrect, because Dan's mother predeceased him. Choices **C** and **D** are incorrect. Les takes nothing for the reasons described above.

4. **A** An adopted child is treated as a natural-born child for purposes of inheritance. (UPC §2-118.) Lisa will inherit equally with Tom because she was adopted by Ellen. The $10,000 will not be treated as an advancement, because the only evidence of Ellen's intent was oral. (Section 2-109(a) requires that if an individual dies intestate, advancements must be established as such either in a writing contemporaneous with the gift signed by the testator or in a written acknowledgment by the heir.) Because the condition upon Tom's gift was oral and not written, Lisa and Tom will each take $75,000. Choice **B** is incorrect because it assumes that the $10,000 will be treated as an advancement against Tom's share of the estate. Choice **C** is incorrect because it assumes that Lisa is not treated as Ellen's child for purposes of inheritance. Choice **D** is incorrect because it fails to provide for inheritance by Tom.

5. **A** A writing that is in existence when a will is executed may be *incorporated by reference*, if the language of the will manifests the intent to incorporate and describes the writing sufficiently to permit its identification. (UPC §2-510.) In this case, the will relies upon an extrinsic document (John's *inter vivos* trust) to identify the devisees. The trust was executed prior to Ann's will and is described sufficiently to allow incorporation. Because Adrian and Kimberly were the only income beneficiaries at the time of Ann's death, they take equally. Choice **B** is incorrect because (contrary to the facts) it indicates that Ann intended to put the bequest in trust. The trust was incorporated merely to identify the beneficiaries under Ann's will. The devisees are given Ann's estate free of trust. Choices **C** and **D** are incorrect. Rita, John, and Lisa do not take any part of the $100,000 bequest.

6. **B** A will may dispose of property by *reference to acts and events that have significance apart from their effect upon dispositions made by the testator* in his or her will (whether they occur before or after the execution of the will, or before or after the testator's death). The execution or revocation of a will of another person is such an event. (UPC §2-512.) The will of Bill's mother is an event of independent significance because the statute expressly provides for the execution or revocation of another individual's will. Because State University was the residuary legatee in the will of Bill's mother, it will get the $500,000 bequest. Choice **A** is incorrect because Bill's mother revoked the will under which Tim and Tom would take. Choice **C** would be correct only if the gift to State University had failed. Choice **D** is incorrect. If the gift to State University had failed, the money would have passed under the residuary clause to the American Red Cross.

7. **A** A specific devisee has the right to *any balance* of the purchase price owing from a purchaser by reason of the testator's sale of the property, together with any security agreement by the purchaser. (UPC §2-606(a)(1).) The devise of the condominium was specific; it can be identified as against all other assets of the testator's estate. Although a gift of specifically devised property is ordinarily adeemed when the property is sold during the testator's lifetime, the balance due and owing to the decedent from the buyer is not adeemed. Choice **B** is incorrect because it gives the account to Tom. Tom's best argument that he is entitled to the account is under UPC §2-606(a)(6), which rejects the identity approach to ademption and adopts the intent approach. But UPC §2-606(a)(6) applies only if the specifically devised property is not in the testator's estate and its value or its replacement is not covered by the provisions of paragraphs (1) through (5). Here, provision (a)(1) applies to give Tom the outstanding balance of the installment sales contract, so provision (a)(6) is not applicable. Choice **C** is incorrect because any property not transferred as a specific or general gift passes via the residuary clause, not intestacy, so the account passes under the residuary clause to Lighthouse University. Choice **D** is incorrect because Tom is entitled to the outstanding balance under the installment sales contract under UPC §2-606(a)(1).

8. **B** Generally, a will is construed in light of the circumstances surrounding the testator when the will is executed. Consistent with that principle, Larry's gift of "my home" to his son Ron will be construed to mean the home that he owned when he executed the will. When Larry later conveyed this home to Ron, the specific gift of "*my* home"

was adeemed. When Larry subsequently purchased the second home, Ron has two arguments to support his claim that he is entitled to the second home as well. First, under UPC §2-606(a)(5), any real property owned by the testator at death that the testator acquired as a replacement for specifically devised real property goes to the devisee of the specifically devised property. Larry arguably acquired the second home as a replacement for the first home, so Ron, the specific devisee, is entitled to the second home. In the alternative, Ron can claim "acts of independent significance." Under acts of independent significance, UPC §2-512, a will may dispose of property by reference to acts and events that have significance apart from their effect upon the disposition made in the will. Under acts of independent significance, Ron will argue that he is entitled to the second home because Larry transferred the first home and purchased the second for reasons independent of the effect upon the dispositions under the will, and therefore, he should be entitled to the second home under the terms of the will.

The issue then becomes whether the conveyance of the first home to Ron, and/or the cash gift to Carolyn, acted as a full or partial satisfaction of the specific bequests to them. A lifetime gift of property to a devisee is treated as a satisfaction only if (1) the will provides for deduction of the gift; (2) the testator declares in a contemporaneous writing that the gifts are in satisfaction of the devise or that their value is to be deducted from the value of the devise; or (3) the devisees acknowledge in writing that the gifts are in satisfaction of the devise or that their value is to be deducted from the value of the devise. (UPC §2-609.) None of these conditions was satisfied as to either the house transfer to Ron or the cash gift to Carolyn. Larry's estate will therefore be distributed according to the terms of his will.

Choice **A** is incorrect because it assumes satisfaction of both gifts. Choice **C** is incorrect because it assumes satisfaction of the gift to Ron. Choice **D** is incorrect because it fails to distribute all of the cash to Carolyn.

9. **D** A person who kills another intentionally and feloniously loses any right to benefit financially from his or her victim's estate, whether the assets are part of the probate estate or pass outside the estate. This principle is codified in UPC §2-803(c)(1), which provides that the felonious and intentional killing of the decedent "revokes any revocable . . . disposition . . . of property made by the decedent to the

killer in a governing instrument...." Both wills and insurance policies are covered by the definition of "governing instrument." (UPC §1-201(18).) The bequest to Sofia and the designation of her as policy beneficiary are both canceled. Therefore, the cash and insurance proceeds pass into Bert's intestate estate.

Under UPC §2-803(c)(2), the felonious and intentional killing also "severs the interests of the decedent and killer in property held by them at the time of the killing as joint tenants with the right of survivorship, transforming the interests of the decedent and killer into tenancies in common." Therefore, Bert's intestate estate holds a one-half interest in the home as tenant in common; this tenancy then passes to the grandchildren equally.

Choice **A** is incorrect in that it assumes the conviction of murder has no effect upon any of the assets owned by Bert. Choice **B** is incorrect in that it assumes that the conviction affects distribution of probate assets only, not the insurance policy or the joint tenancy in the home. Choice **C** is incorrect in that it also assumes the conviction does not affect an insurance policy.

10. **A** When a second will—which revoked the first will—is thereafter revoked by physical act, the first will is *revived* if the testator *intended the first will to take effect* as executed and that intent is evident from (1) the *circumstances* under which the second will is revoked, or (2) the testator's contemporary or subsequent *declarations*. (UPC §2-509(a).) Although the second will expressly revoked the first will, the statements of Jamir that his father should take the estate under the first will evidenced an intent to revive the first will after destruction of the second will. Choice **B** is incorrect because the second will was revoked by physical act. Choice **C** is incorrect because the first will was revived and is in effect. Choice **D** is incorrect because (1) the first will is revived and is in effect, and (2) even if the first will were not revived and Jamir died intestate, his mother and father, not his sisters, would take by intestate succession.

11. **C** As in question 11, the tearing up of the second will was a "revocatory act" that revoked that will. (UPC §2-507(a)(2).) Under these new facts, there are no direct statements by Jamir supporting revival of the first instrument. On the contrary, we have Jamir's statement deriding all wills. That being so, the first will remains revoked by the second will. Therefore, Jamir's estate passes by intestate succession (*i.e.*, to his mother and father equally). Choices **A** and **B** are incorrect

because neither will survives and Jamir died intestate. Choice **D** is incorrect because Jamir's father and mother (rather than his sisters) would take by intestate succession.

12. **D** A will is *revoked* by a subsequent will that is *inconsistent* with the former instrument. (UPC §2-507.) Will #2 revoked Will #1 by inconsistency. Because Will #3 revoked Will #2, but gave no indication that revival of the first will was intended, revival of Will #1 will *not* occur. See UPC §2-509(c). Thereafter, Edgar validly revoked Will #3 by physical act. Under the revival doctrine, where a later will validly revokes a prior will, and thereafter the testator validly revokes the later will by act, the earlier will is revived as long as the testator intended to revive it and that intent is evident from (1) the circumstances under which the later will was revoked, or (2) the testator's contemporaneous or subsequent declarations. (UPC §2-509(a).) There was nothing about the circumstances surrounding Edgar's revocation of Will #3 that evidences his intent to revive Will #1.

The tough issue is whether the unsigned and undated handwritten note found on Will #1 after Edgar died, which read "This is my will," can be used to validate Will #1. The revival doctrine provides that where the testator revoked the later will by act, as long as the testator evidences the intent to revive the earlier will, and that intent is expressed contemporaneously with or subsequent to the revocation, the earlier will is revived. The problem is that the handwritten note cannot be used to evidence the testator's intent to revive Will #1 because it cannot be proved that it was a contemporaneous or subsequent declaration by Edgar—it is undated (it may have been written before Edgar revoked Will #3, and the revival doctrine requires that it be a contemporaneous or subsequent declaration). The unsigned and undated writing cannot be used to give effect to Will #1 under incorporation by reference because the writing would have to qualify as a holographic will. A holographic will requires a writing, signed by the testator, with the material provisions in the testator's handwriting, and testamentary intent. (UPC §2-502(b).) The writing found on the will was not signed. (The unsigned and undated writing cannot be validated as a will under the harmless error doctrine [UPC §2-503] because there is no clear and convincing evidence that the decedent intended that writing to be his last will. There were too many executed wills and revocations, and because the unsigned writing was undated, it is impossible to prove by clear and convincing evidence that Edgar intended this writing to be his last will.) Thus, Edgar died intestate and his estate should be divided between Tom and Wilma.

Choice **A** is incorrect because it assumes revival (or incorporation by reference) of Will #1 and that did not occur for the reasons stated above. Choice **B** is incorrect because Will #2 was expressly revoked by Will #3. Choice **C** is incorrect because the facts stipulate that Will #3 was revoked by physical act.

13. **A** A will, including a holographic will, may refer to a written statement or list to dispose of tangible personal property not otherwise specifically disposed of by the will. To be admissible, the writing must (1) be signed by the testator, and (2) describe the items and the devisees with reasonable certainty. (UPC §2-513.) Even though the list could *not* be incorporated by reference (*i.e.*, it was created after the will) and has no significance apart from its testamentary effect (so acts of independent significance does not apply), inclusion of the list is permitted under the tangible personal property list doctrine. (An argument could also be made that the handwritten list qualifies as a holographic codicil, though it might be difficult to establish testamentary intent, but this argument is unnecessary because it qualifies under the tangible personal property list doctrine). Choice **B** is incorrect because the bequest is effective as written and the items do not fall into the residue. Choice **C** is incorrect; there is no indication that this property was specifically devised to Rusty and Rosa. Choice **D** is incorrect because if the bequests listed in the writing failed, they would pass as part of the residuary gift, not in intestacy.

14. **B** Where a gift (residuary or other) is given to a beneficiary who is the decedent's grandparent or a lineal descendant from the decedent's grandparents, and the beneficiary predeceases the decedent, the beneficiary's issue take the beneficiary's gift unless the instrument expresses a contrary intent. (UPC §2-603.) Here, both Roberta and Ted predeceased the decedent. Roberta was not survived by issue, so her gifts (the piano and her share of the residuary) lapse and pass through the residuary to the other residuary takers. Ted was survived by a son, so he takes Ted's share of the residuary, along with Edwina and Judy. Choice **A** is incorrect because Roberta's gifts lapsed and no one can take through her. (Roberta died without descendants.) Choice **C** is incorrect because Ted's child is entitled to share in the residue as Ted's descendant. Choice **D** is incorrect because the antilapse statute applies only if the predeceased beneficiary is survived by a *descendant*, not a *spouse*.

15. **D** A person who is a devisee under a testamentary instrument may *disclaim* the right to take any property or interest therein by filing a *written* disclaimer. (UPC §2-1105.) Because Albert renounced his gift, he is treated as though he had predeceased the testator. If Albert had predeceased Tim, the antilapse statute would have come into play: Because Albert is a descendant of a grandparent of the testator and was himself survived by a descendant, that descendant (Albert's son) would take the real estate under the antilapse statute. Consequently, Albert's disclaimer means that his son takes the real estate. The remainder of the estate is divided among Tim's brothers and sister. Choice **A** is incorrect because a devisee is permitted to disclaim his or her interest in a devise, and Albert validly did so here. Choice **B** is incorrect because the antilapse statute applies when a devisee is deemed to have predeceased the testator. Choice **C** is incorrect because Tim's children would take the real estate only if the whole will were to fail, which it does not here.

16. **A** A specific devise passes the property, subject to any mortgage interest existing at the date of death, without right of exoneration (regardless of a general directive in the will to pay debts). (UPC §2-607.) Even though this may result in an unequal distribution of assets on these facts, there is no specific directive by Tom to pay the debt secured by the mortgage from the general assets of the estate. Choice **B** is incorrect because there is no specific directive by Tom to pay the debt secured by the mortgage. Choice **C** is incorrect because there is no provision for a gift of stock to Joan in the will. Choice **D** is incorrect; the court must distribute Tom's estate in accordance with terms of the will, not according to its conjectures about Tom's possible motives.

17. **A** Because paternity was established prior to John's death, Jennifer is treated as his child. (UPC §2-117.) Jennifer is a pretermitted child (Jennifer was born after John had made his will). A pretermitted child (the UPC refers to an "omitted" child) takes as if her parent had died intestate. (UPC §2-302.) When testator is unmarried and leaves only one child, that child's intestate share is the entire estate. (UPC §2-103(a)(1).) Therefore, Jennifer receives the entire estate. Choice **B** is incorrect because Jennifer's claim to the intestate share as a pretermitted child supersedes the devise to ABC Charity. Choices **C** and **D** are incorrect because they do not state Jennifer's share correctly—Jennifer is entitled to the entire estate.

18. **B** Relatives of the half-blood inherit the same as if they were of the whole-blood. (UPC §2-107.) Although Kane is a half-brother of Mark (*i.e.*, they share only one common parent), he is entitled to inherit from Mark just as if he were a whole-blood brother. Mark died without surviving issue or parents. (Steve is not Mark's "parent," because that term "excludes any person who is only a stepparent." [UPC §1-201(32).].) Therefore, Will and Kane as Mark's brothers share Mark's estate equally. (UPC §2-103(a)(3).) Choice **A** is incorrect since Kane is entitled to inherit equally with Will. Choices **C** and **D** are incorrect because Steve is not related to Mark in the degree required by the principles governing intestacy.

19. **B** The doctrine of independent significance provides that a testator can change the dispositive scheme in a will without changing the will through a duly executed codicil, if the acts that change the disposition of property under the will have significance outside of merely changing distribution of property at the testator's death. This is an exception to the wills execution formalities requirements. A common example of the doctrine of independent significance is a gift in a will of "the house I live in at the time of my death." The testator can change the value of the gift by selling one house and moving into a much more or less expensive home, but the testator would not do so just to change the size of the gift to the beneficiary. Tanesha's gift in her will can change if she lets some people go and hires new employees, but she would be changing employees based on the needs of the business rather than on who she wants to receive $10,000 at her death. Choice **A** is incorrect because integration refers to the principle that all parts of the document present at the will signing and attached are included as the will. Choice **C** is incorrect because incorporation by reference allows a testator to refer to another document not present at the will signing and to incorporate the provisions of that document into the will as long as the document is already in existence at the time the will is signed. Choice **D** is incorrect because republication by codicil is then principle that a codicil incorporates all the terms of the underlying will that were not changed by the codicil, and the date of the codicil becomes the date of the underlying will.

20. **B** Foster children do not ordinarily inherit from their foster parents. Section 1-201(5) of the UPC defines "child" so as to exclude a "foster child." However, most jurisdictions recognize "equitable adoption/ adoption by estoppel" when there is an unperformed agreement to

adopt. In this case, the statement made to Lisa could reasonably have been interpreted by her as a promise of adoption. Taken together with the fact that Harvey and Ann "held Lisa out as their daughter," most jurisdictions would probably treat Lisa as an adopted child by estopping Harvey's estate from denying that an adoption existed. If there are surviving descendants of the decedent, one or more of whom are not descendants of the surviving spouse, the intestate share of the surviving spouse is $150,000, plus one-half of the balance of the estate. (UPC §2-102(4).) Because Harvey left a descendant, Bob, who is not a descendant of Ann, Ann's intestate share is $150,000, plus one-half of the balance of the estate. Because Lisa would probably be considered Harvey's adopted child and his descendant, she takes one-half of the remainder along with Bob. Choice **A** is incorrect because it would control the distribution only if Harvey had no descendants. Choice **C** is incorrect in that it misstates Ann's share. Choice **D** is incorrect. It applies only if all of the decedent's surviving descendants were also descendants of the surviving spouse. Here, Harvey had a son by a previous marriage.

21. **C** A holographic will requires a writing, signed by the testator, with the material provisions in the testator's handwriting, and testamentary intent. (UPC §2-502(b).) Here, there is a writing, signed by Patricia, which sets forth the material provisions. The intent that this should constitute her will, though a bit ambiguous, is evidenced by the phrase "if I don't return . . . . " The issue is whether the will was intended to be valid *only* if she did not return from the cruise.

    In most jurisdictions, a testator's explanation of her motives in making a testamentary document will not ordinarily be interpreted as a condition to the effectiveness of the document. *In re Taylor's Estate*; *Eaton v. Brown*. The inference here would be that Patricia was prompted to make her will at this time because she was about to make the trip, not that she wished her will to be ignored if she returned. The writing is a valid holographic will that devises her estate to the County Art Museum.

    Choice **A** is incorrect because there is no requirement in the UPC that a holographic will be dated to be enforceable. Choice **B** is incorrect because the will is effective, and, in any event, if the will were not effective, Patricia's mother would inherit the entire estate. (UPC §2-103(2).) Choice **D** is incorrect. There is no interpretation under which the two would share. Either the Art Museum would take (if the will is valid) or the mother would take (if the will is not valid), but *not* both.

22. **A** A contract to make a will or testamentary gift, or not to revoke a will or testamentary gift, can be established only by (1) provisions of a will stating material provisions of the contract; (2) an express reference in the will to an agreement and extrinsic evidence proving the terms of that contract; or (3) a writing signed by the decedent evidencing the contract. (UPC §2-514.) (Note that this section does not preclude one from recovering in *quantum meruit* for the value of services rendered.) Because the agreement here is not evidenced in writing (either in Clay's will or in a separate document signed by Clay), it cannot be enforced by Arnold against Clay's estate. Therefore, Anne will take under the will. Choice **B** is incorrect because the agreement with Arnold was oral and not referred to in Clay's will; therefore, it cannot be proved. Choice **C** is incorrect. Even if the agreement could be proved, Arnold would take to the exclusion of Tom. Choice **D** is incorrect. The will, which is effective, leaves Clay's entire estate to Anne.

23. **D** A contract to make a testamentary gift is generally not enforceable during the testator's lifetime. If the testator, however, either orally or by his actions, repudiates the contract after the promisee has substantially performed or acted in reliance on the contract, the promisee may ordinarily sue for anticipatory breach and seek to impose a constructive trust upon the assets in the hands of a third party. Because Clay has transferred a substantial portion of his assets after promising to leave his entire estate to Arnold, his conduct will probably be viewed as an anticipatory breach. Arnold may sue to have a constructive trust imposed on the assets transferred by Clay to Tom. Tom would probably *not* be deprived of their use during Clay's lifetime, but would be ordered to transfer the assets to Arnold at Clay's death (pursuant to Clay's agreement with Arnold). Choice **A** is incorrect because Arnold has no right to possession of the assets until Clay's death. Choice **B** is incorrect. The assessment of damages before Clay's death would be speculative and difficult. Arnold might die before Clay. Choice **C** is incorrect because Arnold has no right to control Clay's assets until Clay's death.

24. **A** Most jurisdictions recognize revocation by presumption. Under revocation by presumption, if a will was last in the testator's possession, cannot be found after the testator's death, and the testator was competent until death, a rebuttable presumption arises that the

reason why the will cannot be found is that the testator revoked the will by act. Here, the will was last in Toni's possession, she was competent until death, and the will cannot be found after her death. A rebuttable presumption arises that she revoked it by act. However, the conversation Toni had with her attorney just the week before her death, in which she affirmed her will, saying that it represented her wishes, is probably sufficient to overcome the presumption. Even though the will cannot be found, it was not revoked.

A will, the original of which cannot be produced in court, can nevertheless be probated as a "lost" will if its execution and terms can be proved. (UPC §3-402(a).) Most jurisdictions require clear and convincing evidence to prove up the lost will. Here, because Toni's attorney has a conformed copy of the will and the attorney can testify that just a week before she died Toni affirmed that the will, as executed, represented her testamentary wishes, the will should be probated as a lost will.

Answer **B** is incorrect because either the will is probated and First Baptist takes it all, or the will is revoked and First Baptist takes nothing. Under no scenario does First Baptist share the estate with Toni's children. Answer **C** is incorrect because it assumes that the will was revoked and Toni's estate passed through intestacy; but the will is only lost and can be probated. Answer **D** is incorrect because (1) it assumes that the will was revoked (which it was not), and (2) if the will were deemed revoked, under intestacy only Toni's children would take, not her parents.

25. **B** If no members of a class are in existence when a will is executed or at the testator's death, the members of the class (whenever born) ordinarily do not receive their gifts when the designated ancestor of the class dies (this is an exception to the Rule of Convenience). We can assume that Parker knew that his best friend had no children and that he wanted the distribution to Sam's children postponed until all of the class members could be determined. Choice **A** is incorrect in that it does not include all of Sam's children. Choice **C** is incorrect because Parker did not provide for Ann and was not required to provide for her. Choice **D** is incorrect because Parker's estate would pass to his parents only if the will was invalid. (UPC §2-103(a)(2).)

26. **A** Under the Rule of Convenience, a class closes the moment one member of the class is entitled to claim possession of his or her share. Although the doctrine is a rule of construction, not a rule of

law, courts generally follow and apply it. Here, because Sam's eldest son, Bob, was alive when Parker died, Bob was entitled to claim his share the moment Parker died and Parker's will became effective. Bob takes the entire estate under Parker's will. Choice **B** is incorrect. Under the Rule of Convenience, the class closed at Parker's death (after-born class members do not participate). Choice **C** is incorrect because Parker was not required to provide for Ann. Choice **D** is incorrect because Parker's estate would pass to his parents only if the will was invalid. (UPC §2-103(a)(2).)

27. **B** Although Parker's class gift would be completely invalid under the common law approach to the Rule Against Perpetuities, the UPC has adopted the "wait and see" approach to the Rule Against Perpetuities, using a fixed period of 90 years. (UPC §2-901(a).) Under the Rule of Convenience, the class closes when the first member of the class is entitled to distribution. The class would close when Bob reached age 25; only Bob and Ellen were alive when Bob reached 25. Bob's and Ellen's shares would be retained until each reached 25, and would be distributed to him or her as he or she reached that age. If either died before reaching age 25, his or her share would be distributed to the survivor of them. Choice **A** is incorrect because Ellen is a prospective member of the class. Choice **C** is incorrect because Sally was born after the class closed (when Bob reached 25) and therefore is not a member of the class. Choice **D** is incorrect because Bob and Ellen must reach age 25 before he or she takes, and Sally is not a member of the class.

28. **C** When a testator makes specific *per capita* bequests to members of a class and there are no members of the class living at the testator's death, the gift fails. The bequests fail because the amount of each bequest does not vary and the total cannot be determined. Because there were no takers at Parker's death, the gift fails altogether. When no residuary clause is expressed in the will, property not disposed of by the will passes by intestate succession. Here, the entire estate passes by intestacy. Choice **A** is incorrect because (1) it gives property to one of the class members (Bob), but they are not entitled to take; and (2) it gives property to the testator's sister, Ann, who is not entitled to take under either the will or intestacy. Choice **B** is incorrect because it gives property to the class members (Bob, Sally, and Ellen), but they are not entitled to take. Choice **D** is incorrect because it gives property to the testator's sister, who is not entitled to

take, because under the rules governing intestacy only the decedent's parents would take.

29. **D** The mere execution of joint wills or reciprocal wills does not create the presumption of a contract by either testator not to revoke his or her will. There is no evidence of a contract between Edward and Mary not to revoke the original wills. Edward was therefore free to execute a new will. Choice **A** is incorrect in that Edward's first will was revoked by the inconsistent disposition made in his second will. Choice **B** is incorrect in that the second will is valid and that Edward did not die intestate. Choice **C** is incorrect because (1) Edward's second will is valid, and (2) even assuming, *arguendo*, that Edward had died intestate, his estate would have passed by representation one-half to his son, Tim, and one-half to his grandchildren (the issue of his predeceased daughter Lisa).

30. **D** In most states, only "interested parties" may contest a will. An interested party is one who is *adversely affected* by the will's admission to probate. If the second will here is probated, Jim gets $10,000 more than he would have received under the prior will. Because he is not adversely affected, he cannot contest. Only Elizabeth has standing, because she takes everything under the first will, but suffers a $10,000 reduction under the second will. Choices **A** and **B** are incorrect because Jim's interest is not adversely affected under the second will (*i.e.*, he gets more than he would have if the first will remained in effect). Choice **C** is incorrect because neither Jim nor either of Bill's parents is adversely affected by the second will. Bill's parents take nothing under either will, and the first will is conceded to be valid.

31. **A** When a will provision is the product of an insane delusion of the testator, that provision will not be given effect by the probate court. An insane delusion is sometimes described as "a belief that is the product of the imagination and is held tenaciously against all evidence and reason to the contrary." (Haskell, p. 42.) John's belief about Clay's illegitimacy would seem to qualify: There is no evidence that Clay was conceived as the consequence of an illicit relationship; in fact, the evidence (the blood type and resemblance) is to the contrary. The will establishes that John was driven to make his will disinheriting Clay by his irrational belief. On the other hand, there is no evidence that John was otherwise irrational or incompetent to make a will. The court will attempt to admit the will to probate without enforcing the clause relating to Clay. However, because excision of

the clause will not remedy the wrong to Clay (Clay still won't get anything), the court will probably refuse to admit the whole will to probate on these facts. This will produce a more just result (Clay takes in intestacy). Choice **B** is incorrect. Compliance with correct formalities is assumed when a will is admitted to probate, but a will (or a provision of the will) will not be enforced when the testator is laboring under an insane delusion. Choice **C** is incorrect because there is no indication that anyone unduly influenced John. Choice **D** is incorrect. Although a testator may disinherit a child, the court will intervene to prevent an inequitable bequest when it is prompted by the testator's insane delusion. Although John may have the legal right to disinherit Clay, his insane delusion prevented him from executing a document that will be admitted to probate.

32. **C** Under UPC §2-101(b), a decedent "by will may expressly exclude or limit the right of an individual or class to succeed to property of the decedent passing by intestate succession." "Will" is defined in UPC §1-201(55) to include "any testamentary instrument that merely ... expressly excludes or limits the right of an individual or class to succeed to property of the decedent passing by intestate succession." So a document that does nothing more than disinherit an individual can nonetheless be a valid "will." The document here is entirely in the testator's handwriting, it was signed by him, and it expresses testamentary intent (the intent that it be his will—as indicated by his intent to disinherit his child), so it is a valid holographic will. (UPC §2-502(b).) Therefore, it will be admitted to probate. Choice **A** is incorrect because the document is a valid will for the reasons just discussed. Choice **B** is legally incorrect (a natural father may disinherit his child). Choice **D** is incorrect because a mistake in the "inducement" to a will (*i.e.*, a mistake as to the surrounding facts or circumstances) will not be cause to refuse probate, unless the mistake is evident on the face of the will or is the product of an insane delusion, neither of which circumstance applies here.

33. **D** First, a beneficiary designation on an insurance policy cannot be changed by will. The change must be accomplished according to the terms of the policy, which would require a change of beneficiary sent to the insurance company. The will provisions therefore had no effect to change the beneficiary. However, most states have statutes that would revoke a designation of a spouse as beneficiary of a life insurance policy upon dissolution of the marriage. If such a statute was applicable, it would revoke the designation of Bob as the

beneficiary. The proceeds would then be payable to Ashley's estate, and the will would give the proceeds (along with all of Ashley's other assets) to Hector. Such a statute would not apply in this case, however. According to the U.S. Supreme Court in *Egelhoff v. Egelhoff*, 532 U.S. 141 (2000), if life insurance is issued as part of an employee benefit plan governed by ERISA, then ERISA preempts state revocation on divorce statutes and a designation of a former spouse as beneficiary of such a policy is *not* revoked upon divorce. Bob therefore receives the insurance proceeds. Choice **A** is incorrect because one cannot change a life insurance beneficiary by will. Choice **B** is incorrect because the insurance was provided by her private employer and presumably governed by ERISA, so the subsequent divorce had no effect on the beneficiary designation. Choice **C** may be technically correct but ignores the potential application of the revocation of divorce statute so it is overly simplistic.

34. **A** When an attorney prepares a will in which he or she is a beneficiary and supervises its execution, the majority view is that a rebuttable presumption of undue influence arises. Although there is no showing that Jones actually influenced Ellen, the facts that (1) the attorney-client relationship is a confidential one, and (2) the lawyer who prepared the will was employed by Jones, raise a presumption that must be rebutted. Choice **B** is incorrect. The question asks which argument is most likely to be successful. Because the party asserting fraud bears the burden of proof, fraud would be more difficult to establish under these facts. A presumption of undue influence arises in many jurisdictions any time an attorney takes a gift from his client's will (as is the case here). In contrast, there is no evidence that the attorney misrepresented any facts to the testator (as would be necessary to prove fraud in the inducement) or that the attorney fraudulently inserted the gift into the will (as would be necessary to prove fraud in the execution). Choice **C** is incorrect. There is no evidence that Ellen lacked testamentary capacity. Choice **D** is incorrect. A probate judge would not be likely to invalidate a will for this reason. The judge might refer Jones to the proper disciplinary authorities, but he or she would be more likely to use undue influence as the basis for rejecting the will.

35. **C** This question depends on applicable state law. First, the reference to "my car" may be interpreted as "my car owned by me now" or "my car owned by me at the time of my death." The ambiguity will need to be resolved, but because the only car Fernanda owned at either

point in time was the Volvo, it should be read to mean the Volvo she owned at the time the will was signed. The fact that the car has been sold during Fernanda's lifetime means that the gift has adeemed, and in a state that follows strict identity theory, Billy would receive nothing. Assuming that the UPC applies, Billy can be paid the value of the Volvo under two different sections. First, §2-606(b) provides that if specifically bequeathed property is sold by a conservator or attorney in fact, the beneficiary is entitled to the sales price of the item sold. Also, §2-606(a)(6) provides that the specific legatee is entitled to a pecuniary bequest equal to the value of the item that has been disposed of if it can be established that the testator did not intend ademption, which could be established in this case. Some states have adopted the UPC position, and other states would compensate Billy under a statute similar to 2-606(b). Choice **A** is not correct because the reference to "my car" can be clarified. Choice **B** is incorrect under the UPC approach (and in states that have statutes that compensate beneficiaries when a specific gift is sold by a conservator or attorney in fact), but would in fact be correct in a state that follows the traditional strict identity theory. Choice **D** is incorrect because even in a strict identity theory state, Celeste acted reasonably in selling the car. Billy could argue that because she knew about the specific gift, selling it amounted to tortious interference with his inheritance. However, he would have to establish that her sale of the car was wrongful. See Restatement 2d Torts section 774B.

36. B Fraud occurs when the testator is willfully deceived as to facts that are material to his or her testamentary scheme, and these facts actually induce him or her to make, alter, or refrain from making a testamentary gift. Robin had a duty to obtain a divorce before she remarried, and Craig had a right to believe that Robin was in fact divorced. When she declared her marital status as single, she committed a fraud upon Craig. The fraud will only matter, for probate purposes, if the court concludes that the fraud "caused" the gift — that is, that the gift would not have been made had the fraud not been committed. Because the gift was made to Robin as "my wife," there is at least strong evidence that the gift was the product of Robin's fraud, so the court will probably conclude that the requisite causal connection between fraud and gift is established. The best remedy in light of Craig's dispositive language is to probate the will and impose a constructive trust upon Robin's share in favor of Aunt Martha. Otherwise, Robin's one-half would be distributed by intestacy. This would result in Craig's children taking part of his estate—a result that he obviously did not want. Answer **A** is incorrect. Although a true general statement, it does not provide for the effect of fraud by a beneficiary. Answers **C** and **D** are incorrect. Both would result in Aunt Martha's receiving nothing and in the distribution of Craig's entire estate to his children, a result Craig expressly did not want.

37. **A** A general power of appointment is one that is exercisable in favor of the donee, his or her estate, his or her creditors, or the creditors of his or her estate. There are no limits on the persons to whom Ted can appoint, and so the power is a general one. Because there is no condition precedent, Ted is authorized to exercise the power during his lifetime by deed, and it is therefore "presently exercisable." Choice **B** is incorrect because Ted is not prohibited from appointing to himself, his estate, his creditors, or the creditors of his estate. Choice **C** is incorrect because Ted can exercise the power by deed during his life. Choice **D** is incorrect both (1) because Ted can appoint to himself, and (2) because Ted can exercise the power by deed.

38. **C** Where (1) a testator holds a power of appointment, and (2) the instrument creating the power does *not* require that the exercise of the power reference the power, a general residuary clause in a will exercises the power only if (a) the power is a general power and the instrument creating the power does not contain an express gift in the event the power is not exercised, or (b) the will manifests the intent to include the property subject to the power. (UPC §2-608.) Ted's power was a general power, and John's will contains a gift to John's heirs if Ted failed to exercise the power, so test (a) is not satisfied. Further, Ted's will did not refer at all to the power of appointment bestowed upon him in John's will or the property subject to the power, so test (b) is not satisfied either. The residuary clause of Ted's will probably will not be construed as an exercise of the power. John's estate consequently passes to John's heirs. Choice **A** is incorrect; the residuary clause did not exercise Ted's power. Choices **B** and **D** are incorrect. The property subject to Ted's power passed to John's heirs by virtue of Ted's failure to exercise the power.

39. **B** The word "heirs" is usually taken to refer to those persons who, at the decedent's death, are entitled to succeed to the estate under the rules of intestate succession. (UPC §2-711.) Art predeceased John and was not survived by issue. Thus, his share lapsed (and antilapse does not apply to save the gift because Art has no surviving descendants to take his share). (UPC 2 §2-603(b)(1).) Bob and Charles

(John's "heirs") both survived John. Their shares *vested at John's death*, subject to being divested by Ted's exercise of the power over John's estate. Because Ted did not exercise the power, their shares passed by their wills to their wives. Choice **A** is incorrect because Art predeceased John. Art was not within the class of "heirs" at John's death. Choice **C** is incorrect, because (1) Bob's share vested prior to his death, and Bob's wife was entitled to his share under his will, and (2) Charles's share passed to Marcy by will. Choice **D** is incorrect because the interests of Bob and Charles vested at John's death. They could dispose of their shares to their wives by will.

40. B Under the *capture* doctrine, whereby the donee of a general power of appointment makes an ineffective appointment, the property not effectively appointed will go to the donee's estate, not the default takers, *if* the donee manifested an intent to assume control over the appointive property for all purposes (and not simply for the limited purpose of the attempted appointment). The most common evidence of the donee manifesting an intent to assume control over the appointive property for all purposes is when the donee's will has a *blending* residuary clause—a residuary clause that blends the appointive property with the donee's own property. Here, Ted's will contains a *blending* residuary clause that purports to combine the rest of his property with the property over which he has the general power of appointment. Inasmuch as the attempted appointment is ineffective (the appointed beneficiaries are dead and antilapse does not apply because none left surviving descendants), and inasmuch as Ted's blending residuary clause shows his intent to exercise control over the appointive property for all purposes, the appointive property becomes part of Ted's residuary clause and will be distributed to Ann. Choice **A** is incorrect because it assumes the capture doctrine does not apply, but it does. Although choice **C** applies the capture doctrine, it is nonetheless incorrect because it assumes that the appointive property would pass under intestacy to Ted's heirs. While the part of the residuary clause trying to appoint the appointive property was ineffective, the part giving the rest of his estate to Ann is valid and effective. Where only part of a residuary clause is invalid, the property is distributed to the other takers in the residuary clause, not through intestacy. (UPC §2-604(b).) Choice **D** is invalid because Bill has no right to all of the appointive property under either the will or intestacy.

41. C If, after executing a will, the testator is divorced from the spouse who is a beneficiary under the will, the divorce revokes any disposition made by the will to the former spouse. (UPC §2-804(b).) The divorce automatically revoked the gift to Doris, and therefore, she will receive nothing. Choices **A**, **B**, and **D** are all incorrect because Doris takes nothing from T's estate.

42. D When a spouse marries the testator after the testator makes his or her will, the will is treated as a premarital will and the spouse is treated as an "omitted" spouse. The omitted spouse will receive his or her intestate share of that portion of the estate that the testator did not bequeath to his or her children from another marriage or relationships, unless (1) it appears from the will or other evidence that the will was made in contemplation of the marriage; (2) the will expresses the intent that it should be effective notwithstanding any subsequent marriage; or (3) the testator provided for the spouse outside the will, and that gift was intended to be in lieu of the spouse taking under the will. (UPC §2-301(a).) T's total estate was $180,000. After first deducting the specific bequest of $15,000 to Mike, Kay's share will be $150,000 plus one-half of the balance of $15,000, for a total of $157,500. The bequests to Ben will not be honored (see answer 46 below). Choice **A** is mathematically incorrect. Choice **B** is incorrect both because it is mathematically incorrect and because the bequest to Ben will not be honored. Choice **C** is incorrect because Kay is an omitted spouse.

43. D If one or more children of the testator were living when he or she executed his or her will and the will devised property to one or more of those children, then a pretermitted child would be entitled to a pro-rata share of the gifts to such child or children. (UPC §2-302(a)(2).) Because Liz was born after the will was executed, she is a pretermitted child and she will receive one-half of the $15,000 gift to Mike ($7,500). Choices **A** and **B** are mathematically incorrect under the required formula. Choice **C** is incorrect because Liz is a pretermitted child.

44. B Any person who *kills* another *feloniously* and *intentionally* is not entitled to any benefit under the victim's will, and the decedent's estate passes as if the killer had disclaimed all provisions. (UPC §2-803(c).) A person who commits *voluntary* manslaughter is deemed to have intended to kill or seriously injure the decedent (in contrast to a person who commits involuntary manslaughter). Therefore, Ben satisfies the "feloniously and intentionally kills" definition, and will receive nothing from T's estate. Choice **A** is incorrect. Even though the gift of Rex, Inc., stock was adeemed, the $1,000 gift was not, but Ben is not entitled to it because of the homicide doctrine. Choices **C** and **D** are incorrect because Ben receives nothing from T's estate.

45. **B** First, the gift of the diamond bracelet was adeemed by satisfaction when she gave it to Brenda, and even in a state following the UPC, which under §2-606 would allow a beneficiary the value of an adeemed item if there is proof that the testator did not intend ademption, Brenda would get nothing because the gift indicates that Tallulah did not intend for Brenda to receive anything else. The gift of the home to Aiden lapsed because Aiden did not survive Tallulah. However, because Aiden was related to Tallulah and left a descendant, Augusta, there is most likely an applicable antilapse statute that would give the house to Augusta rather than having it lapse into the residue and be distributed to Edna. See UPC §2-603. However, even in states with an antilapse statute, the relationship of aunt and nephew may be too remote to trigger the antilapse statute, so the answer is dependent on applicable state law. Because Calista was not related to Tallulah, and she predeceased Tallulah, her gift lapses, the antilapse statute would most likely not apply, and the Picasso will drop into the residue and be distributed to Edna. As for the Mercedes, under UPC §2-606(a)(3), which gives a specific legatee the proceeds of insurance payable for damage to the item given, Daniel would receive the proceeds of the insurance policy. Even with a state that follows the strict identity theory of ademption, the car did not adeem because it was not disposed of during Tallulah's life but simultaneous with her death. Choice **A** is incorrect because Augusta and Daniel have claims as discussed above. Choice **C** is incorrect because Calvin cannot claim the Picasso and Brenda cannot claim the value of the bracelet as discussed above. Choice **D** is incorrect because Calvin has no claim to the Picasso.

46. **A** *Powers of appointment* are generally *releasable*. Upon the release of a power of appointment, the property passes to previously designated takers in default: in this case, to Linda's living issue, per stirpes. Linda's release of the power was effective when delivered to Sam. Her attempt to exercise the power in her will was ineffective. The result is that the property held by Sam in trust passes to Linda's surviving issue, per stirpes. Choice **B** is incorrect because the attempted exercise of the power is ineffective after the power has been released. Choice **C** is incorrect because Martha is entitled to Karen's share

under the per stirpes approach. Choice **D** is incorrect because Ralph provided for default takers in the event the power was released or not exercised by Linda, so the property in question does not pass through intestacy.

47. C A testamentary power may not be encumbered by or made subject to a contract with the holder of the power. Because contracts encumbering a *testamentary* power of appointment are unenforceable, Linda's exercise of the power is valid. Thus, Adam, Ron, and Martha take equally. Choice **A** is incorrect because the contract between Linda and Adam is unenforceable. Adam may, of course, sue Linda's estate for restitution. Choice **B** is incorrect because Martha was specifically included among the appointees. Choice **D** is incorrect because Linda exercised the power through her will.

48. C/A A trust is created only if (1) the settlor has the intent to create a trust *when the property is transferred to the trustee*, and (2) the settlor appropriately manifests his or her intent to the outside world. Although the key is the settlor's intent at the moment he or she transfers the property in question, evidence of the intent can include acts or statements that occur *after* the act that purportedly creates the trust. (Restatement 3d of Trusts, §13, Comment b.) Here, Alice made no statement when she initially transferred the property to Jim, but only two weeks later she clearly expressed her intent that the property was being transferred in trust. Alice's subsequent statements are relevant to the issue of her intent at the time of transfer and would be considered by a court. The magnitude of the gift, Alice's subsequent unequivocal assertion that the property was to be held in trust, Jim's initial acquiescence to Alice's trust assertion, and the fact that Alice has surviving children—all of these considerations support a finding that Alice intended a trust when the initial transfer occurred. The key, however, is what Alice intended *at the time of the transfer*; a subsequently formed intent would not count. This is a close call. If the court were to conclude that Alice had the intent to form a trust at the time of the transfer, choice **C** would be correct. Choices **A**, **B**, and **D** would then all be incorrect because they all assume that no valid trust was created. If, however, the court were to conclude that Alice did not have the intent to form a trust when she transferred the money to Jim, choice **A** would be correct. (Choice **B**, **C**, and **D** would then be incorrect because if there is no trust, Jim gets to keep the property and no one else has any right to it.)

49. B When a trustor manifests an intent that a trust take effect at some *future point in time*, no trust is created. (Restatement 3d of Trusts, §15, Comment b.) Because Stephanie manifested an intent that the trust be created only upon her return from Europe, no valid trust was created. The farm was still part of her estate and passed to Rick pursuant to the will. Choice **A** is incorrect, because no trust was created by the letter to Sam. The letter expressed only an intent to create a trust in the future. Choice **C** is incorrect. Stephanie's death did not in itself have any testamentary effect. No trust was ever created because the letter to Sam manifested only the intent to create one in the future. Choice **D** is incorrect in that the farm passed pursuant to Stephanie's will, not by intestacy.

50. D A trust must *identify the beneficiaries* or provide a standard by which the beneficiaries can reasonably be ascertained. If the beneficiaries are indefinite, and there is no reasonable way to identify them, the trust fails. (Restatement 3d of Trusts, §46.) The designation of "my three best friends" is probably an insufficient description of the beneficiaries, as evidenced by the fact that John, who was also Christina's friend, was unsure who her three best friends were. Thus, the trust probably fails, and Christina's entire estate passes to her mother. Choices **A** and **B** are incorrect because the trust failed. Choice **C** is incorrect. Christina never manifested any intent that Ann, Barbara, and Cary should take anything outright.

51. B A formal will must ordinarily be signed by the testator and at least two persons, each of whom witnessed either the signing of the will or the testator's acknowledgment of his or her signature on the will. (UPC §2-502.) Note that the current version of the UPC allows a notary in lieu of the witnesses. Although at common law and under many state statutes the witnesses must sign in the presence of each other, the UPC does *not* require that the two witnesses sign in each other's presence. The UPC does require, however, that each witness sign within a reasonable time of witnessing the testator sign or acknowledge the will. Although X and Y did not sign the will in front of each other, because each signed shortly after having witnessed T execute her will, T has a valid testamentary writing. Choice **A** is incorrect because the will was typed, and the "material provisions" were not in the testator's handwriting. Choice **C** is incorrect because there is no requirement under the UPC that the witnesses sign the will in each other's presence. Choice **D** is incorrect because there is no requirement that an attested will be dated to be valid.

52. B Because T signed and acknowledged the will in the presence of X and Y, and they signed within a reasonable time thereafter, the writing is valid. (UPC §2-502.) Choice **A** is incorrect because the will was typed, and the "material provisions" were not in the testator's handwriting. Choice **C** is incorrect because there is no requirement under the UPC that witnesses sign the will in the testator's presence. Choice **D** is incorrect because there is no requirement that witnesses actually read, or know the provisions of, the testator's will.

53. C The traditional and general rule is that to be valid, a trust must have (among other requirements) a named or *ascertainable beneficiary* capable of enforcing the trust. Traditionally, in most states, this beneficiary must be a *human* (or organization), not an animal. Although the modern trend is to recognize honorary trusts (a trust with no definitely ascertainable human beneficiary and with only a specific noncharitable purpose), the traditional approach to the law of trusts does not recognize honorary trusts. Trusts for the care of specific animals are honorary trusts. Under the traditional approach to the law of trusts, the trust for Rusty's care will fail. (Note that the UPC has optional provisions, §2-907(a) and (b), and the Restatement (Third) of Trusts has a provision, §47, which validate a trust for a "designated domestic or pet animal." [UPC §2-907(b).] The trust is enforceable by a trustee designated in the trust instrument or one appointed by the court. In a jurisdiction with this type of provision in force or that adopts the Restatement (Third) of Trusts approach, the correct answer would be choice **A**.) Choice **A** is incorrect in most jurisdictions; there must be a named or reasonably identifiable *individual* who could enforce the trust. Choice **B** is incorrect because Bruce manifested no intent that Selma take the property in her own right. Choice **D** is incorrect because there is a right answer—choice **C**.

54. C A condition in a trust unreasonably restraining marriage is usually not enforced. (Restatement 3d of Trusts, §29, Comment j.) A gift over to an alternate beneficiary upon *remarriage* of the settlor's *surviving spouse* is usually viewed as only a *partial* restraint upon marriage. (*Id.*) On the other hand, the condition imposed upon the children that they not marry constitutes a *complete* restraint on marriage and is likely to be deemed unreasonable. This condition should be stricken, and the gift for their benefit should be without this restraint. (Restatement 3d, §29, Comment i.) The condition imposed upon Will that he not receive anything if he remarried is probably enforceable. Choice **A** is incorrect because the condition that Will forfeit his interest if he remarried is probably enforceable. Choice **B** is incorrect. The court is likely to find the condition imposed upon Will reasonable and enforceable. On the other hand, the conditions imposed upon the children will be deemed unreasonable and will be stricken. Choice **D** is incorrect. If a condition is deemed invalid, it is stricken and the trust is otherwise enforced.

55. **B** A secret trust arises when a will makes an outright gift in reliance upon the devisee's *oral promise* to hold the property as trustee for others. The agreement here is unenforceable as an express trust, because the oral agreement did not comply with the statutory formalities for wills (*e.g.*, the requirement that the terms be in writing). However, a *constructive trust* may be imposed in favor of the intended beneficiary to prevent the devisee's unjust enrichment, provided that the court is convinced by extrinsic evidence that the decedent relied on the devisee's promise to hold the property in trust for another. Here, Judith relied upon Earl's oral promise to hold the funds in trust for Grace. Although Earl's promise is unenforceable as an express trust, it may be enforceable as a constructive trust to prevent Earl from being unjustly enriched. Choice **A** is incorrect in that a testamentary express trust cannot be created orally; it must be executed in accordance with the requisite formalities of a valid will. Choice **C** is incorrect; a resulting trust could not result because there was no *express* intention on the face of the will to create a trust. Choice **D** is incorrect; a majority of states would impose a constructive trust in this situation.

56. **C** Where the express language of a will expresses the intent to create a trust, but the trust fails for want of adequate terms (*i.e.*, failure to identify the beneficiary or failure to set forth the terms of the trust), the failed attempt at a testamentary trust is called a *semisecret* trust. The traditional and still majority rule is to impose a *resulting trust* on the failed trust, and the property in question falls to the residuary clause of the will. Because Judith indicated in the will that the gift was made in trust, but failed to name the beneficiary in the will, the trust is a resulting one for the residuary legatees. A constructive trust will ordinarily not be imposed, because the will indicates on its face that Earl is taking the property as trustee and there's no opportunity for unjust enrichment by him. Choice **A** is incorrect. Grace will probably not be permitted to enforce the trust because the trust fails for want of ascertainable beneficiaries—she was not specifically named in the will. Choice **B** is incorrect because

the majority rule is to impose a resulting trust where the failed testamentary trust is a semisecret trust; a constructive trust is imposed, as a general rule, where the failed trust is a secret trust (though there is a modern trend to apply the constructive trust to both the secret and the semisecret trust—in which case choice **B** would be the correct choice). Choice **D** is incorrect because Judith's will expressly stated that Earl was to take the bequest in trust, not outright, so the failed trust is a semisecret trust and a resulting trust is the appropriate remedy to keep Earl from taking the bequest.

57. A A bank or savings account in the name of "X, in trust for Y" is called a "Totten trust," and is viewed as a type of informal will. Upon the death of X, the funds in a Totten account will be deemed to belong to Y. See UPC §6-212(b) and the Comment thereto; see also §6-201(8)(ii). This construction will not apply where there is clear evidence that X did not intend a death benefit to Y, but there is no such evidence here. Therefore, Karen takes the funds in the account. Choice **B** is incorrect because there was a valid Totten trust. If no trust existed, choice **B** would be the correct answer because Amy left all her property to Ed. Choices **C** and **D** are incorrect because the account is a valid Totten trust in favor of Karen alone; and even if the trust were invalid, the account would pass under the residuary clause of Amy's will to only Ed.

58. C A Totten trust is automatically revoked upon the death of the beneficiary prior to the death of the settlor. See UPC §6-212(b)(2), last sentence. The contents of the account then belong to the settlor free of the trust. Therefore, the trust res passes to Ed under the terms of Amy's will. Choice **A** is incorrect in that the interest of Karen was divested when she predeceased Amy. Karen could not dispose of the account by her will. Choice **B** is incorrect because Karen's interest in the Totten trust was extinguished by her death before Amy. No one could take any interest in the account through Karen. Choice **D** is incorrect because Amy's will disposed of her estate to Ed.

59. D The beneficial interest in a trust is *alienable*, unless the trustor specifically imposes some restraint upon alienation. Because no restraint upon the alienation of Carl's interest was stipulated in the trust, the assignment was valid. However, Carl could assign only his own equitable interest in the trust (*i.e.*, the trust continues in accordance with its terms). Choice **A** is incorrect; Carl's interest was alienable because the trustor did not specifically restrain his right to alienate. Choice **B** is incorrect; both income and remainder interests are alienable.

Choice **C** is incorrect; although Carl's interests may be assigned, the assignee can receive only an interest that is coextensive with that enjoyed by Carl as the beneficiary-assignor.

60. **A** In most jurisdictions, the first assignee in point of time prevails, regardless of who first gives notice to the trustee. (Restatement 3d of Trusts, §54.) Because Carl's interest is an equitable one, he retained no interest that he could assign subsequently. (If Ted could successfully assert estoppel against Sam, Ted would prevail under the Restatement (Third) of Trusts approach. [Restatement 3d of Trusts, §54.] However, it is unclear whether Ted could prevail under these facts.) Choice **B** is incorrect; consideration is not a pertinent factor here (the bona fide purchaser rule is not applicable in this context). Choice **C** is incorrect as a statement of law (priority of ownership is ordinarily not based upon the order of notification to the trustee). Choice **D** is incorrect in that consideration is not pertinent on these facts.

61. **C** Although the existence of a spendthrift clause makes it impossible for a beneficiary to make a legally binding transfer of his or her interest, (1) the trustee *may* choose to honor the beneficiary's purported assignment, and (2) the beneficiary can revoke the transfer at any time as to future payments. (Uniform Trust Code [UTC] §502.) Here, assuming the trustee decides to honor the purported transfer, the direction is valid, but revocable by Beatrix. The trustee may pay the income to Karen until such time as (1) the trustee decides to recommence distributions to the beneficiary Beatrix, or (2) Beatrix revokes the transfer (as to future payments only). Choice **A** is incorrect because the transfer is not *per se* void—it is valid to the extent the trustee decides to honor it and the beneficiary does not revoke it. Choice **B** is incorrect because the phrase that the trustee "*must*" pay the income to Karen fails to recognize (1) that trustee does not have to honor the purported transfer, and (2) that the beneficiary can revoke the purported transfer (as to future payments). Choice **D** is incorrect because (1) the purported transfer is not *per se* void, and (2) the debt to Karen is not satisfied until completely paid.

62. **A** Under the majority rule, and the Uniform Trust Code (UTC §503), certain classes of creditors are not restrained by a spendthrift clause. The claims of the federal government for unpaid taxes under the Internal Revenue Code are usually within this group. (UTC §503(b)(3).) Choice **B** is incorrect; Beatrix's interest is only an income interest, which does not enable the government or anyone else to reach

the trust principal. Choices **C** and **D** are incorrect because a spendthrift clause is *not* valid against a judgment by the United States.

63. **B** The interest of a beneficiary that is subject to the discretion of the trustee may not be subjected to the claims of his or her creditors, until that discretion has been exercised. The creditor could levy upon Larry's remainder interest, because this interest is *not* subject to the trustee's discretion. However, a court would order that *no* amount be paid to the creditor until the last of Kathy's children died. Until that time, it would not be possible to determine Larry's *per capita* interest precisely. Choice **A** is incorrect. Larry's income interest is subject to the trustee's discretion (and therefore not attachable). Choice **C** is incorrect; it includes Larry's income interest, which is subject to the trustee's discretion and not subject to the creditor's claim. Choice **D** is incorrect because Larry's remainder interest may be attached by creditors, subject to the restriction discussed above.

64. **D** Most states have statutes that protect life insurance from creditor claims. The money in the 401(k) account is protected from creditors under the Employee Retirement Income Security Act (ERISA). Most states will also give the surviving spouse the right to claim a homestead amount of equity in the residence that would not be available to pay creditors. The amount of homestead varies significantly from state to state. Svetlana will be able to enforce her debt only against the stock account and the equity in the house that exceeds the amount of the state's homestead exemption. In some states, Caleb's surviving wife may be able to protect part of the stock account from Svetlana's claim under some sort of family support award that supplements homestead protection. Choice **A** is incorrect because the life insurance and the 401(k) account are protected from creditors, and the home equity will have some protection under homestead laws. Choice **B** is incorrect because the stock account should be available for satisfaction of claims, and equity in the house over the state homestead award is also available. Choice **C** is incorrect because the 401(k) and a portion of the equity in the home will also be protected from creditor claims.

65. **C** In most states, a trustor cannot create a spendthrift trust in favor of himself or herself. His or her interest is subject to the claims of creditors (present or prospective). Therefore, Ted may not create a spendthrift trust in favor of himself. Insofar as he retains an interest (*i.e.*, the income interest, in this case), it is subject to the claims of his creditors. Mae's interest, however, is not subject to the claims of

Ted's creditors, unless the transfer constituted a fraud upon his creditors (*i.e.*, Ted was insolvent when the transfer of funds was *initially* made). Choices **A** and **B** are incorrect because Ted is not permitted to create a spendthrift trust in favor of himself. Choice **D** is incorrect because Mae's interest in the trust cannot be attached by Ted's creditors.

66. **A** A trust qualifies as a charitable trust as long as its purpose is charitable. Charitable purposes include (1) the relief of poverty, (2) the advancement of education, (3) the advancement of religion, (4) the promotion of health, (5) governmental or municipal purposes, or (6) other purposes the accomplishment of which is beneficial to the community. Moreover, a charitable trust must benefit either society as a whole or a substantial segment of the community. If the purpose is a valid charitable purpose, and a broad segment of the community benefits (either directly or indirectly), the trust is usually a valid charitable trust, even though the trust funds may be distributed to only a limited number of recipients. The benefits of a charitable trust are that (1) the beneficiaries do not have to be ascertainable (and in fact should not be because it is to benefit a large segment of society), and (2) the trust is not subject to the Rule Against Perpetuities. Here, because the purpose of the trust is to discover a cure for cancer, and the benefits of this accomplishment will be shared by a large segment of society, the trust, most likely, is a valid charitable trust. Choice **B** is incorrect because a large segment of society will benefit indirectly and that is good enough for a charitable trust. Choices **C** and **D** are incorrect because charitable trusts are not subject to the Rule Against Perpetuities.

67. **D** Courts have enforced trusts "for charitable purposes" even though the trustee was authorized to select any charitable purpose. The trustee can probably use the money for any purpose that comes within the definition of "charitable" as that term is defined under the applicable law. Choice **A** is incorrect because the beneficiaries need not be ascertainable as long as the trust qualifies as a charitable trust. In addition, the courts have held that a trust for "charitable purposes" authorizes the trustee to select a particular charitable purpose and is a valid charitable trust. Choice **B** is incorrect because charitable trusts are exempt from the Rule Against Perpetuities. Choice **C** is incorrect; the trustee is not limited in his choices but may utilize the trust res for any charitable purpose.

68. B When the particular charitable purpose specified by a trustor has become impossible, or impracticable to accomplish, and it is determined that the trustor had a general charitable intent, a court may modify the trust so as to carry out the trustor's purpose to the extent that it is possible to do so. The theory permitting such modification is called the *cy pres* doctrine. Although Terry's alma mater was chosen as the recipient of the gift, it may be argued that Terry's primary purpose was to benefit "worthy students from Arizona." Thus, the *cy pres* doctrine should be used to allow the gift to be given to another charitable institution whose primary purpose is education and whose students include students from Arizona. Choice **A** is incorrect in that a charitable gift cannot be made to a profit-making organization. Choice **C** is correct only if the charitable gift is held to fail. In this instance, the broader purpose of educating Arizona students can be carried out without destroying the trust. Choice **D** is incorrect because *cy pres* should be applied before the trust is deemed to fail; and even if the trust were to fail, a resulting trust would be imposed and the money would go to the residuary clause where it would pass to Terry's parents.

69. B This is a very difficult question.. There has been much litigation over whether a gift that contains provisions that discriminate on the basis of race or gender constitutes illegal discrimination. Here, there are no public entities involved in the immediate administration of the trust, but if Delphi balks at applying the terms of the trust and is sued, there would be an issue as to whether the court's enforcement of the original terms constitutes impermissible state action. The problem is that Delphi cannot accept the gift as intended, so the trust purpose has become impossible/impractical. From a doctrinal perspective, the general rule is that where the problem can be solved using administrative deviation, administrative deviation is preferred to *cy pres* because the former retains the settlor's original intent as to the trust's core, dispositive provisions. That would support the position that choice **B** is correct because it solves the trust problem by changing the administrative provisions — substituting another institution that can adhere to the settlor's original restrictions. On the other hand, many courts find such discriminatory restrictions abhorrent, if not illegal, and to avoid issues of state action, apply *cy pres* to strike the offending provision. That would support the position that choice **C** is correct because it solves the trust problem by striking the discriminatory provision and permitting Delphi to continue to administer the trust. On the other hand, some courts, though probably a minority, are reluctant to apply *cy pres* to such discriminatory restrictions and prefer simply to terminate the trust—although this is counter to the strong public policy in favor of sustaining charitable gifts whenever possible. That reasoning would support choice **D**. But although choice **D** is defensible, it arguably is incorrect in light of the call of the question, which asked what a court would "probably" do and this is a minority approach. Choice **A** is incorrect because the settlor clearly expressed strong feelings against using the funds for the education of atheists, which does not raise the same constitutional and statutory concerns as discrimination based on race and gender, and it would be inconsistent with his charitable intent to repudiate this constraint.

70. **B** A trustee is ordinarily prohibited from any type of self-dealing, which constitutes a breach of fiduciary duty, and under the "no further inquiry rule" the trustee's good faith or the reasonableness of the transaction is irrelevant. See also UTC §802(b). The trustee cannot personally purchase trust property even for its fair market value. (Restatement 3d of Trusts, §78, Comment b.) Although Edward had an implied right to sell the trust asset, the sale of trust property *to himself* was prohibited. Choice **A** is incorrect because, although Edward had an implied power to sell the trust assets under these circumstances, he did not have the right to sell them to himself. Choice **C** is incorrect because under the "no further inquiry" rule, where the trustee breaches the no self-dealing rule, the reasonableness of the transaction is irrelevant. Choice **D** is incorrect because absent express authorization by the settlor or consent by all the beneficiaries following full disclosure, a fiduciary cannot engage in self-dealing. (The Uniform Trust Code adopts an exception to this traditional approach, but that exception is beyond the scope of this question.)

71. **A** Under traditional trust principles, a trustee has no implied power to *borrow funds* or to encumber trust property. A trustee cannot ordinarily borrow funds against trust assets or against the general credit of the trust, unless he has been specifically granted that power. Choice **B** is incorrect. Edward violated his duty whether or not the net income was reduced. Choice **C** is incorrect; a trustee has no implied power to borrow funds against trust property. He or she must have the express authority to borrow. Choice **D** is legally incorrect. Edward did breach his fiduciary duty by exercising a power which he did not possess.

Under the Uniform Trust Code, a trustee is granted broad powers over the trust property. The Code expressly grants each trustee "all powers over the trust property which an unmarried competent owner has over individually owned property;" and "any other powers appropriate to achieve the property investment, management, and distribution of the trust property . . . ." (UTC §815(a)(2)(A) and (B).) The code goes on to expressly grant each trustee the power to "borrow money, with or without security, and mortgage or pledge trust property . . . ." (UTC §816(5).) The call of the question, however, expressly asked how the fact pattern would be resolved under traditional trust principles.

72. **B** A trustee has a duty to diversify trust assets. Section 3 of the Uniform Prudent Investor Act, adopted by most states and incorporated into the UTC as Article 9, provides that a trustee must diversify unless there are special circumstances that would indicate diversification was not the best investment option for the trust. Some states allow a trustee to retain inception assets (assets placed into the trust by the trustor) but even under those circumstances, a trustee must monitor the investment and diversify if prudent. Under the circumstances in the question, there was no reason to hold on to buildings in the same area, and there were signficant indications that the trustees should have sold the buildings and reinvested. The bank also violated its duty of impartiality. Trustees have a duty to act impartially with regard to multiple beneficiaries of a trust when investing, managing, and distributing trust property. UTC §803. The Bank violated that duty by not preserving the value of the principal. It did not reinvest the trust property when the value of the buildings began to fall and it did not invest enough of the rent income to maintaining the buildings in a way that they could retain their value. Instead, all rent was distributed to the income beneficiaries. Therefore, the bank favored the income beneficiaries' interests over the remaindermen's interests. The bank also failed to protect the trust property—by insufficiently maintaining it—and failed to invest prudently by leaving the trust assets in one type of investment that was dropping in value. Choice **A** is not correct because there is no indication that the bank did not segregate the trust assets (which would have been done by titling the buildings in the name of the trust). Choice **C** is incorrect because there is no indication that the bank delegated its duties to a third party without careful selection and oversight of such third party. Choice **D** is incorrect because it includes the two duties (to

delegate responsibly and to segregate assets) that were not violated under the facts of the question and it did not include the duty to invest prudently.

73. **C** A trustee must act within the bounds of reasonable judgment in carrying out the purpose of the trust. (Restatement 3d of Trusts, §87 Comment d; UTC §814(a).) The grant of sole, absolute, or uncontrolled discretion does not completely insulate the trustee from judicial review. Even though "sole, absolute, and uncontrolled" discretion was granted to the trustee, she was required to carry out the purpose of the trust in a good faith, nonarbitrary manner. The favoring of one beneficiary over another without reason would be arbitrary, and an abuse of discretion, for which the court could impose liability. Choices **A** and **B** are incorrect in that the court does have the power to review the decisions of the trustee in these circumstances (*i.e.*, making income payments only to the oldest child, who might be the least needy); and there is no presumption that the trustee has acted reasonably when the facts (preferring one child to the others) would support a contrary presumption. Choice **D** is incorrect in that the court is not permitted to substitute its own judgment, but may impose liability for actions that are so unreasonable as to amount to an abuse of discretion by the trustee.

74. **D** Because real property values historically fluctuate greatly, a trustee is generally not authorized to invest in *unimproved land* for resale or appreciation. However, a trust instrument may specifically authorize the trustee to make such an investment. Here, Ted had no such authority. Choice **A** is incorrect; although a trustee is governed by the prudent investor rule, investment in unimproved land for appreciation or resale is generally deemed imprudent by its very nature. Even under the modern portfolio approach, absent special circumstances investment of *all* of the trust's assets in one parcel of unimproved real estate is probably too risky and inconsistent with the settlor's intent. Choice **B** is incorrect in that the applicable rule is not mitigated by an appraisal that happens to support the trustee's judgment. Choice **C** is incorrect; an otherwise improper investment may be specifically authorized by the trust instrument.

75. **D** Historically, once a trustee accepted the position, he or she could not resign without court approval. Under the Uniform Trust Code, the trustee can resign (1) with court approval, or (2) by notice to the beneficiaries, settlor (if living), and all cotrustees. (UTC §705(a).)

Here, Karl has done none of the above—though he arguably is not "resigning" but only delegating his responsibilities while temporarily away. But the law is equally demanding with respect to a trustee's ability to delegate his or her powers. At common law, a trustee could only delegate ministerial powers at best, not discretionary powers. Here, Karl has purported to delegate all powers and duties—a clear breach of his common law duties as trustee. Under the Uniform Trust Code, a trustee is given greater authority to delegate powers and duties, but even then the trustee must exercise reasonable care (1) in selecting the agent, (2) in establishing the scope and terms of the delegation, and (3) in periodically reviewing the agent's actions. (UTC §807(a).) There is no evidence here that Karl has exercised reasonable care in selecting Edward, and more importantly, there is no evidence that Karl has exercised reasonable care in establishing the scope and terms of the delegation or in monitoring Edward. Under both the traditional approach and the modern-trend approach, Karl has breached his fiduciary duty. Choice **A** is incorrect because Karl is not permitted under these facts to relieve himself of his duties as trustee during the year and would be liable for any resulting damages. Choice **B** is incorrect because Karl has not properly delegated his powers under either the traditional approach or the modern trend. Choice **C** is incorrect under the traditional approach because the trustee could delegate ministerial duties and powers, but not discretionary duties and powers; and it is incorrect under the modern trend because while it may be permissible to delegate discretionary duties and powers under the modern trend, it is permissible only under limited conditions that Karl has not established here.

76. **B** Under traditional trust principles, a trustee may employ agents to perform services for the trust, so long as the trustee exercises the care of a reasonably prudent person in selecting the agents and continues to oversee the performance of their assigned services. The duty to make investment decisions is not *totally* delegable. Karl was required to inquire of Edward his reasons for investing in particular stocks and the likelihood of their financial success. After these inquiries, Karl was required to make the investment decision himself. If Karl failed in either duty, he would be strictly liable for any loss (even if a reasonably prudent investor might have made the same investment decision as Edward). Choice **A** is incorrect; Karl is liable even if the stock would have been purchased by the prudent investor. Choice **C** is incorrect in that Karl was obliged to oversee,

inquire into, and approve Edward's decisions. Choice **D** is incorrect; even if Karl exercised reasonable care in selecting Edward, he was still obliged to "supervise" and review all of Edward's investment recommendations.

[Under the Uniform Trust Code, a trustee is granted greater authority to delegate powers over the trust property as long as the trustee exercises reasonable care (1) in selecting the agent, (2) in establishing the scope and terms of the delegation, and (3) in periodically reviewing the agent's actions. (UTC §807(a).) It is a closer call whether Karl has breached his duty under the Uniform Trust Code, but a strong argument can be made that Karl has not periodically reviewed the agent's actions in order to monitor the agent's performance. The call of the question, however, expressly asked how the fact pattern would be resolved under traditional trust principles so this latter discussion is moot.]

77. **B** Absent authorization in the terms of the trust, it is a breach of a trustee's fiduciary duty to borrow funds from the trust for his or her personal use. (Restatement 3d of Trusts, §78, Comment d.) In addition to repaying the principal and interest of the loan, Karl must forfeit all profits that he made as a consequence of his loans from the trust. (Restatement 3d of Trusts—Prudent Investor Rule, §§205-206.) Choice **A** is incorrect; Karl is legally obliged to remit any profits to the trust. It is immaterial to the central issue of trust that no damage occurred. Choices **C** and **D** are incorrect. It's plain and simple—Karl has breached his fiduciary duty to the trust. It was improper for him to borrow funds from the trust under any circumstances and he is liable whether or not the trust suffered any losses and whether or not he repaid his loans.

78. **C** The majority rule is that beneficiaries may compel termination of a trust if all the beneficiaries are legally competent and agree to the termination and termination will not defeat a material purpose of the trust. See Restatement 3d of Trusts, section 65; see also UTC §411. This rule is known as the Claflin doctrine. Because the purpose of the trust was to support Selena in light of her husband's impecunious state, and they are both now billionaires, the trust no longer has a purpose to carry out. Courts frequently hold that the inclusion of a spendthrift clause in the trust, protecting a beneficiary's interest from creditors, is a material purpose and a trust with such a clause cannot be terminated early. The facts of the question do not mention whether there is a spendthrift clause. If the trust

agreement included one, then a court may in fact find that the trust cannot be terminated. The Restatement Third of Trusts takes a more modern approach to trust termination and will allow termination if the reasons for terminating the trust outweigh the remaining purpose. Under this standard, particularly because it would be more economical for the family to invest the trust property themselves and avoid the trustee fees, the trust could be terminated. Choice **A** is incorrect because a trust can be terminated after a trustor's death as long as certain requirements are met. Choice **B** is incorrect because the beneficiaries' consent is insufficient if there is a material purpose of the trust still outstanding. Choice **D** is incorrect because the trustee's consent is not relevant.

79. **D** A valid exculpatory clause in a trust is sufficient to excuse ordinary negligence; as a matter of public policy, however, it is not ordinarily construed as relieving a trustee for losses resulting from bad faith, intentional wrongs, or *gross* negligence. (Section 1008(a) of the Uniform Trust Code provides that despite a valid exculpatory clause a trustee remains liable for breaches committed in bad faith or "with reckless indifference to the purposes of the trust or the interests of the beneficiaries"—reckless indifference arguably includes intentional wrongs and gross negligence.) The exculpatory clause here would therefore be sufficient to excuse Amy from liability based upon ordinary negligence, but not gross negligence. Choice **A** is incorrect in that Amy would be liable for the consequences of her gross negligence—that is, if she had invested in the new business without conducting any investigation at all. Choice **B** is incorrect in that if Amy were liable at all, the loss of income resulting from her negligence might affect the other beneficiaries of the trust as well as Amy herself. (Amy was entitled only to that portion of income necessary for her own support, maintenance, and education.) Choice **C** is incorrect; if Amy's omission constituted gross negligence, she would be liable to the other beneficiaries for lost principal.

80. **A** Under traditional trust principles, a trustee is ordinarily *personally liable* for breach of contract regarding trust assets. Under the traditional approach, a trustee held liable for breach of contract has a right of indemnification from the trust, so long as he or she acted in good faith. Although Laura is personally liable as trustee under the traditional approach, she has a right to indemnification, assuming she acted in good faith and assuming there are sufficient assets. Choice **B** is incorrect; Laura is personally liable under the traditional

approach. Choice **C** is incorrect; Laura probably has a right to indemnification under the traditional approach because she appears to have acted in good faith. Choice **D** is incorrect; Laura has a right of indemnification whether or not the trust document contains an exculpatory clause.

[It should be noted that the modern trend is that the trustee is *not* personally liable on contracts properly entered into in his or her fiduciary capacity in the course of trust administration as long as the trustee discloses his or her representative capacity and the identity of the trust. (UPC §7-306; UTC §1010 requires only disclosure acting in representative capacity.)]

81. **C** Under traditional trust principles, a trustee is ordinarily personally liable for all torts he or she commits during his or her administration of the trust, whether or not he or she is personally at fault. Furthermore, a trustee cannot obtain *indemnity* from the trust when he or she is personally at fault. Because Bill was personally at fault (*i.e.*, he was driving negligently), he may *not* receive indemnity from the trust estate. The fact that Bill was arguably acting in the course of administering the trust is irrelevant. Choice **A** is incorrect because Bill may not indemnify himself under these circumstances under the traditional approach. Choice **B** is incorrect because Bill is personally liable under the traditional approach. Choice **D** is incorrect because an exculpatory clause ordinarily insulates a trustee from responsibility to reimburse a trust for diminishing its assets by his or her errors in judgment—it does not authorize indemnity for the personal negligence of the trustee in causing injury to third parties. (It should be mentioned that the trust assets are ordinarily not available to pay claims for torts personally committed by the trustee in the course of administering the trust. Even if Bill is judgment proof, Phyllis will probably not be able to recover against the trust's assets.)

[It should be noted that the modern trend is that the trustee is personally liable for torts committed in the course of trust administration only if the trustee is personally at fault. (UPC §7-306(b); UTC §1010(b).)]

82. **B** Under traditional trust principles, a trustee is ordinarily personally liable for all torts committed by employees of the trust while acting within the scope of their employment. The trustee is, in fact and in law, the employer. The trustee is ordinarily entitled to indemnity under traditional trust principles as long as he or she was not

personally at fault. Bill is personally liable under the principle of respondeat superior; but because he was not personally at fault he may seek indemnity from the trust property. Bill's recovery, however, is limited to the trust assets; he cannot seek indemnity from the trust beneficiaries themselves. In this case, he must personally pay the excess damages ($100,000). Choice **A** is incorrect; a trustee may *not* ordinarily seek indemnity from the beneficiaries individually. Choices **C** and **D** are incorrect in at least one respect—Bill is personally liable under traditional trust principles.

[It should be noted that the modern trend is that the trustee is personally liable for torts committed in the course of trust administration only if the trustee is personally at fault. (UPC §7-306(b); UTC §1010(b).)]

83. A Under traditional trust principles, in most states, *stock dividends* are always treated as principal, and thus allocated to the *corpus* of a trust. Choices **B, C,** and **D** are all incorrect because stock dividends are usually allocated exclusively and entirely to the corpus of a trust.

[It should be noted that the modern trend is to adopt the portfolio approach to trust investments, which favors overall trust return as opposed to specific classification of the return as income or principal. Under the Principal and Income Act, §104, the trustee is granted the power of equitable distribution to reallocate the total return between the income and principal beneficiaries to ensure that the two groups are treated fairly while paying particular attention to the larger rate of return regardless of how the return is classified (income vs. principal).]

84. D When there is an income interest in a trust separate from the principal interest, the trustee is generally obligated to *sell unproductive property* within a reasonable time period. (Restatement 3d of Trusts, §240.) (This rule also applies to "underproductive" assets—*i.e.*, those that produce so little current income, compared with what could be earned from an alternative investment having the same principal value, that it is unfair to the income beneficiary to keep the low-income assets.) Under the modern trend, the trustee has an obligation to apportion the proceeds between the income beneficiaries and the principal where the sale is delayed. The facts here imply that the trustee did not immediately sell the unproductive parcels of land. Therefore, the trustee has a duty to sell the property within a reasonable period of time and, in light of the delay in selling the parcels of land, to apportion some of the sale proceeds to the income beneficiaries. Choice **A** is incorrect because it does not acknowledge the trustee's duty to sell under these circumstances and it incorrectly allocates all of the sale proceeds to the principal. Choice **B** is incorrect because it fails to acknowledge the trustee's duty to sell under these circumstances. Choice **C** is incorrect because it fails to acknowledge the trustee's duty to apportion some of the sale proceeds to the income beneficiaries.

85. **D** Under traditional trust principles, *maintenance, taxes,* and *insurance* pertaining to trust assets are paid, in the first instance, *from income* (even though these expenditures protect both income and remainder interests). Under the traditional approach, all three expenditures are charged to the income beneficiaries. Choice **A** is incorrect in that taxes and insurance are also charged against trust income. Choice **B** is incorrect in that insurance is also charged against trust income. Choice **C** is incorrect in that the maintenance of trust assets is also charged against income.

86. **D** Under traditional trust principles (and still the Restatement 3d of Trusts approach, §63) the settlor has the power to revoke or modify a trust only to the extent the terms of the trust so provide. Because the facts indicate that Ellen did not expressly retain a power to revoke or modify, she can do neither. Choices **A**, **B**, and **C** are incorrect because Ellen did not explicitly retain the power to modify or revoke the trust.

    [It should be noted that the Uniform Trust Code provides that a settlor retains the power to revoke or modify the trust unless the trust expressly provides otherwise. (UTC §602.)]

87. **C** UPC §2-1106(b)(3)(A) provides that "the *disclaimed interest* passes as if the disclaimant had died immediately before the time of distribution" (emphasis added). If Ashley had not disclaimed, she would have been entitled to 50 percent of the estate. Ashley might have hoped that by disclaiming, then she would be treated as having predeceased her mother so that UPC §2-106(b) would apply and division of the estate would begin at the level of "living" descendants. Under this approach, the shares of her four children would be equal to the shares of Drew and Derek. However, the language of the disclaimer section refers to the "disclaimed interest." Ashley's interest was 50 percent, so her share is divided among her four children, and Drew and Derek receive 25 percent each. The statute therefore prevents Ashley from increasing her family's share of the estate by

disclaiming. Choice **A** is incorrect because Drew and Derek are at a different generational level from Ashley and would have to share their mother's share of the estate. Choice **B** would be correct if Ashley had not disclaimed, but because of her disclaimer she receives nothing. Choice **D** may have been the result Ashley was hoping for, but as explained previously, it is not the result under the UPC.

88. **D** Because Naomi had no children at the time the interest was created, their interest is contingent on being born. If Naomi has any children, then each child upon being born or adopted would have a vested remainder, subject to partial divestment because his or her share would be reduced if Naomi had any other children. A vested interest must follow a contingent interest, so Andrew retained a reversion. He left his residual estate, which would include the reversion, to the Home. Choices **A**, **B**, and **C** are all incorrect because the unborn children cannot have a vested interest.

89. **A** The first will is presumed revoked because it was in T's possession and cannot be found at his death. The presumption is bolstered by his comments to others that he had torn up his will. The second document cannot be probated because it was not witnessed or notarized and was not in his handwriting. Choice **B** is incorrect because none of the material portions were in his handwriting. Choice **C** is incorrect because there is no evidence that T intended the second document to be his will. Presumably, he had previously had a properly executed will and knew what was necessary. Choice **D** is incorrect because the first will was torn up at least two years before the second document was drafted. In order for dependent relative revocation to apply, T would have had to revoke the first will under the belief that the second document was effective. Because the two acts were two years apart, dependent relative revocation cannot revive the first will.

90. **C** UPC §2-804 does not directly address the situation of the remainderman slaying the life tenants, but §2-804(f) does provide generally that property should be distributed in accordance with the equitable principle that a killer cannot profit from his wrong. Charlotte received the remainder from Olive and should not be affected by the killing. However, Charlotte should not be able to receive the remainder early because of her act. The life estates would have been held by Agnes and Boyd if Charlotte had not killed them, so for the period of time that Charlotte presumably would have had to wait, the heirs of Agnes and Boyd should benefit from the use of the property. Choice

A is incorrect because Charlotte willfully killed Agnes and Boyd and should not benefit. Choice B is incorrect because Charlotte should not have to forfeit a property interest that she already held. Choice D is incorrect because Olive did not retain an interest in the property.

91. **B** Because both Arnold and Beatrice predeceased Terry, their shares in the estate lapsed. (UPC §2-702.) The question then arises whether the antilapse statute (UPC §2-603) applies. Arnold is a descendant of Terry's grandparents, and he left a descendant, Gina, so Arnold's interest is given instead to Gina. Beatrice, however, is not related to Terry so her share lapses. The question is then what becomes of Beatrice's lapsed share of the residue. Under the common law "no residue of a residue" rule, her share would pass via intestacy. However, UPC §2-604(b) overrules the common law rule and provides that a lapsed portion of the residue passes to the other residuary takers. Gina therefore takes all. Choice **A** is incorrect because the antilapse statute and the statutory rule giving lapsed residuary gifts to other residuary takers prevents intestacy. Choice **C** is incorrect because the antilapse statute does not apply to Beatrice, and choice **D** is incorrect because Beatrice's lapsed share is absorbed by the other residuary taker.

92. **C** This is an extremely complex fact pattern. First, the one-half of the farm that passed under Abigail's will to Uriah for life, remainder to Neil, gave Neil a vested remainder. The fact that Neil died during Uriah's life estate did not change that. Because Neil left his estate to his wife, she is entitled to Abigail's one-half now that Uriah is deceased. As for Uriah's one-half, he made a written contract to leave it to Neil upon the death of the survivor of himself and Abigail, and he has breached that contract. Arguably, there is no breach because Neil predeceased and cannot take under Uriah's will. UPC §2-514. However, because Neil and Uriah were related, and Neil left descendants, the antilapse statute would save his interest for his children. (UPC §2-603.) The children can therefore make a claim in Uriah's estate for his one-half. Choice **A** is incorrect because Neil's wife would not have received Uriah's half because of the timing of Neil's death. Choice **B** is incorrect because it is incomplete, and choice **D** is incorrect because Neil's family already had a vested interest in Abigail's half.

93. **C** Under UTC §409 and Restatement Third of Trusts §47, a trust without ascertainable beneficiaries and with a noncharitable purpose can be enforced for a period of up to 21 years as long as the purpose

is not capricious or illegal. This trust has no ascertainable beneficiary but the trust purpose is legitimate, so it should fall under this rule. Traditionally, however, the trust would fail. Choices **A** and **B** would be correct under traditional common law because the trust has no designated beneficiary and it would violate the common law Rule Against Perpetuities because there is no measuring life and it may take more than 21 years to find the killer. Choice **D** is incorrect because this does not fit the common law definition of a charitable purpose.

94. B Because Mom signed the will without knowing it was an actual will, this is fraud in the execution. Choice **A** is incorrect because fraud in the inducement would require Sarah to make fraudulent misrepresentations to Mom to get her to sign a will with provisions based on Mom's belief in those misrepresentations. Choice **C** is incorrect because undue influence would require Sarah to have coerced Mom to sign the will, but this was just trickery. Choice **D** is incorrect because there is no evidence that Mom lacked testamentary capacity.

95. B The document does not satisfy the requirements of a will in any jurisdiction because it is not witnessed, and it is typewritten so it cannot qualify as a holographic will. The Tiny Tim Foundation can try to argue that the document created a valid trust. The critical issue is whether the language "I intend" demonstrates sufficient intent to create a trust. Specific language designating the arrangement as a trust is not necessary. The arrangement specifies a trust res and beneficiaries. A trustee is necessary, but Tess could be considered the trustee because she retained control of the assets. Choice **A** is incorrect because the language used by Tess could be construed as creating a trust. Choice **C** is incorrect because the document clearly contemplates that the foundation would not receive the property until her death, and a gift requires delivery of the property. Choice **D** is also incorrect because the document could not be considered a gift.

96. D Although some states allow a trustee to keep inception assets, which are assets that the trustor placed into the trust, the trustee must always monitor the performance of all trust assets, including inception assets, and diversify if prudent. Leaving the entire trust in a company that is exposed to certain risks does not appear to be prudent, even if there was no prior indication that the company would be sued. It was therefore a breach of the trustee's duty of care and duty to diversify. The exculpatory clause appears to present a problem because it relieves the trustee from liability except for acts that amount to willful misconduct, and the trustee's breach was one of negligence because the trustee just did not get around to evaluating the investments. This is the type of breach covered by the exculpatory clause. However, the trustee is the one that inserted the clause into the agreement and did not discuss the clause with Selma. Exculpatory clauses are strictly construed, and under the UTC §1008, an exculpatory clause is invalid if the trustee caused the clause to be included and the trustee cannot prove that the clause is fair under the circumstances and was adequately communicated to the trustor. Choice **A** is incorrect because in this instance it was a breach of the duty to diversify, and the loss is directly related to that breach. Choice **B** is incorrect because the exculpatory clause was not explained to the trustor and is therefore unenforceable. Choice **C** is incorrect because the trustee was merely negligent and did not deliberately intend to avoid diversifying the trust.

97. **C** This requires a close reading of the relevant sections of the UPC. The starting point is that the joint tenancy designation presumptively gives the property to Tom, and that designation trumps the provisions of the later will. Choice **B** is therefore incorrect. (UPC §6-213.) However, George set this up only for convenience of bill paying rather than for the purpose of giving Tom full rights to the property upon his death. UPC §6-212 Comment clarifies that the drafters intended to give a court the ability to implement the intentions of parties if the account was set up for convenience rather than to give a death benefit. Because Tom's siblings can show that was George's intention, the funds in the account should pass into George's estate and under the terms of his will. Choice **A** is incorrect because that is inconsistent with George's intent, and choice **D** is incorrect because there is no evidence that Tom unduly influenced George to put his name on the account.

98. **C** First, the deed on its own does not give Alberta the farm because a deed requires delivery in order to be effective and there was no delivery. Therefore, choice **A** is incorrect. Second, the deed cannot be saved by UPC §6-101, which authorizes nonprobate transfers, because such nonprobate instruments must be otherwise effective and this is an undelivered deed. See *First Nat'l Bank v. Bloom*, 264 N.W.2d 208 (N.D. 1978). Therefore, choice **B** is incorrect. However, under UPC §2-514, the agreement with Sally should be enforceable

because the deed was a writing signed by the decedent. If a court deems that the deed is insufficient evidence of the contract, however, then the farm would pass by intestacy to Alberta and her siblings, as provided in choice **D**.

99. D UPC §2-509(b) provides that if a later "will" that partially revokes a prior will is itself revoked, then the provision of the prior will that was revoked is revived. Under this rule, revocation of the codicil revived the gift of the home to Judy. Taping the codicil pieces together is insufficient to revive it. The will in its original form is therefore enforceable. Choice **A** is incorrect because revoking a codicil does not revoke the underlying will, and choice **B** is incorrect because taping together the pieces is not a testamentary act. Choice **C** is incorrect because the revocation of the codicil revived the terms of the original will.

100. D Delia violated her duty to delegate responsibly because she delegated investment decisions to a friend, albeit a professional, without investigating the friend's suitability for this particular trust or the friend's general track record. She also has not educated herself on how to read the statements so she cannot adequately monitor what the friend is doing. She is violating her duty to keep beneficiaries informed by refusing to give Doris an accounting: Doris is a remainder beneficiary of the trust and is therefore entitled to information. She is violating her duty to invest prudently because she does not even know how the funds are invested, $1 million in a savings account earning virtually no interest seems imprudent, and the investment in the home seems imprudent because of the cost of the upkeep and Steve's inability to use the property fully, although the home may be a good investment depending on the local real estate market. She has also breached her duty of loyalty because she is paying herself a six-figure salary even though she has delegated most of the responsibilities to others (who are also being paid by the trust), and she purchased a lavish residence with trust funds that is not appropriate for Steve's needs but that she gets to enjoy. Choice **A** is incorrect because she has diversified among cash, real estate, and stocks. Choice **B**. is incorrect because it does not include the duty of loyalty or the duty to invest prudently and does include the duty to diversify. Choice **C** is incorrect because it does not include the duty of loyalty and does include the duty to diversify.

101. A A person's heirs are usually determined as of the time of the person's death, although for the purpose of determining a future interest, it may be determined as of the time the interest vests. In this scenario, the time of Viola's death and the vesting of the interest in Viola's heirs is the same. Viola's children will have to survive to Viola's death in order to take, so their interest is contingent. Choices **B** and **C** are incorrect because the children's interest would not vest until they survived Viola and became her heirs. Choice **D** is incorrect because an executor interest only follows a vested remainder, and the interest preceding the children's interest is a life estate.

Table of References to the Uniform Probate Code (UPC)

§1-201(5).............. 83, 116, 211
§1-201(11) 78
§1-201(18) 207
§1-201(23) 81
§1-201(24) 79
§1-201(32) 211
§1-201(55) 217
§2-101(b) 99, 140, 204, 217
§2-102(1)..................... 142
§2-102(1)(ii)................. 117
§2-102(4).............. 60, 118, 212
§2-103(1).................... 203
§2-103(2).................... 212
§2-103(a).................... 127
§2-103(a)(1) 56, 88, 103, 140, 210
§2-103(a)(2) 214, 215
§2-103(a)(3) 121, 127, 140, 204, 211
§2-103(a)(4) 204
§2-104 .... 127, 203
§2-106 127
§2-106(b) 56, 88, 241
§2-107 211
§2-109(a).................... 204
§2-117 210
§2-118 .... 90, 204
§2-118(a).................... 116
§2-202 60
§2-203 60

§2-301 .... 60, 92, 117, 142
§2-301(a).................... 222
§2-302 .... 70, 78, 81, 92, 103, 210
§2-302(a)(2) 222
§2-502 .... 53, 58, 69, 96, 101, 102, 105, 119, 225, 226
§2-502(a).................... 119
§2-502(a)(3) 101
§2-502(b) 69, 81, 92, 93, 101, 119, 138, 208, 212, 217
§2-502, Comment 102
§2-503 .... 70, 81, 101, 110, 111, 120, 123, 125, 139, 208
§2-505 .... 82, 141, 203
§2-505(b) 58, 69, 81, 96, 100
§2-505, Comment 79
§2-506 81
§2-507 .... 69, 96, 208
§2-507(a)(1) 53, 101
§2-507(a)(2) 59, 96, 102, 207
§2-507(b) 54
§2-507(c).................. 54, 92
§2-509(a).................... 207
§2-509(c).................... 208
§2-510 .... 90, 106, 125, 138, 204
§2-512 .... 117, 123, 129, 205, 206
§2-513 .... 90, 209
§2-514 .... 113, 213, 245
§2-601 203
§2-603 .....97, 117 203, 209, 223, 243

§2-603(2) 132	§2-711 . . . . 132, 220
§2-603(b) 90, 116, 130, 203	§2-803(c) 222
§2-603(b)(1) 79, 140, 220	§2-803(c)(1) 206
§2-603(b)(2) 131	§2-803(c)(2) 207
§2-604(a) 64	§2-804 . . . . 141, 142, 242
§2-604(b) 221, 243	§2-804(b) 77, 88, 203, 222
§2-605 . . . . 91, 111, 142	§2-804(f) 242
§2-605(a)(1) 77, 116, 139	§2-901(a) 215
§2-606 223	§2-907(a) 226
§2-606(a) 82, 88, 139	§2-907(b) 226
§2-606(a)(1) 205,	§2-1105 210
§2-606(a)(3) 139	§2-1106(b)(3)(A) 241
§2-606(a)(5) 206	§3-402(a) 214
§2-606(a)(6) 66, 139, 205, 219	§3-902 102
§2-606(b) 219	§6-101 . . . . 89, 245
§2-607 210	§6-201(8)(ii) 228
§2-608 220	§6-212 68
§2-609 . . . . 83, 206	§6-212(b) 228
§2-702 . . . . 135, 245	§6-212(b)(2) 228
§2-707 . . . . 76, 145	§6-212(b), Comment 228
§2-708 . . . . 130, 131, 132	§6-213 245
§2-709 131	§7-306 239
§2-709(b) 132	§7-306(b) 239, 240

Table of References to the Uniform Trust Code

§402, Comment 75	§802(b) 72, 233
§411 .... 136, 237	§807(a) 236, 237
§411(c) 137	§813 150
§413 142	§813, Comment 147
§502 229	§814(a) 235
§503 .... 136, 229	§815(a)(2)(A) 234
§503(b)(3) 229	§816(5) 234
§602 241	§1002 152
§602(a) 135	§1005 152
§602(c)(1) 135	§1008 245
§602(c)(2) 135	§1008(a) 238
§705(a) 235	§1010 239
§801 151	§1010(b) 239, 240
§802 147	

Table of References to the Restatement (Second) of Trusts

§55, Comment h................ 98	§330, Comment j............. 135
§157(a)..................... 136	§337, Comment l............. 137
§330 135	§338(1) 79

Table of References to the Restatement (Third) of Trusts

§8	98
§13, Comment b	224
§15, Comment b	225
§29, Comment i	226
§29, Comment j	226
§46	225
§47	226, 243
§54	229
§63	241
§63, Comment h	135
§63, Comment i	135
§65	136
§65, Comment e	137
§78, Comment b	233
§78, Comment d	237
§87, Comment d	235
§205	237
§206	237
§240	240

Index

References are to the number of the question raising the issue. "E" indicates an Essay Question; "M" indicates a Multiple-Choice Question.

Ademption by extinction
   Generally, E4, E10, E12, E18, E24, M7, M35, M45
   By act of Fiduciary, M35
   Presumption against ademption, E4

Ademption by satisfaction, E10, M9, M45

Adopted children
   Generally, E12, E21, M4
   Adoption by estoppel, intestate succession, M20

Advancements, E10, E30, M4

Age, competence to make will, M

Alcohol, testator under influence at time of execution of will, E15

Alienation of beneficial interest in trust, E7, E9, E23, M59, M60, M61, M62

Ambiguous provisions, construction of wills, E1, E22

Amendment of Trust, E5

Animals, honorary trusts, M53

Antilapse statutes, E9, E12, E14, E18, E22, E24, M2, M3, M14, M15, M39, M45, M58, M91, M92

Assignment of beneficial interest in trust, E7, E9, E23, M59, M60, M61, M62,

Attestation of will
   Generally, E1, E2, E18, E19, M3, M51, M52

Interested witnesses, E2, E6, E9, E15, M2
Signature of witness, E1, M51, M52

Attorney malpractice, E5, E25

Bank accounts, joint, E5, M97

Bank accounts, Totten trusts, E12, M57, M58

Beneficiaries
   Charitable trusts, E11
   Inter vivos trusts, E4, E8, M93
   Testamentary trusts, E29, M50, M53

***Bona fide* purchasers, breach of duty of loyalty,** E7

Borrowing of funds, trustees, M71, M77

Burden of proof of execution and contents of missing will, E2, M24

Charitable gifts, "mortmain" statutes, E13

Charitable trusts
   Generally, E11, E29, M66, M67
   Beneficiaries, E11, M93
   Cy pres, E11, M68, M69
   Delivery, E11
   Intent, E11
   Res, E11
   Resulting trusts, E11
   Trustees, E11

Children and minors
  See also Adopted children; Illegitimate children; Intestate succession
  Generally, E8
  Competence to make will, M3
  Grandchildren as pretermitted heirs, E10
  Guardian *ad litem*, consent to termination of trust, E24
  Pretermitted children, E6, E9, E10, E13, E15, M17, M43
  Spendthrift trusts, child support, E23
  Stepparents and stepchildren, M18

Class gifts, E22, M15, M25-M28

Codicils
  See also Holographic wills and codicils; Revocation of wills and codicils
  Generally, E13
  Holographic codicils, E19, E26
  Republication of prior will, E13, E20

Conditions on gifts
  Generally, E4
  Divorce, encouragement of, E4
  Marriage, restraint of, E4, M54
  Motivation, expression of, M21

Consent to termination of trust, E23

Construction of wills
  Ambiguous provisions, E1, E22
  Extrinsic evidence, E13
  Intent of testator, E1, E22

Constructive delivery, E11

Constructive trusts
  Generally, E6-E7, M55, M56
  Repudiation of contract to make will or gift, M23

Contest of will, interested parties, M30

Contract to make will or gift, E17, M22, M23, M92

Convenience, Rule of, M26, M27

Creditors
  Exemption for certain nonprobate assets, M64
  Fraud upon creditors, E9
  Spendthrift trusts, E7

***Cy pres*, charitable trusts,** E11, E25, E26, M68, M69

Delegation of powers by trustees, M75, M76

Delivery
  Charitable trusts, E11
  Constructive and symbolic delivery, E11, E26, M95
  Inter vivos trusts, E4, E8

Dependent relative revocation, E1, E3, E6, E15, E20, M10

Depletion of trust res, E1

Destruction of specifically devised property, insurance proceeds for, E24

Disclaimers, M15, M87

Diversification, investments, M72, M96, M100

Divorce
  See also Marriage
  Condition on gift that encourages divorce, E4
  Revocation of testamentary gift, E8, E12, M2, M41
  Revocation of nonprobate beneficiary designation on divorce, M33

Index

Drafting Will Provisions, E29, E30

Employees, hiring by trustees, M75, M76, M82

ERISA, M64

Events of independent significance, E9, E10, E18, E19, M6, M8

Exculpatory clauses, trusts, M80, M96

Exoneration, specific devise as subject to mortgage, M16

Extinction, ademption by

See Ademption by extinction

Extrinsic evidence

Construction of wills, E13

Revocation of wills and codicils, E14

Failure of trust, E21

Foster children, intestate succession, M20

Fraud

Generally, M34, M36

Constructive trusts, E22

Creditors, fraud upon, E9

In the execution, M94

Marriage, M36

Furniture as passing with house in which it is contained, E16

Gender restrictions, charitable trusts, M69

General vs. specific devise, E24, M7

Good faith, trustees, M73, M80

Government functions, charitable trusts, E11

Grandchildren as pretermitted heirs, E10

Gross negligence, exculpatory clauses in testamentary trusts, M80

Guardian ad litem, consent to termination of trust, E23

Half-blood, relatives of, M18

Harmless error,

Correction of mistakes, E17

Lack of formalities as, E6, E15, E16, E19, E24

Heirs, determination, M101

Holographic wills and codicils

Generally, E3E4, E6, E10, E12, E13, E15, E16, E18, E19, E24, M21

Interested persons, E10, E14

Place of signature, E14

Homestead, M64

Honorary trusts, M53

Illegitimate children

Inheritance from father, M17

Impartial, Trustee duty to be, M72

Income taxes, recovery from spendthrift trusts, M62

Incorporation by reference, E9, E12, E16, E18-E20, E24, M5, M13, M19

Indemnification, trustees, M80-M82

Independent significance, events of, E9, E10, E18, E19, M6, M10, M19

Infants

See Children and minors

Initials as signature, E6, E18

Insane delusion, will provision as product of, M31

Insurance

Destruction of specifically devised property, proceeds for, E24

Murderer, disposition of property to, M9

Premiums, payment from trust income, M85

Proceeds of policy, E24

Integration, M19

Intent
    Generally, E15
    Charitable trusts, E11
    Construction of wills, E1, E22
    Inter vivos trusts, E4, E8
    Trusts, E20, M48, M49, M63, M95

Interested persons
    Attestation of will, witnesses, E2, E6, E9, E15, E21, M2
    Holographic wills and codicils, E10, E14

Interpretation of wills
    See Construction of wills

***Inter vivos* trusts**
    Generally, E4, E23, M86
    Beneficiaries, E4, E8
    Creation, E28
    Delivery, E4, E5, E8
    Intent, E4, E5, E8
    Modification, E9
    Res, E4, E8

Intestate succession
    Generally, E1, E2, E12, E14, E18, E20, E21, E24, M3, M28, M32
    Adoption by estoppel, M20
    Foster children, M20
    Half-blood, relatives of, M18
    Illegitimate children, M17
    Partial intestacy, E14

Intoxication at time of execution of will, E15

Investments
    Generally, ,M72, M74, M100
    Delegation of powers, M76, M100
    Diversification, M72, M100
    Reasonably prudent investor, M72, M74
    Unimproved land, M74
    Unproductive and underproductive property, M84

Joint wills, M33

Killer, disposition of property to, M12, M46, M93

Lapse of gifts, E9, E12, E14, E18, E21, E22, E24, M2, M3, M14, M15, M39, M45 M58, M91

Libraries, charitable trusts, E11

Life estates, E20

Life insurance, E25, M33, M64

Loyalty, duty of trustees, E7

Maintenance, payment from trust income, M85

Manslaughter, disposition of property to murderer, M44

Mark as signature, M3

Marriage
    See also Divorce
    Condition on gift that restrains marriage, E4, M54
    Fraud, M36

Remarriage of surviving spouse, gift over to alternate beneficiary on, M54

Minors
    See Children and minors

Misrepresentation
    See Fraud

Missing wills
    Burden of proof of execution and contents, E2, M24

Presumption of destruction from inability to find will, E1

Proof of contents, E1, E2, M24

Mistake
Revocation of wills and codicils, E13
Wills, E17, E22, M32

Modification of *inter vivos* trusts, E9

Mortgage, specific devise as subject to, M16

"Mortmain" statutes, E13

Motivation, expression of, M21

Municipal functions, charitable trusts, E11

Murderer, disposition of property to, M12, M44

Mutual wills, M29

Negligence, exculpatory clauses in testamentary trusts, M80

Noncharitable Trust, E29

Nonprobate transfers, M33, M98

Omitted children, E6, E9, E10, E13, E15, M17, M43

Omitted spouse, E2, E13, E17, E18, E25, M42

Operation of law, trusts by
See Constructive trusts; Resulting trusts

Paternity, pretermitted children, M17

Perpetuities, Rule Against, M66, M67

Personal effects, E18

Personal liability of trustees, M80-M82

Per stirpes vs. per capita distribution, E1, E20-E22, M1, M28

Pets, honorary trusts, M53

Place of signature, holographic wills and codicils, E14

Place where will was executed or where testator was domiciled, E10

Power of appointment
Generally, M37-M40, M46, M47
Special powers, E26, M51

Power of attorney, M35

Precatory words, testamentary trusts, E6, E20

Presumptions
Ademption, E4
Destruction of missing will, E1

Public Policy, E29

***Quantum meruit*, breach of contract to make will or gift,** M22

Racial restrictions, charitable trusts, M69

Reciprocal wills, M29

Release of power of appointment, M46

Religious restrictions, charitable trusts, M69

Remarriage of surviving spouse, gift over to alternate beneficiary on, M54

Republication of prior will, codicils, E13, E19, M19

Repudiation of contract to make will or gift, M23

Res
Charitable trusts, E11
Inter vivos trusts, E4, E8
Testamentary trusts, E17

Rescission for breach of duty of loyalty, E7

Resulting trusts
  Generally, E8, E14
  Charitable trust, failure of purpose, E11
  Semisecret trusts, E14, M56

Revival of wills
  Generally, E1, E2, E21, M12, M99
  Dependent relative revocation, E1, E6, E15, E20, M10
  Physical act, revocation of later will by, E2

Revocation of trust
  Generally, E8, E23
  Totten trusts, M58

Revocation of wills and codicils
  See also Revival of wills
  Generally, E1, E2, E3, E13, E15, E19, E20, E21
  Divorce, E8, E12, M2, M41
  Earlier will as revoked by later will, E1, M11, M12
  Extrinsic evidence, E14
  Holographic revocation, E15
  Joint and reciprocal wills, M29
  Mistake, E13
  Partial revocation, E6
  Physical act, revocation by, E2, E3E14, E21, M10, M11
  Presumption of destruction from inability to find will, E1, M89

Rule Against Perpetuities, charitable trusts as exempt from, M66, M67

Rule of Convenience, closing of class, M26, M27

Savings accounts, Totten trusts, E12, M57, M58

Secret trusts, E6, M55

Self-dealing by trustees, E7, M70, M77

Semisecret trusts, E14, M56

Signature of witness to will, E1, M51, M52

Simultaneous death, E22, M3, M4

Slayer, disposition of property to, M9, M44

Specific vs. general devise, E24, M7

Spendthrift trusts, E7, E9, E23, M59, M61, M62, M65

Spousal support, spendthrift trusts, E23

Statute of Wills
  Generally, E9
  Secret trusts, E6

Stepparents and stepchildren, M18

Stock
  Accretions, addition to original bequest, E8, E12, E16, E24
  Trust, allocation of dividends to corpus, M83

Substitute gifts, E8, E22, M3

Taxes
  Income of trust, payment from, M85
  Spendthrift trusts, recovery from, M62

Termination of trust, E23M78

Testamentary trusts
  Generally, E5, E6, E21
  Beneficiaries, E17, M50, M53
  Discretionary distributions, recovery by creditor against, M63
  Exculpatory clauses, M80
  Precatory words, E6, E20,

Index

Torts, personal liability of trustees, M81, M82

Totten trusts, E12, M57, M58

Trustees

See also Investments

Borrowing of funds, M71, M77

Breach, damages, E28

Breach, statute of limitations, E28

Breach of contract, personal liability for, M80

Charitable trusts, E11

Delegation of powers, M75, M76

Employees, hiring of, M75, M76, M82

Good faith, M73, M80

Indemnification, M80-M82

Loyalty, duty of, E7, E27, E28

Notice to beneficiaries, E27, E28, M100

Personal liability, M80-M82

Reasonably prudent investor, E17, E27, E28, M72, M100

Sale of trust assets, E7, E27, E28

Self-dealing, E7, E27, E28, M70, M77, M100

Testamentary trusts, E17

Torts, personal liability for, M81, M82

Undue influence

Generally, E6, M34

Drafter of will as beneficiary, M34

Unimproved land, investments, M74

Unproductive and underproductive property, investments, M84

Voluntary manslaughter, disposition of property to murderer, M44